# COMPARATIVE LAW IN PRACTICE

This book provides a comparative study of contract law, examining the interaction of common law and civil law approaches to contract law. Drawing extensively upon English, French and European law, the book explores how the law of contract of Jersey, Channel Islands, has been influenced by both civil law and common law sources. It is argued that this jurisdiction is a striking example of comparative law in action, given that Jersey contract law is made up of a blend of common law and civil law approaches. Jersey law is premised upon a subjective approach to contracts, in which civil law concepts such as cause (rather than consideration) and *vices de consentement* are the foundational aspects, but is nonetheless highly influenced by the common law in areas such as remedies (damages, termination, etc).

The book analyses a series of key issues from a comparative and European perspective, including the principles underlying contract law (comparing and contrasting civil and common law approaches), the formation of contract, requirements of reciprocity (cause vs consideration), the structure and approach of precontractual liability, the role of good faith in a mixed system, the architecture of remedies, and more.

**Volume 17 in the series Hart Studies in Private Law**

# Comparative Law in Practice

## Contract Law in a Mid-Channel Jurisdiction

Duncan Fairgrieve

BLOOMSBURY
NEW DELHI • LONDON • OXFORD • NEW YORK • SYDNEY

BLOOMSBURY INDIA
Bloomsbury Publishing India Pvt. Ltd
Second Floor, LSC Building No. 4, DDA Complex, Pocket C–6&7,
Vasant Kunj, New Delhi 110070

BLOOMSBURY, BLOOMSBURY ACADEMIC INDIA and the Diana logo are
trademarks of Bloomsbury Publishing Plc

**First published in India 2023**
First published 2016



This edition published with permission from Bloomsbury Publishing Plc,
50 Bedford Square, London, WC1B3DP, UK



British Library Cataloguing-in-Publication Data
A catalogue record for this book is available from the British Library

Library of Congress Cataloging-in-Publication Data
A catalog record for this book is available from the Library of Congress

ISBN: 978-93-56403-60-4

Typeset by Compuscript Ltd, Shannon
Printed at Manipal Technologies Limited, Manipal

To find out more about our authors and books
visit www.bloomsbury.com and sign up for our newsletters

# PREFACE

The genesis of this book is to be found in my teaching and research at the Institute of Law in Jersey, and I would therefore at the outset like to record my gratitude for the support of the Institute in this project.

I have also incurred debts of gratitude in preparing this work, and would therefore like to thank Sir Philip Bailhache, Ghislain Guillaume, Nicole Langlois, Dr David Marrani, Fraser Robertson and Dr Solène Rowan.

Thanks also go to all those at Hart Publishing who have been thoroughly efficient and helpful in steering the text towards publication.

Duncan Fairgrieve

# CONTENTS

# 1

# Introduction

The objective of this book is to undertake a comparative law study of contract law, examining the interaction of common law and civil law approaches to contract law. Drawing extensively upon English, French and European law, the book explores the law of contract of Jersey, Channel Islands, as a unique subject of comparative law study.

The Channel Islands, hitherto overlooked by scholarly analysis,[1] provide a fascinating subject of study for the comparative lawyer. The jurisdictions of both Jersey and Guernsey are striking examples of comparative law in action, and Jersey contract law is a particularly illustrative example. The contract law of Jersey is a subtle and complex blend of common law and civil law, based first and foremost upon Norman customary law but influenced also by modern French law as well as English law: one thus finds Norman law notions coexisting cheek by jowl with common law concepts and approaches. The Jersey law of contract is premised upon a subjective approach to contracts,[2] in which civil law concepts such as consent and *volonté*,[3] the notion of *cause* (rather than the doctrine of consideration),[4] and *vices de consentement*[5] are the foundational aspects. Despite this civil law baggage, the law of Jersey is nonetheless highly influenced by the common law, and one finds extensive use of common law concepts and jurisprudence in areas such as remedies.[6]

The Jersey lawyer is thus a comparative lawyer of the most unusual variety: a practising comparative lawyer. This is not solely an issue of substantive law, though as we shall see, the content of Jersey contract law draws upon myriad different sources and a Jersey practitioner will thus need to master Jersey

[1] Note, however, that there is a law journal dedicated to the laws of Jersey and Guernsey, the *Jersey and Guernsey Law Review* (www.jerseylaw.je/Publications/jerseylawreview/) (last accessed 18 February 2016)

[2] *O'Brien v Marett* [2008] JCA 178. Though for the continuing debate concerning this topic, see Chapter 3 pp 38–47.

[3] See further Chapter 3 below.

[4] See further Chapter 4 below.

[5] See further Chapter 5 below.

[6] In particular in respect of damages: see further Chapter 7 below.

customary law, including concepts such as *voisinage*[7] or *quasi-contracts*.[8] We shall also see, and this is perhaps one of the most unusual aspects of the study, that the hybrid of civil and common law sources has also affected mindsets or *mentalités*. The outlook of a Jersey advocate, who will generally have received his or her initial legal training in a common law system, has been shaped by the hybrid Jersey context. This has given rise to a distinctive method of legal reasoning (premised upon a principle-based approach), a very open approach to norms and sources of law, a specific attitude to law-making and the evolution of case law with—for a dyed in the wool English common lawyer—a surprisingly flexible approach to precedent. As a result, it will thus be argued that a mid-Channel lawyer has a very particular mindset or *mentalité*.[9]

Through the analysis of this unusual, but under-explored jurisdiction, a series of comparative law themes will be examined in this book. First and foremost, Jersey provides a fascinating example of comparative law in action through the functioning of a hybrid legal system, in which civil law and common law influences continue to follow an evolutionary process within a micro-jurisdiction context. The Jersey legal system is an extremely open one, with foreign, external sources having a direct impact on the law, and is therefore an unusual subject of study from a comparative law perspective. Issues such as hybrid sources, the efficacy of transplants and the practical use of comparative law during the forensic process will be examined in this book. Comparative law reflections will thus be a prominent feature of the study.

Second, there is the perspective of European private law. Although Jersey is not part of the European Union, this legal system paradoxically provides many lessons for European private law. In one sense, Jersey might be seen as a laboratory for European private law. The relevance of the European comparative law backdrop is examined throughout the book and informs the discussion of broader comparative law issues in the conclusions.

Third, there is the issue of the reform of the law of obligations. Drawing upon the author's experience teaching at the Jersey Institute of Law,[10] consideration is given of the challenges confronting policy-makers in Jersey, and this book examines the reform issues and options. It is argued that a bold approach to reform, embracing the dual common and civil law heritage as an advantage, would provide for greater consistency and legal certainty in this core area of private law. Such a reform might also provide a significant reference point for national and international projects.

[7] Whereby a neighbour must not use his property so as to damage neighbouring property: see *Rockhampton Apartment Limited v Gale and Clarke* 2007 JLR 332; *Fogarty v St Martin's Cottage Limited* [2015] JRC 068.

[8] Related to the concept of unjust enrichment: see *Classic Herd Limited v Jersey Milk Marketing Board* 2014 (2) JLR 487.

[9] See Chapter 2.

[10] The author is a Visiting Professor at the Jersey Institute of Law.

# I. The Importance of Comparing

A word will first be said about the exercise of comparative legal studies. In both England and France, comparative law has traditionally been underrated as a discipline. From a historical perspective, comparative law was at best seen as a likeable eccentricity, at worst a frivolous distraction from serious intellectual pursuit. In France, François Lichère has referred to comparative law as being considered traditionally as 'a purely intellectual exercise' without any practical utility and undertaken by a select group 'inhabiting ivory Chateaux'.[11] On the other side of the Channel, Professor Otto Kahn-Freund joked in his inaugural lecture for the Chair of Comparative law in Oxford that: '[T]he Professor of Comparative Law suffers from the problem that the subject he professes has by common consent the somewhat unusual characteristic that it does not exist.'[12] One of his successors at Oxford, Professor Sir Basil Markesinis, complained that the English comparatists of the twentieth century had led their students and successors into an isolated and enclosed intellectual ghetto with little prospect of escape.[13]

It should, however, be remarked that, despite these statements, the resort to foreign law has actually been relatively commonplace in English law—at least before the courts. The inherent characteristics of the common law have perhaps served to mask the fact that judicial decision-making has often been based upon a series of comparative law exercises. Citations of, and to, other common law jurisdictions are of course frequent before the English courts, a practice reinforced by the comparative law jurisdiction par excellence the Privy Council, which on a day-to-day basis applies foreign law—sometimes even of a civil law nature.[14] In many ways, the common lawyer has, like Monsieur Jourdain, been deploying comparative law without knowing it.

It is true, however, that there has *recently* been a major shift in the role that courts play, and the sources which are now applicable in judicial decision-making. Domestic courts are deliberately and explicitly making use of comparative law to an unprecedented extent.[15] Many factors can be seen as having influenced this process. Primary amongst these is the breakdown of traditionally closed and hierarchical national legal systems. Another factor is the increasingly complex and polycentric issues which modern courts are required to consider and in respect of which ethical and moral issues are increasingly prominent. The polycentric nature

[11] See D Fairgrieve and F Lichère, 'Comparative Law and the Forensic Process: A Franco-English Comparison' in O Moreteau, *Comparative Law and … / Le droit comparé et …* (Aix-Marseille, Presses Universitaires d'Aix-Marseille, 2016).

[12] O Kahn-Freund, 'Comparative Law as an Academic Subject' (1966) 82 *LQR* 40, 40.

[13] B Markesinis, *Comparative Law in the Courtroom and the Classroom* (Oxford, Hart Publishing 2003) 25–26.

[14] See, for instance, *Snell v Beadle* [2001] UKPC 5, concerning … the Jersey law of contract.

[15] See more generally M Andenas and D Fairgrieve, *Courts and Comparative Law* (Oxford, OUP, 2015).

of these issues poses challenges to traditional judicial approaches and explains a whole host of changes, in terms of procedures, personnel and outlook. Comparative law plays a role in developing the substantive law in different areas, including in finding normative solutions to questions of a more technical kind.

No one can be under the illusion that all the challenges of using foreign-law materials have been resolved. Indeed, the methodological discussions are still very much in play, and much remains to be determined.[16] An engaging and important debate thus continues about the methodology, role and function of comparative law in the study of the law.[17] It is now commonly appreciated and accepted that legal systems are not simply about *formal legal rules*, but are also highly influenced by other factors such as the institutional context as well as cultural or socio-legal influences. The rule-making method of studying foreign jurisdictions needs thus to be supplemented by placing the different approaches in their specific context, drawing upon historical, cultural and constitutional perspectives.[18] These factors contribute to creating distinctive 'mindsets' or '*mentalités*'[19] and there is great importance in taking into account these differences when undertaking comparative law study. It is argued in this book that Jersey lawyers have a very distinctive mindset, which is a product of the particularities of the socio-legal context of their system, including the hybrid approaches to sources as well as the micro-jurisdiction context of this legal system.[20]

Another aspect of this contextual approach is that in comparing the position of English, French and Jersey law, account will be taken of the specific procedural context. We will thus record how the patterns, trends and structures of civil procedure impact upon substantive law. This is a particularly acute consideration for Jersey which, having inherited an adversarial system of civil procedure, draws heavily upon the English common law, whereas the character of French

[16] See in particular on this, P-G Monateri (ed), *Methods of Comparative Law* (Cheltenham, Edward Elgar, 2012); G Samuel, *An Introduction to Comparative Law Theory and Method* (Oxford, Hart Publishing, 2014).

[17] For an excellent introduction to this topic, see Samuel (n 16) and Monateri (n 16). For developments of these themes, see especially G Cuniberti, *Grands Systèmes de Droit Contemporains* (Paris, LGDJ, 2007); P Legrand, *Fragments on Law-as-Culture* (Tjeenk Willink, Deventer, 1999); B Markesinis, *Foreign Law and Comparative Methodology: A Subject and a Thesis* (Oxford, Hart Publishing, 1997); id, *Always on the Same Path: Essays on Foreign Law and Comparative Methodology* (Oxford, Hart Publishing, 2001); K Zweigert and H Kotz, *An Introduction to Comparative Law* (3rd edn, Oxford, OUP, 1998); M Siems, *Comparative Law* (Cambridge, CUP, 2014).

[18] See generally Samuel (n 16) ch 8. See also for a stimulating account of different law-making regimes in a transnational arena, G-P Calliess and P Zumbansen, *Rough Consensus and Running Code* (Oxford, Hart Publishing, 2010).

[19] See P Legrand, 'European Systems are not Converging' (1996) 45 *ICLQ* 52; R Sacco, 'Legal Formants, A Dynamic Approach to Comparative Law (I)' (1991) 39 *American Journal of Comparative Law* 1; id, 'Legal Formants, A Dynamic Approach to Comparative Law (II)' (1991) 39 *American Journal of Comparative Law* 343.

[20] There is a growing scholarly interest in microjurisdictions and small states. See, eg, the Oxford Brookes University Small Jurisdictions Service (www.sjs.brookes.ac.uk) and the Centre for Small States at Queen Mary University of London (www.smallstates.qmul.ac.uk).

civil procedure is very different and is characterised by a predominantly written procedure which is heavily reliant on documentary evidence.[21] We will see that this has an important impact on Jersey law, for instance within the context of the adoption of a subjective approach to contract law, whereby the actual intentions of the parties are taken into account, rather than the objective, external interpretation commonly associated with the common law.[22]

In understanding these difficulties, resort is often made to other systems which have long since juggled with heterogeneous sources and competing reference points.[23] Mixed systems such as the Province of Quebec in Canada or Louisiana in the United States have sometimes been taken up as such an example.[24] And yet, there are examples closer to home, which illustrate, over and above geographical proximity, similarities from a cultural and socio-legal perspective. In this book, it will be shown that the jurisdiction of Jersey, with its mixed origins, deriving from Norman customary law but highly influenced in recent times by the common law, can be seen as a fruitful subject of comparative law study in and of itself.

## II. Scope of the Study

A word must also be said about the scope of this book. As is well known, civil law systems commonly categorise a broad swathe of private law under the umbrella of 'the law of obligations'. Stemming back to Roman law classification, one finds the French civil law topics of contracts, delict and restitution (known as *quasi-contracts*) grouped together within the category of 'obligations' in a way that is not necessarily natural for a common lawyer.[25] The influence of the civil law categorisation may be detected in the law of Jersey, and reference will thus be made across the scope of obligations, including tort law and *quasi-contracts*. The focus of this book, however, is upon one discrete part of the law of obligations, namely the Jersey law of contract.

[21] See generally J Bell, S Boyron and S Whittaker, *Principles of French Law* (2nd edn, Oxford, OUP, 2008) ch 4; J Beardsley, 'Proof of Fact in French Civil Procedure' (1986) 34 *American Journal of Comparative Law* 459.

[22] See pp 44–47 below.

[23] S Farran, E Orucu, and S Patrick, *A Study of Mixed Legal Systems: Endangered, Entrenched or Blended* (Farnham, Ashgate, 2014).

[24] VV Palmer, *Mixed Jurisdictions Worldwide: The Third Legal Family* (Cambridge, CUP, 2012); S Farran, E Orucu and S Patrick, *A Study of Mixed Legal Systems: Endangered, Entrenched or Blended* (Farnham, Ashgate, 2014). See also the stimulating analysis of I Castelluci, 'How Mixed Must a Mixed System Be' (2008) 12(1) *Electronic Journal of Comparative Law*, May.

[25] This, however, is changing: see, eg, the structure of A Burrows (ed), *English Private Law* (3rd edn, Oxford, OUP, 2013) in respect of which Part IV is entitled 'The Law of Obligations'; and more recently, A Burrows (ed), *Principles of the English Law of Obligations* (Oxford, OUP, 2015).

As we shall see in the next chapter, the sources of the Jersey legal system are somewhat heterogeneous, making it a strikingly open legal system,[26] and comparative law is thus an accepted and important part of the development of the law.[27] Following this tradition, copious reference will be made to just such external sources. Analysis will thus be made of the English law of contract. The French law of contract is of course primarily to be found, as one would expect in a codified system, in the French Civil Code. Whilst this is true for the core aspects of contract law, it should not be overlooked that a number of important issues related to contract law are included in other codes such as the Code de commerce or the Code de la consommation. In order to address this fragmentation, and also to modernise codified provisions which in many ways have not evolved since the original version of the French Civil Code in 1804, a strong movement in France has developed in favour of an update and clarification of the French law of contract and, more broadly, the law of obligations. Different projects have emerged. First, the 'Avant-projet de réforme du droit des obligations et de la prescription' (also known as the 'Rapport Catala')[28] was undertaken by a team of academics, directed by Professor Pierre Catala, and was handed over to the French Minister of Justice, Pascal Clément, in September 2005. Second, the Terré report, headed up by leading academic Professor François Terré under the auspices of the Académie des Sciences morales et politiques was published in 2008.[29] This had a significant influence on the third reform effort, launched by the French Ministry of Justice in 2015, and finalised in early 2016. This project has resulted in a radical overhaul and modernisation inter alia of the contract law provisions of the French Civil Code.[30] A draft reform by means of Ordonnance was published in February 2015, with a consultation period running until April 2015; after the review process before the Conseil d'Etat, the Ordonnance was implemented in February 2016 and is due to enter into force in October 2016.[31] This book will therefore draw upon the new provisions of the Civil Code as part of the comparative exercise. Over and above these purely domestic French reform projects, we will also refer to the various international projects, as an interesting reference point for current thinking on contract law reform, which draw upon sources from a number of legal families.

[26] On this notion, see R David and C Jauffret-Spinosi, *Les Grands Systèmes de Droit Contemporains* (Paris, Éditions Dalloz, 2001) paras 270 et seq.

[27] S Nicolle, *The Origin and Development of Jersey Law: An Outline Guide* (5th edn, St Helier, Jersey and Guernsey Law Review, 2009) para 1.2.

[28] *Avant-projet de réforme du droit des obligations et de la prescription*, sous la direction de P Catala (La documentation française, 2006). An electronic version is accessible on the French Ministry of Justice's website in French, English, German, Spanish and Italian versions: www.justice.gouv.fr/index.php?rubrique=10047&ssrubrique=10049&article=11944 (last accessed 18 February 2016).

[29] F Terré, *Pour une Réforme du Droit des Contrats* (Paris, Dalloz, 2008).

[30] See more generally: www.textes.justice.gouv.fr/textes-soumis-a-concertation-10179/reforme-du-droit-des-contrats-27897.html (last accessed 18 February 2016). Plans are now afoot for a reform of the tort law provisions of the Civil Code http://www.textes.justice.gouv.fr/art_pix/avpjl-responsabilite-civile.pdf.

[31] Ordonnance No 2016-131 du 10 février 2016 portant réforme du droit des contrats, du régime général et de la preuve des obligations.

# 2

# A Mid-Channel Jurisdiction—Jersey as a Mixed Legal System

## I. Introduction

It is difficult to appreciate the contemporary position of a legal system without knowing about its origins. This is very much the case of the common law, evolving as it does in its characteristically incremental way over time. The historical dimension is also imperative in the Channel Islands, as the hybrid nature of the sources of law there is attributable to the particular history of those islands. We will here first analyse the historical background. This historical analysis will be followed by an overview of the current approach to sources in Jersey, and then more specifically the sources of the law of contract. A final section will then be given over to the analysis of the particular mindset or *mentalité* of a Channel Island lawyer.

## II. Historical Background

The sources of law in Jersey are of an unusual and heterogeneous nature. The customary law of Jersey is based upon that of the Duchy of Normandy, and this continues to be the foundation of Jersey law.[1] The significance of Norman law is a product of the history of the Channel Islands, and whilst this is not the place for an exhaustive historical account of the sources of law in the Channel Islands,[2] it is important to place the discussion of the Jersey law of contract within its broader historical context.

[1] See *Snell v Beadle* [2001] UKPC 5, [17]–[18.]

[2] For an excellent overview, see S Nicolle, *The Origins and Development of Jersey Law: An Outline Guide* (5th edn, St Helier, Jersey and Guernsey Law Review, 2009); J Kelleher 'The Sources of Jersey Contract Law' (1999) 3 *Jersey Law Review* 17. See also the very informative discussion in G Dawes's introduction to G Terrien, *Commentaires du Droict Civil tant public que privé Observé au Pays & Duché de Normandie* [1574] (Guernsey Bar, 2010).

As is well known, the Channel Islands were, until the thirteenth century, part of the Duchy of Normandy, and thus subject to Norman customary law. That long association between continental and insular Normandy ceased in 1204 on the occasion of the historical separation between Jersey and Normandy when King John was deprived of the Duchy of Normandy by Philippe Augustus, King of France, thereby putting an end to the English sovereigns' historical connection with continental Normandy, stretching back to William the Conqueror's conquest of England. Whilst the Channel Islands became a dependency of the English Crown after the separation, the customary law of Jersey continued to be drawn from Norman customary law,[3] which itself developed and evolved over time.[4] In terms of sources of law, purists would therefore argue that the starting point for any analysis of Jersey law is the position of Norman customary law as at 1204. As we shall see, however, if that was the case, then there would be little, if any, content to the Jersey law of contract.

Norman law had formed into a cohesive oral body by the late eleventh century[5] and was eventually expressed in written form very early in the thirteenth century in the form of a text entitled *Le Très Ancien Coutumier de Normandie*, an unofficial compilation of Norman customary law.[6] Local Jersey practitioners were naturally drawn to this account of customary law.[7]

In understanding Jersey law at the time, reference must thus be made to the various sources of Norman customary law during that period. Over and above the aforementioned *Le Très Ancien Coutumier de Normandie*, these sources include *Le Grand Coutumier de Normandie*,[8] the work of an unknown practitioner and thought to date between 1235 and 1258,[9] and used extensively in the Island, as well as the various *Styles de Procéder*[10] and a commentary on the Grand Coutumier known as the *Glose*. This collection of customary law texts, referred to as the *Ancienne Coutume*, was followed in the sixteenth century by an official revised version of Norman customary law produced on royal authority.[11] Appearing in 1583, the *Coutume Reformée* drew together the local customs of Normandy (including the *Ancienne Coutume* and later developments), but also cast its net

[3] Although it might have been thought that the English common law would naturally be extended to the Channel Islands, Norman customary law continued to apply, which documentary evidence suggests was at the acquiescence of Kings John and Henry III: see R Falle and J Kelleher, 'The Customary Law in Relation to the Foreshore' (2010) 14 *Jersey and Guernsey Law Review* 124, 125–28.

[4] Nicolle (n 2) para 11.7.

[5] On this, see further Kelleher (n 2).

[6] See further Nicolle (n 2) s 4.

[7] As was noted in the leading modern Jersey case of *The State of Qatar* (1999) 3 *Jersey Law Review* 118, 123.

[8] Also known in Jersey as the Summa of Mansel (variously spelt as Mancael or Maukael).

[9] Kelleher (n 2).

[10] Including the fourteenth-century *Ancien Style*, the *Nouveau Style* and the *Le Style de 1515* which are contained in Le Rouillé's 1539 edition of the *Grand Coutumier*, and were subsequently cited by the two influential seventeeth-century commentators Le Geyt and Poingdestre.

[11] Stemming back to a 1453 Order of Charles VII of France.

wider to draw from the *ius commune*.[12] Whilst there are legitimate concerns about how authoritative the *Coutume Reformée* is as a source of law within the Island's legal system,[13] due to the fact that by this time the paths of Normandy and Jersey had diverged for a period of almost four centuries, it should not be overlooked that much of the content of the *Coutume* had been assimilated into Jersey customary law.[14]

The *Ancienne Coutume* was also supplemented by various commentaries, relied upon by the jurists in the Channel Islands, which is another striking and distinctive feature of the Channel Island's approach to sources. Prominent amongst these local commentaries is Terrien's elegant sixteenth-century commentary on Norman customary law.[15] As Dawes notes: 'Terrien was not just the last and principal authority for unreformed Norman customary law; but he also paved the way for its reform.'[16] The relevant authorities reaffirm the specific position of Terrien in elucidating the unreformed Norman customary law.[17] Dawes thus concludes that:

> Terrien continues to be an important authority for Jersey law in those areas where Jersey law continues to look to customary law, whilst taking account also of later commentators of the reformed custom, Pothier, the *Code civil* itself and, again when appropriate, modern French law.[18]

Other commentators have been influential in Jersey, including the 'distinguished duo of Lieutenant Bailiffs'[19] Poingdestre and Le Geyt in the late seventeenth and early eighteenth centuries, as well as the French jurist Robert-Joseph Pothier and, more recently, Charles Le Gros.[20] The first two of these commentators provide an understanding of how Jersey law had developed in the early seventeenth century. Jean Poingdestre was born in 1609, and was appointed Lieutenant Bailiff in 1669, a post he held until 1676 and continued thereafter as a Jurat (lay judge of the Royal Court). He was the author of a number of texts on Jersey law, including *Les Commentaires sur l'Ancienne Coutume de Normandie*[21] and *Les Lois et Coutumes*

[12] As did Scotland: see Lord Hope, 'The Role of the Judge in Developing Contract Law' (2011) 15 *Jersey and Guernsey Law Review* 6, 7.

[13] R Southwell, 'The Sources of Jersey Law' (1997) 1 *Jersey Law Review* 221.

[14] See eg *Report of the Civil Law Commissioners* (1861) para iii.

[15] Terrien (n 2).

[16] Dawes' introduction to Terrien (n 2) 33.

[17] In *La Cloche v La Cloche* [1870] UKPC 14, a case concerning the construction of a will of a testator domiciled in Jersey at the time of death, and thus subject to the law of Jersey, the Privy Council commented that: 'The commentary of Terrien, therefore, may be reasonably regarded as the best evidence of the old custom of Normandy, and also of the Channel Islands before the separation of Normandy from the English Crown.'

[18] See Dawes's introduction to Terrien (n 2) 53.

[19] Ibid, 111.

[20] C Le Gros, *Traité du Droit Coutumier de L'Ile de Jersey* [1943] (St Helier, Jersey and Guernsey Law Review, 2007).

[21] Published in 1907 by the Jersey Law Society, and available at: www.jerseylaw.je/Publications/Library/JerseyLawTexts/poin01/default.aspx (last accessed 29 January 2016).

*de l'Ile de Jersey*.[22] Poingdestre's work has been cited in a number of Jersey cases, such as *Gallichan v Gallichan*[23] (on cause), *West v Lazard Brothers*[24] (on *dol*) and *Steelux Holdings Ltd v Edmonstone*[25] (on *dol par reticence*). Philippe Le Geyt was born in 1635. He was successively a Greffier (Officer of the Royal Court) and then Jurat before being appointed Lieutenant Bailiff in 1676 as successor to Poingdestre. His principal works were *Constitution, Lois et Usages*[26] and *Privilèges, Loix et Coustumes*.[27] These works were only published well after his death, and have been cited in a number of cases such as *Deacon v Bower*[28] (on nullity) and *Gallichan v Gallichan*[29] (on cause), and have been attributed with a certain authority on Jersey law matters.[30]

Charles Le Gros was born in Jersey in 1867. He was educated at the University of Caen, and returned to the island to practise law first as a Jersey solicitor, and then as a Jersey advocate, later serving as the Bâtonnier, the chair of the Jersey Bar. In 1929, Le Gros entered public service in Jersey and was appointed as Vicomte, and then Lieutenant Bailiff in Jersey. In parallel to his professional life, Le Gros was a scholar of the laws and customs of the island, and this gave rise to the *Traité du Droit Coutumier de l'Ile de Jersey*, published in 1943.[31]

In the rich constellation of sources of Jersey law, greater space must be given over to the eighteenth-century French jurist Robert-Joseph Pothier, as we shall see below.

## III. Sources of Law in Jersey: The Particular Position of Jersey Contract Law

### A. Introduction

If the definitive position for the law of contract in the Channel Islands is to be taken as 'the separation' in 1204, then any analysis of the Jersey law of contract

[22] Published in 1928 by the Jersey Law Society, and available at: www.jerseylaw.je/Publications/Library/JerseyLawTexts/poin02/default.aspx (last accessed 29 January 2016)

[23] *Gallichan v Gallichan* (1954) JJ 57, 62–63.

[24] *West v Lazard Brothers* 1993 JLR 165, 302.

[25] *Steelux Holdings Ltd v Edmonstone* 2005 JLR 152, at 157.

[26] P Le Geyt, *La Constitution, les Lois, et les Usages de Cette Ile*, tomes 1–4 (reprinted 1846, St Helier), available at: www.jerseylaw.je/Publications/Library/JerseyLawTexts/legeyt01/default.aspx (last accessed 29 January 2016).

[27] P Le Geyt, *Privilèges, Loix et Coustumes de l'Ile de Jersey* (reprinted 1953, St Helier), available at: www.jerseylaw.je/Publications/Library/JerseyLawTexts/legeyt02/default.aspx (last accessed 29 January 2016).

[28] *Deacon v Bower* (1978) JJ 39, 51.

[29] *Gallichan v Gallichan* (1954) JJ 57, 62–63.

[30] Described by the Privy Council 'as high an authority as can be produced on the local law of Jersey' (*Godfray v Godfray (Jersey)* [1866] UKPC 7, 14).

[31] Le Gros (n 20).

would be very thin indeed. At first blush, Norman customary law would not appear to be of great assistance in terms of the rules of Jersey contract law. Indeed, one authoritative commentary of French customary law undertaken by Charles Giraud notes that: '[T]he customs did not have ... a general theory of obligations nor a specific theory of different contracts, with the exception of certain particular rules relating to the sale of ... certain merchandise.'[32] Indeed, the *Très Ancien Coutumier* contains very little on contract law.[33] Kelleher thus observes in a Channel Islands' context, '[i]f we are to be restricted to pre-1204 customary law we are left without a theory of contract law, without even a concept of consensual obligations'.[34]

That initial position should, however, be nuanced. A French writer, Jean Yver, has, in an interesting exercise of legal archaeology, examined the position of contracts in eleventh- to thirteenth-century Normandy.[35] In a detailed study, working from primary sources, including Charters, case law compilations and customary documents, as well as the *Etablissements de Rouen*,[36] Yver traces the evolution of contractual mechanisms during the period. Whilst there was clearly no general theory of contracts, Yver's work shows that there was nevertheless a series of specific, ad hoc instruments, corresponding to the conception of a contract. These covered both contracts subject to specific formalities, such as the instrument of *fides*, as well as a series of embryonic consensual contracts, often linked to credit and security. Yver's study shows the importance of the canon law influences. However, it is also clear that Roman law had an important place as well. Indeed, Giraud's study concluded that, in the absence of a general theory of contract, 'everything was—in part at least—governed by Roman law'.[37] The resort to Roman law is also confirmed by Poingdestre.[38]

The aforementioned commentaries thus illustrate the importance of Roman law within the traditional sources relied upon to shape the Jersey law of contract. The Privy Council even asserted in the case of *Benest v Pipon*[39] that: 'The Roman law relative to prescription has been adopted into the law of Normandy, which prevails in Jersey.'[40] In the case of *Mendonca v Le Boutillier*[41] the Royal Court held that Jersey 'takes its authority in the matter of contract from Roman law'.[42]

[32] C Giraud, *Précis de l'Ancien Droit Coutumier Français* (Durand, Paris, 1852) 61.

[33] On this issue, see the detailed analysis of J Yver, *Les Contrats dans le très ancien droit Normand* (Paris, Domfront, 1926) 17. Yver notes, however, that more information on contracts is to be found in the *Grand Coutumier de Normandie*, albeit the text is of not great clarity on this point, and is described by Yver as 'the worst part of all the tome' (ibid, 17).

[34] Kelleher (n 2).

[35] Yver (n 33).

[36] Dating from around 1180, and which Yver describes as 'governing matters of debts' and which represented the 'only official regulation of the law of obligations ... in Normandy' (ibid, 14).

[37] Giraud (n 32) 61.

[38] As noted by Nicolle (n 2) para 13.4.

[39] *Benest v Pipon* (1829) 1 Knapp 60, cited in Nicolle (n 2) para 13.12.

[40] *Benest v Pipon* (1829) 1 Knapp 60, 69.

[41] *Mendonca v Le Boutillier* 1997 JLR 142, 150. See also *Maynard v Public Services Committee* [1995] JLR 65, 78.

[42] *Mendonca v Le Boutillier* 1997 JLR 142, 145. References were made to the importance of Roman law in *Attorney General v Foster* 1989 JLR 70, 83.

The Roman law influences are also complemented by the relevance of the *ius commune* within the Channel Islands. Indeed, the *ius commune* was particularly influential within Jersey, supplementing the *Coutume Reformée*, as well as influencing the purely local customary law.[43] As was noted in the decision of the Privy Council in *Snell v Beadle*, '[l]ike other customary law systems, Jersey law had recourse to the *ius commune* for areas not covered by municipal customary law'.[44]

However, in the spectrum of various sources of law in Jersey, the most visible sign of civil law influences is the reliance placed upon civil law writers. Domat's writings[45] have thus been referred to on many occasions by the courts.[46] The example par excellence of reliance upon French civil law commentators is, however, that of Pothier. The influence of Pothier has been considerable, and his writings have—in some ways quite surprisingly—developed to become one of the primary sources of the Jersey law of contract.

## B. The Overaching Influence of Pothier

A word will first be said about Pothier, and his work, before examining his impact in Jersey.[47] The eighteenth-century French jurist Robert-Joseph Pothier[48] was a writer on both customary and civil law who, as is well known, greatly influenced French law. Pothier's primary activity was as a judge. At the age of 21, Pothier was appointed *Conseiller du roi, juge magistrat au bailliage* and *siège présidial d'Orléans*. He carried out his judicial role for over fifty years and was particularly engaged in striving to make the justice system more efficient, swifter and more humane. Following the death of Professor Prévost de la Jannès, Pothier was designated in 1750 by Louis XV, to occupy the Professorship of French Law *(Chaire de droit français)*, at the Orleans law faculty. The King also allowed him to carry on his judicial functions. Pothier was acclaimed for his teaching, and he is said to have developed innovative teaching methods based upon concrete examples drawn from everyday life in eighteenth-century Orléans.[49]

Pothier never adhered to the Enlightenment philosophy,[50] and he was, not during the Revolution, quoted in the Revolutionary Assemblies' debates, nor is he mentioned within the preliminary reports to the first two projects of the Code civil written respectively in 1793 and 1794. It is likely that he was perceived as

[43] Nicolle (n 2) para 13.8.

[44] *Snell v Beadle* [2001] UKPC 5, [20].

[45] Such as *Traité des Lois Civiles* of 1689.

[46] See eg *Benest v Pipon* (1829) 1 Knapp 60, 69 (Privy Council).

[47] See the elegant analysis in C MacMillan, *Mistakes in Contract Law* (Oxford, Hart Publishing, 2010) ch 5.

[48] 9 January 1699–2 March 1792.

[49] J-L Sourioux, 'Aperçu de la vie de Robert-Joseph Pothier' in J Monéger, J-L Sourioux et A Terrasson de Fougères (eds), *Robert-Joseph Pothier, d'hier à aujourd'hui* (Paris, Economica, 2001) 19.

[50] J-L Halperin, 'La lecture de Pothier par la doctrine du XIXème siècle', in ibid, 66.

being emblematic of the *Ancien droit*.[51] Nevertheless, the name of Pothier was quoted during the presentation of the third Civil Code project in 1796 and it is likely that this growing influence was explained by the gradual evolution of the codification movement towards a compromise between the *Ancien droit* and the revolutionary approach.

The true impact of Pothier commenced during the Restoration period.[52] Pothier is perceived as being one of the most important sources for the drafting of the Code civil for at least two reasons. First, much of the content of the Code civil was inspired by his publications. Second, and contrary to the oft-perceived view of the Code civil as a clean break from the past, there was a real desire to attempt to bridge the *Ancien droit* and the Code civil, and thus his works were a natural reference point.

### *(i) Pothier's Influence on the Common Law*

Pothier's role in the civil law is well documented. Less recognition has, however, been given to Pothier's influence beyond the borders of France, and yet his writing has had a profound impact on English as well as American law.[53] Pothier's first publications were recognised and appreciated from an early date in England and United States,[54] and particularly from the time when his works were translated into English.[55] The most striking example of his impact on US law is the Supreme Court decision of *Laidlaw v Organ*.[56] Even though Chief Justice John Marshall did not ultimately adopt the principles laid down by Pothier concerning the existence of precontractual disclosure obligations, and preferred the notion of caveat emptor, Pothier's approach was extensively cited. Pothier has been cited more than a hundred times in the Case Reports of the US Supreme Court, and he is officially recognised in the US House of Representatives as one of those figures, amongst whom are Justinian and Blackstone, who established 'the principles that underlie American law'.[57]

The impact of Pothier on English law is also considerable. Ibbetson thus notes that:

> [I]n the last decade of the eighteenth century there started to appear a steady stream of treatises on the law of contract. … The model from which judges and writers derived

[51] The law under the *Ancien Régime* (ie before the Revolution—see Tocqueville's 1856 essay entitled *L'Ancien Régime et la Révolution* was made up of customary law in the north (and central France), and Roman-inspired written norms in the south.

[52] Marking the return of the French monarchy in 1814.

[53] See MacMillan (n 47) 104–06.

[54] Sir William Jones, *An Essay on the Law of Bailments* (1781, US edition) 29–30.

[55] His renown came in the common law world with a translation of his *Traité des Obligations* in two volumes undertaken by William David Evans, published in London in 1806 and in the US in 1826, 1839 and 1853.

[56] *Laidlaw v Organ* 15 US 178; 2 Wheat 111 (1817).

[57] See http//:aoc.gov/capitol-hill/relief-portrait-plaques-lawgivers/robert-joseph-pothier (last accessed 4 January 2015).

their inspiration was the *Traité des obligations* of the French jurist Robert-Joseph Pothier.[58]

Zimmerman observes similarly that: 'Pothier's treatises, accessible to English lawyers in translated versions, became one of the most influential sources [of the modern law of contract].'[59] Baker attributes to Pothier 'the seeds of the English law of offer and acceptance, mistake, frustration, and damages'.[60] The draftsman of the Sale of Goods Act, Sir Mackenzie Chalmers, was profoundly influenced by Pothier's *Traité du Contrat de Vente*.[61] Judges also cited Pothier as an authority. Best J stated that Pothier's *Treatise on the Law of Obligations* was, as an authority, 'the highest that can be had, next to a decision of a court of justice in this country'.[62]

### (ii) Pothier and the Jersey Law of Contract

In Jersey, the works of Pothier have been particularly influential. His civil law treatise *Traité des Obligations* is much cited in the case law on the law of contract, and his customary law works such as the *Coutume d'Orléans* are also influential. Indeed, such is the prestige of this writer that he has metamorphosed into a quasi-authority of Jersey law. The reasoning behind this unusual process of evolution—from foreign treatise-writer to source of law in a mid-Channel jurisdiction—is explained by a number of factors. Pothier's role both in explaining and tracing the customary law of Orléans, and his pioneering work in restating the law of obligations, through his *Traité des Obligations*, provides dual reasons of particular relevance within the Jersey legal system. As Nicolle has explained:

> Pothier thus serves as authority in two fields. Where in accordance with the usual principles of customary law interpretation, the local (Norman/Jersey) customary law requires assistance from other customary law systems … recourse may be had to his writings on the Coutume d'Orléans. … In those areas of law, eg contract, where Jersey, like other customary law systems, had little or nothing of its own and drew upon civil law … recourse may be had to his non-customary, civilian influenced works.'[63]

In the sphere of contract law, the Jersey courts have often described Pothier as the 'surer'[64] or 'surest guide'[65] to the Jersey law of contract. His works have been influential in structuring many elements of contract law. Indeed, in *Golder*,[66]

[58] D Ibbetson, *A Historical Introduction to the Law of Obligations* (Oxford, OUP, 1999) 220.

[59] R Zimmermann, *The Law of Obligations: Roman Foundations of the Civilian Tradition* (Oxford, OUP, 1996) 336–37.

[60] JH Baker, *An Introduction to English Legal History* (4th edn, Oxford, OUP, 2002) 352–53.

[61] See eg Zimmermann (n 59) 336.

[62] *Cox v Troy* (1822) 5B & Ald 474, 4808.

[63] Nicolle (n 2) para 14.12.

[64] See eg *HM Viscount v Treanor* (1969) JJ 1243, 1245.

[65] *Selby v Romeril* [1996] JLR 210, 218.

[66] *Golder v Société des Magasins Concorde* (1967) JJ 721.

the Royal Court went as far as ruling that: '[T]he principles stated by Pothier we believe to be the principles of our law.'[67] Concrete examples of Pothier's influence on Jersey case law abound, including the definition of the basic aspects of a contract,[68] the *vice de consentement* of *dol*, the notion of the *objet* of a contract,[69] the latent defect warranty (*vices cachés*),[70] the rules concerning penalty clauses[71] amongst others. Indeed, Kelleher has calculated that Pothier has been cited in approximately half of the contract law cases before the Jersey Royal Court since 1950![72]

It might seem unusual for a legal system to rely upon a doctrinal writer in such an extensive way as a source of law. Pothier is moreover a commentator from a different era, a different legal system and to some extent a different legal tradition. Indeed, even the language of Pothier's texts are foreign to a great many Jerseymen and women. However, there is, as we have seen, an intellectual and legal argument underpinning the role of Pothier in Jersey. We have already seen above the twin pillars for this influence.[73] The clarity of Pothier's civil law works, as well as their format akin to restatements, and the accessible English translations, helps explain the enduring relevance.[74] The influence of Pothier on the common law world is also of relevance, but the key factor is the way in which Pothier represents a direct and accessible route into a structured and coherent presentation of the civil law of obligations which corresponds well with the pre-existing structure and approach of Jersey law.

## C. Assessing the Relevance of Modern French Law

Much debate has occurred about the relevance of modern French law within the formal hierarchy of sources of Jersey law. From one perspective, the adoption of the French Code civil in 1804 can be seen as an obstacle to the reception of modern French law in the Jersey system, traditionally founded, as we have seen, upon the pre-existing customary law. According to such an approach, the rupture with the *Ancien Droit* as symbolised by the adoption of the Napoleonic Code meant that, from a Jersey perspective, the evolutionary process from its Norman customary origins was broken. It is true that the unification of the French systems

[67] Ibid, 730. More recently, in the case of *Flynn v Reid* [2012] JRC 100, the Royal Court acknowledged the relevance of Pothier's statements of general application (at [103]).

[68] *Golder v Société des Magasins Concorde* (1967) JJ 721; *Selby v Romeril* 1996 JLR 210.

[69] *Groom v Stock* (1965) JJ 429.

[70] *Kwanza Hotel Limited v Sogeo Company Limited* (1983) JJ 105.

[71] *Viscount v Treanor* (1969) JJ 1243; *Doorstop Ltd v Gillman and Lepervier Holdings Ltd* [2012] JRC 199.

[72] Kelleher (n 2).

[73] Namely the proximity of the customary law of Orléans with that of Normandy, and Pothier's pioneering work in restating the law of obligations.

[74] Moreover, Jersey is not the only legal system that has adopted commentaries as formal sources of law: see, for instance, the institutional writers in Scotland.

of *pays de droit écrit* in the south and *pays de droit coutumier* in the north during the post-revolutionary codifications was an important turning point in European legal history.[75] By bringing an end to the pre-existing customary law systems, including that of Normandy, a link to the Channel Islands was thus undoubtedly brought to an end. From that perspective, it could thus be argued that modern French law is merely a reference point for the law of Jersey, to be used, along with other systems, out of merely comparative law interest.

The foregoing analysis is, however, an overly simplistic one. A contrary argument can be made that as the Code civil drew upon the *Ancien Droit*, and that the writing of Pothier was of great influence on the drafting of the Code, the reference to the Code and to modern French law may therefore be a legitimate source of Jersey law. Moreover, as Dawes argues (in respect of the law of Guernsey), the '*Code civil* maintains the *esprit* of customary law to a much greater extent than English law and thereby derives its right to be consulted and cited by Guernsey lawyers'.[76]

Indeed, there is an established tradition in Jersey of looking to modern French law to supplement the understanding of concepts which are rooted in the civil law, but on which there is little Jersey authority. A number of examples may be given. In formulating the doctrine of latent defect warranty,[77] known also as the doctrine of *vices cachés* (itself deriving from the Roman law remedy of *actio redhibitoria*),[78] the Jersey courts explicitly drew upon modern French law in formulating the law. Thus, in the case of *Kwanza Hotel Limited v Sogeo Company Limited*, the Court of Appeal referred explicitly to the French Civil Code, as well as commentaries.[79] In doing so, the court noted that there was a practice in Jersey of 'referring to the law of France in commercial matters'.[80] In the earlier case of *Wood v Wholesale Electrics Ltd*,[81] on the same issue of defective goods, the Royal Court had similarly relied upon modern French authority to supplement Pothier's writings. In the case of *Benest v Pipon*,[82] the Privy Council noted, on an issue relating to prescription, that '[t]he Code Napoleon makes use of nearly the same expressions on this subject'.[83]

In a different area of contract law, in the case of *Fort Regent v Regency Suite*,[84] which concerned the issue of waiver/*renonciation*, the Royal Court looked to

[75] For a description of the period leading up to the codification process, see A von Mehren and J Gordley, *The Civil Law System: An Introduction to the Comparative Study of Law* (2nd edn, Little, Brown and Company, 1977) 48.

[76] G Dawes, 'From Custom to Code—The Usefulness of the *Code Civil* in Contemporary Guernsey Jurisprudence' (2004) 8 *Jersey Law Review* 255.

[77] Which entails that, on the sale of property or goods, there is an implied warranty that there are no hidden defects in the item sold.

[78] See Zimmermann (n 59) 317.

[79] *Kwanza Hotel Limited v Sogeo Company Limited* (1983) JJ 105, 116–18.

[80] Ibid, 113.

[81] *Wood v Wholesale Electrics Ltd* (1976) JJ 415.

[82] *Benest v Pipon* (1829) 1 Knapp 60.

[83] Ibid, 69.

[84] *Fort Regent v Regency Suite* 1990 JLR 228.

modern French authorities[85] (as well as to Nicholas's *French Law of Contract*),[86] and indeed opined that: 'We are quite satisfied that we can draw sufficient from the French authorities which have been stated time and time again in this court to be preferred.'[87] In the case of *Warner v Hendrick*,[88] on the doctrine of *réception* in contract law, the court looked to modern French law sources, in determining the contours of this doctrine.[89] Other areas of contract law have also been affected. In the case of *In the Estate of Father Amy*, Deputy Bailiff Birt recognised that the Jersey courts had drawn upon modern French law in some areas such as cause or in respect of penalties.[90] In the recent case of *O'Brien v Marett*, the French Civil Code was referred to as a reference point for understanding the notion of *erreur*.[91]

A case seen as particularly important for the relevance of modern French law is that of *Selby v Romeril*,[92] in which the Royal Court held that:

> It is true that Pothier has often been treated by this court as the surest guide to the Jersey law of contract. It is also, however, true that Pothier was writing two centuries ago and that our law cannot be regarded as set in the aspic of the 18th century. Pothier was one of those authors upon whom the draftsman of the French Code Civil relied and it is therefore helpful to look at the relevant article of that Code. … In our Judgment it may now be asserted that by the law of Jersey, there are four requirements for the creation of a valid contract, namely, consent, capacity, objet and cause.[93]

Clearly, this statement was an important one. Kelleher has summarised the impact as follows:

> The effect of this statement was to take the three requirements of a valid contract established by Pothier which had been followed in Jersey (see *Osment v Constable of St Helier*) and to recast them in the mould of Article 1108 of the Code Civil. The full implications of this extension are yet to be seen, but it cannot be other than to invite from counsel submissions based on the interpretation of this and other articles in the Code Civil made by modern French courts and writers.[94]

However, in other cases, the Jersey courts have counselled caution. The Court of Appeal thus held in *Public Services Committee v Maynard*:

> However, care has to be taken in referring to French legal texts in connection with the law of Jersey. After the Channel Islands were severed from the rest of the Norman

[85] Ibid, 232.
[86] Ibid, 233.
[87] Ibid, 233.
[88] *Warner v Hendrick* 1985–86 JLR 366.
[89] Ibid, 370–72.
[90] *In the Estate of Father Amy* 2000 JLR 80, 93.
[91] *O'Brien v Marett* [2008] JCA 178, [55]–[57].
[92] *Selby v Romeril* 1996 JLR 210.
[93] Ibid, 218.
[94] Kelleher (n 2). The judge in that case has recounted how, on the handing down of that judgment, 'some shock waves were felt in the legal profession' (P Bailhache, 'Jersey: Avoiding the Fate of the Dodo' in S Farran, E Orucu and S Patrick (eds), *A Study of Mixed Legal Systems: Endangered, Entrenched or Blended* (Farnham, Ashgate, 2014) 100).

> territories in what is now France, Norman customary law continued to develop in Jersey, Guernsey and Normandy in parallel, but not with identical developments. In Normandy, development was naturally affected by doctrines prevailing in other parts of France. The Napoleonic Codes embodied much of the pre-existing laws of the French provinces, but with some material changes. After the Napoleonic Codes came into existence, French law developed independently of developments in Jersey and Guernsey, under the direction or influence of French statutes, French jurisprudential writers and the case law of the French courts. Accordingly, no great weight can be placed on French law as it exists today in ascertaining what is Jersey law, except perhaps on a comparative basis as showing how the same problems have been treated in another legal system.[95]

In the later case of *Re Esteem Settlement*,[96] the Royal Court cited this passage with approval, and went on to say that:

> We would add respectfully that modern French law may also be of assistance if it is clear that the principles being considered originated in the old customary law and have not been subject to great change. More detailed exposition of the old principles than was undertaken by the writers on customary law is sometimes available. … the Court must always be careful, when considering writers on modern French law, to ensure that it is not inadvertently incorporating some aspect of French law which is not the same as that from which the law of Jersey is derived.[97]

However, as Nicolle has pointed out, the concluding phrase of the passage in *Maynard*[98] may be misleading:

> The history of French influence on Jersey law over the centuries suggests that the conclusion embodied in the final sentence of the above extract is an over-simplification. The continuous grafting of post-separation developments in Norman law onto the Jersey legal system, where they took root and flourished, was a recognised feature of Jersey's legal development from an early date, see Le Geyt's comments … on the assimilation of parts of the Coutume Reformée, while the assimilation of provisions from customary law systems of other parts of the *pays de droit coutumier*, from French writers on the civil law, and from post-revolutionary French law are all equally well attested and too well established to be reversed now save by legislation.[99]

Richard Southwell QC, who gave judgment of the Court of Appeal in *Maynard*,[100] has responded extra-judicially to the points made by Stéphanie Nicolle QC. In an article in the *Jersey Law Review*,[101] supplementing a previous article,[102] Southwell argues that:

> Stéphanie Nicolle is right to emphasise that throughout the period since 1204, despite the separation of mainland Normandy and these Islands, there has been a continuing

[95] *Public Services Committee v Maynard* 1996 JLR 343, 350.
[96] *Re Esteem Settlement* unreported, 17 January 2002 (reissued 11 March 2002).
[97] Ibid, para 253.
[98] *Public Services Committee v Maynard* 1996 JLR 343, 350.
[99] Nicolle (n 2) para 14.2.
[100] *Public Services Committee v Maynard* 1996 JLR 343.
[101] R Southwell, 'A Note on Sources of Jersey Law' (1999) 3 *Jersey Law Review* 213.
[102] R Southwell, 'The Sources of Jersey Law' (1997) 1 *Jersey Law Review* 221.

> influx into Jersey law of doctrines developed on the mainland of France. The law of Jersey would be far poorer if this influx had not continued after the Napoleonic Codes had replaced the customary laws of France, and down to recent times. ... However, the Court of Appeal was perhaps right to warn in *Maynard* against arbitrary dipping into French law by the courts of Jersey to use whatever titbits they might think suitable. In each case it is for the courts to ascertain what is the law of Jersey, and to rely on the French Codes and jurisprudence in their modern form only to the extent that they are shown to be continuous with the customary law before codification as stated by for example, Domat or Pothier, or by way of comparative analysis as in *Snell v Beadle*.

The Privy Council seemed to lend some support to this view in the case of *Snell v Beadle*[103] (concerning the civil law doctrine of lesion in Jersey)[104] and expressed a preference for resorting to Roman law, declaring—in rather summary fashion—that 'French law as it exists today in the French Codes or the current jurisprudence is unlikely to be of direct assistance'.[105]

In her writings, Nicolle has given a number of reasons why the Code civil and decisions made under it are of relevance.[106] She has pointed out that the Code civil in many ways perpetuated the pre-existing law and thus both the relevant provisions and related decisions provide useful light on the interpretation of the pre-existing law, applicable in Jersey.[107] Moreover, she argues that up to the end of the nineteenth century, the customary law of Jersey assimilated features of contemporary French law.[108] Finally, she points out that the Code civil has on occasion been the basis for certain Jersey legislation.[109]

Other commentators have supported such an approach. Hodge has written eloquently about, and in favour of, 'the value of the civilian strand',[110] arguing that the civil or Roman law heritage is important, and that this is a fundamental distinction from English law, which 'has developed from different origins and has relied on statute to discard inconvenient relics from the past'.[111] Dawes points out that it is wrong to view the Code civil as representing some sort of rupture with what went before, and argues that:

> If there is no obvious customary law solution to a customary law problem, then it is entirely appropriate to see what modern French law provides. ... It is striking how familiar the provisions of the Code Civil can appear to a Channel Island lawyer familiar with customary law.[112]

103 *Snell v Beadle* [2001] UKPC 5.
104 See generally Chapter 5 below.
105 At para 21, with reference to Southwell (n 101).
106 See generally Nicolle (n 2)
107 Ibid, para 14.17.1. See also *Selby v Romeril* 1996 JLR 210, 218.
108 Ibid, para 14.17.3.
109 Ibid, para 14.17.2. The references given by Nicolle do not, however, include statutes relating to contract law.
110 P Hodge, 'The Value of the Civilian Strand' in P Bailhache (ed), *A Celebration of Autonomy: 1204–2004, 800 Years of Channel Islands' Law* (St Helier, Jersey Law Review, 2005).
111 Ibid, 44.
112 G Dawes, 'Citation from other Legal Systems: A Reply' (2004) 1 *Jersey Law Review* 69.

It should moreover be observed that the Jersey Law Commission in its *Final Report on the Jersey Law of Contract* underlined the importance of modern French law, subject to certain safeguards:

> French law has played, and still does play, a significant role in the development of Jersey contract law. Given the origins of Jersey law it is of no surprise that the Ancienne Coutumier, the Coutumé Reformée, French writers or the Code Civil are frequently used as authority.[113]

From many perspectives, it is not surprising that Jersey continues to draw upon civil law concepts. The very genetic structure of Jersey contract law is that of a civil law system, deriving from Norman customary law. This is not merely a historical feature, but it can be seen from the basic building blocks of the Jersey law of contract, which include concepts such *la convention fait la loi des parties*, the notion of *cause*, the notion of consent/*volonté*, and the corollary concept of *vices de consentement* (to mention but a few). Within this context, the resort to modern civil law influences is understandable. If the DNA of a system is of a civil law provenance, then it is likely that transplants from a similar culture will be appropriate. From that perspective, it is logical that the courts and commentators should look to modern French law, albeit simply as *persuasive* rather than binding authority, for guidance as to the development of the law of contract.

In parallel with the civil law, another other legal system which, in recent times, has had a marked influence on the Jersey law of contract is that of England and Wales.

## D. The Impact of English Law of Contract

Traditionally, the impact of the common law in Jersey contract law was minimal[114] as the historic links to the Norman customary law, and the reliance on civil law writers, such as Pothier, posed a natural barrier to the transplantation of English law. A distinction could thus be drawn with other areas of Jersey law, such as criminal law or tort law, where the influence has traditionally been much greater.[115] More recently, however, a shift in approach to contract law occurred, with an increased influence of the English common law.

Nicolle detected signs of the influence of English law during the nineteenth century, as the Jersey courts started to regard it 'of relevance, if not as authority'.[116]

[113] At para 7.

[114] See on this, *Fort Regent v Regency Suite* 1990 JLR 228, 233; *Wood v Wholesale Electrics Ltd* (1976) JJ 415, 425.

[115] Although this can lead to uncertainty in borderline cases, most notably between tort and contract, eg the issue of precontractual liability which under French law sounds in delict—see Chapter 3 below, at 52–58.

[116] Nicolle (n 2) para 15.16.

Initially, resort to English law may not have been born from a conscious and deliberate shift in approach to the formal sources. As Nicolle explains:

> The 1960s and 1970s saw sporadic reliance upon English principles of contract law. It is at times difficult to escape the feeling that this owed as much to inability or disinclination of counsel to cite proper authority to the courts as to any considered conviction that English law was the appropriate authority to cite.[117]

Indeed, this is borne out by judicial statements. There are a number of cases in which Jersey judges have expressed disappointment at the fact that counsel has relied solely upon English law,[118] to the detriment of either French law,[119] or, more strikingly, to Jersey authority itself.[120]

In other cases, the courts have simply assumed that English law has 'much in common' with Jersey law,[121] and then went on to apply the relevant English authorities. Indeed, in the case of *Kwanza Hotels Ltd v Sogeo Co Ltd*,[122] the Royal Court went as far as to state that it has 'been the practice of the Court for many years to have regard also to the law of England in cases where no clear precedent was to be drawn from the law of Jersey'.[123] This approach may in part explain why the issue in question, the doctrine of *vices de consentement* (factors vitiating consent), has evolved into such a confused state, a suspicion perhaps confirmed by the assertion of the Royal Court in *Kwanza* that 'the principles enunciated by Domat and Pothier have much in common with the law of England relating to misrepresentation'!![124] Difficulties also arose in *Scarfe v Walton*,[125] another case where it was asserted that English law has 'much in common' with Jersey law,[126] as the excerpts from Domat's *Les Loix Civiles* cited by the Royal Court in that case related to the circumstances in which an *action redhibitoire* (*vices cachés*) may be brought, rather than the issue of *vice de consentement*.[127]

In a number of other cases, it is recorded by the courts that the parties agreed on the application of English law, but without explaining why. A recent Jersey

[117] Ibid, para 15.17.

[118] See *Incat Equatorial Guinee Ltd v Luba Freeport Ltd* 2010 JLR 28, para 24.

[119] In the case of *La Motte Garages Ltd v Morgan* 1989 JLR 312 the Court underlined that it was somewhat disappointing that the parties had relied on English law, rather than 'mine the rich lodes of our ancient French law'.

[120] In *Donnelly v Randalls Vautier Ltd* 1991 JLR 49 counsel's preference for citing English case law and thereby omitting Jersey case law was lamented: 'The court, although entitled to rely heavily upon English authorities, particularly in this kind of case, must always have regard first and foremost to Jersey law and it is disappointing to note that neither counsel has deemed it appropriate to cite Jersey authority' (57).

[121] See eg *Scarfe v Walton* (1964) JJ 387, 393; *Kwanza Hotels Ltd v Sogeo Co Ltd* (1981) JJ 59, 65.

[122] *Kwanza Hotels Ltd v Sogeo Co Ltd* (1981) JJ 59. The case was subject to appeal to the Court of Appeal: (1983) JJ 105.

[123] *Kwanza Hotels Ltd v Sogeo Co Ltd* (1981) JJ 59, 65.

[124] Ibid. See further discussion of this topic below.

[125] *Scarfe v Walton* (1964) JJ 387.

[126] Ibid, 393.

[127] See discussion at p 106 below.

decision has, however, addressed this issue openly. The case of *Toothill v HSBC Bank plc*[128] concerned proceedings brought by a bank against Mr and Mrs Toothill for the repayment of loans and an overdraft. Mrs Toothill resisted repayment on the basis that the bank was guilty of misrepresentation by conduct and *dol par réticence* (or misrepresentation by non-disclosure) by failing to inform her that the loans did not conform to its lending guidelines. She also claimed that she had entered two of the loans and the overdraft under the undue influence of her husband. On the issue of sources of law, counsel for the plaintiff[129] conceded during the hearing that as she was not aware of any Norman or French principles which might assist, she would have to rely upon the English law principles laid down in the well-known cases of *Barclays Bank PLC v O'Brien*[130] and *Royal Bank of Scotland plc v Etridge (No 2)*.[131] Counsel for both parties thus accepted that on this issue, the law of Jersey should be similar to that of England as outlined in these two cases.[132]

In the decision, the Court approved this position and went on to articulate pragmatic reasons why resort should be had to English law in such a case. The Court explained that this position was consistent with the underlying policy factors:

> There are strong policy grounds for thinking that the law in this jurisdiction should be the same as in England. The majority of banks who lend money on the security of immovable property in the Island are UK-owned. Their guidelines and procedures have been established in accordance with the clear judicial guidance offered in Etridge and their personnel will have been trained accordingly. Furthermore, the competing policy considerations referred to by Lord Nicholls in the passage quoted in para 24 above are equally applicable in Jersey and a solution which addresses both considerations needs to be found. In our judgment, the position established in Etridge achieves a proper balance between these competing considerations and we hold the law of Jersey to be of like effect.[133]

In practice, there are now areas of the Jersey law of contract where English authorities are regularly cited. As we shall see below, this clearly is the case in respect of the remedy of damages. English law has also exercised an important influence in another sphere of remedies, that of *résolution*.[134] On the other hand, however, in respect of the adjacent topic of the remedy of specific performance, the Jersey courts have not been prepared to adopt the principles of English law, holding on

[128] *Toothill v HSBC Bank plc* 2008 JLR 77.

[129] The terminology of 'plaintiff' continues to be used in Jersey and so will be adopted here throughout.

[130] *Barclays Bank PLC v O'Brien* [1994] 1 AC 180, [1993] 3 WLR 786, [1993] 4 All ER 417, [1994] 1 FLR 1.

[131] *Royal Bank of Scotland plc v Etridge (No 2)* [2002] 2 AC 773.

[132] *Toothill v HSBC Bank plc* 2008 JLR 77, 89.

[133] Ibid.

[134] The Royal Court in *Hamon v Webster* (unreported, 19 July 2002) held that, except in relation to leases where special rules apply, the Jersey courts prefer the English law approach (para 67).

the contrary that '[i]n our view, the word "equity" in Jersey corresponds mainly to the French *équité*'.[135] This has led the Jersey Law Commission to describe this area of the law as illustrative of the 'uncertainties that are inherent in seeking to ascertain the Jersey law of contract'.[136] This cherry-picking approach to the sources of the law of contract has caused complexity and has not advanced the cause of legal certainty.

## E. Brief Conclusion on Sources

The sources of the Jersey law of contract remain a somewhat contested issue. As we have seen, the civil law was traditionally a source of influence. However, more recent Jersey cases have illustrated a strong gravitational pull towards English law. The enactment of the Supply of Goods and Services (Jersey) Law 2009 reinforces this tendency, given the fact that the 2009 Law is based upon English statutes.[137] The close ties with the UK provide cultural and economic reasons to draw upon the stock of ideas and concepts of the common law, as does the fact that the members of the Jersey legal profession (as well as a majority of Jersey Court of Appeal judges) are primarily educated at English universities and law schools.[138] The tendency to draw upon English law has, however, been questioned, sometimes by prominent sources. For instance, the Jersey Law Commission in its Consultation Paper on the Jersey law of contract observed that:

> [I]t is noteworthy that English law has in recent years influenced Jersey contract case law. It is questionable, however, from a strict jurisprudential view, whether there are any circumstances when English law should be followed.[139]

Indeed, in some recent cases, the Jersey judiciary has indicated a more sceptical attitude to the use of English law. In the case of *Incat Equatorial Guinee Ltd v Luba Freeport Ltd*, Deputy Bailiff William Bailhache (as he then was) responded robustly to an attempt by one party to rely upon English sources:

> The Defendant submitted that it was useful to look at *Chitty on Contracts*, a textbook on English Contract Law and the authorities referred to therein. There seems little doubt that if one were seeking to ascertain the English Law of Contract, Chitty would be a good place to start. It may indeed be a helpful textbook in assisting the Royal Court in construction cases, where the language of a particular contract which is under consideration in the Royal Court is similar to the language which has been under consideration in the English courts. Nonetheless, it is clearly a textbook which is to be approached with some

[135] *Trollope v Jackson* 1990 JLR 192, 198. See also *Ex parte Viscount Wimborne* (1983) JJ 17, 19–22.

[136] Jersey Law Commission, *Consultation Paper: The Jersey Law of Contract* (Consultation Paper No 5, February 2002) para 10. Available at: www.lawcomm.gov.je/Contract.htm (last accessed 4 January 2015).

[137] T Hanson and C Marr, 'An Introduction to the Supply of Goods and Services (Jersey) Law 2009' [2009] *Jersey and Guernsey Law Review* 347.

[138] See generally A Binnington, 'The Law of Contract—Which Way?' in Bailhache (n 110) 61.

[139] Jersey Law Commission (n 136) para 7.

> caution insofar as the law of Jersey is concerned, as the basic principles of our law do not have the same provenance.[140]

In another decision, *Sutton v Insurance Corporation of the Channel Islands Limited*, a similar point was made:

> Of course, we accept that the paucity of contract cases coming before the Royal Court means that there will be fewer precedents available to the Court than would be perhaps desirable; but it appears to us that the Court should be cautious to declare the Law of Jersey by abstracting principles from the Law of England which have been drawn fundamentally from a different approach to the law of contract.[141]

It is true that such legal transplants from English law, if taken in isolation, can present disadvantages. The original DNA of the law of Jersey is that of Norman customary law. Jersey contract law clearly has its origins in the civil law. This is not just a historical specificity, but also impacts on language, concepts, legal reasoning and structures of the Jersey law of contract, as we shall see throughout this book. Clearly there are issues relating to accessibility of materials,[142] which are particularly acute for Norman customary law, but which also apply to modern French-language materials, given that the familiarity with French language is decreasing, even within the Jersey legal profession. However, it is difficult to escape the conclusion that, given the background, Jersey contract law has a good deal in common with the civil law (as well as in many areas with the common law). Indeed, it is quite difficult to see how Jersey lawyers can properly look to the common law for guidance on topics such as the classification and categorisation of contracts, given the presence of distinctions between lucrative/onerous transactions,[143] the notion of potestative contractual conditions (*condition potestative*),[144] or more fundamentally when the doctrine of consideration is absent from Jersey law. Similar comments could also be made about the distinctively subjective civilian approach[145] which is premised upon the parties' own consent, a notion that was again underlined recently by the Court of Appeal as adopted by Jersey law.[146] This is very different to the common law approach, as we shall see, and on which there is a good deal of debate.

[140] *Incat Equatorial Guinee Ltd v Luba Freeport Ltd* 2010 JLR 28, para 24.

[141] *Sutton v Insurance Corporation of the Channel Islands Limited* [2011] JRC 027

[142] See generally P Hodge, 'The Value of the Civilian Strand' in Bailhache (n 110).

[143] See *Re Esteem Settlement*, unreported, 17 January 2002, in which the Royal Court explained that a lucrative transaction (*'aliénations faites pour cause lucrative'*) consisted of an alienation to a volunteer, whereas an onerous transaction concerned 'an alienation made for value' (*'aliénations faites pour cause onéreuse'*) ([298]).

[144] Namely contractual obligations which depend for their fulfilment purely on the will of one of the parties. See *Groom v Stock* (1965) JJ 429, 434.

[145] See pp 38–48 below.

[146] The Court of Appeal in *O'Brien v Marett* was unambiguous on this point: '[T]he Jersey law of contract determines consent by use of the subjective theory of contract' (*O'Brien v Marett* [2008] JCA 178, [55]). See, however, the recent decision of the Jersey Court of Appeal in *Home Farm Developments Ltd v Le Sueur* [2015] JCA 242, which has generated some uncertainty on this issue. See discussion below in Chapter 3, pp 45–46.

One aspect, however, which remains a majority view is that the Jersey law of contract currently lacks the necessary coherence and clarity as to sources which is a fundamental requisite of a modern legal system.[147] We will thus examine the reform options below.[148]

## IV. The Mindset or *Mentalité* of a Channel Island Lawyer

We have seen from the perspective of sources of law that Jersey provides a fascinating example of the functioning of a hybrid legal system in a small jurisdiction, in which civil law and common law influences continue to affect the evolutionary process of the law. This unique combination of sources has had an impact on the substantive law of obligations in the Channel Islands, as we shall see. The impact has not been restricted to the substantive angle, however: there has also been a considerable impact on the mindset or *mentalité* of the Channel Island lawyer. In many ways, this impact has been as profound as the substantive dimension, and it will be argued in the following section that the traces of the hybrid approach can be seen in the following areas: the process of law-making and the evolution of case law; an open-textured approach to norms and sources of law; the methods and patterns of legal reasoning; and the role of the judge.

### A. Evolution of the Law: The Doctrine of Precedent or *Jurisprudence Constante*?

As we have already seen, not only is Jersey a civilian system without a code, but it is as a corollary a legal system in which many areas of the law are a construct of case law. In this respect, the law of obligations is no exception, with legislation only occasionally supplementing the case law on this topic. Whilst that might seem to run contrary to traditional perceptions of civil law jurisdictions, it should be recognised that, in reality, the role of case law has been important in the civil law systems as exemplified by French law,[149] particularly in terms of the law of obligations.[150]

[147] Jersey Law Commission (n 136).

[148] See Chapter 8 below, pp 176–185.

[149] Laquièze thus refers to the 'rapid rise of judicial power' in contemporary France: A Laquièze, 'Etat de Droit and National Sovereignty in France' in P Costa and D Zolo (eds), *The Rule of Law: History; Theory and Criticism* (Berlin, Springer Verlag, 2007) 281.

[150] The entirety of French tort law, expounded by a handful of succinct articles in the Civil Code, is premised upon the detailed *jurisprudence*. Note however the recent Governmental proposals to reform tort law : http://www.textes.justice.gouv.fr/art_pix/avpjl-responsabilite-civile.pdf

This therefore begs the question as to the rules governing the *evolution* of case law in Jersey. The first point to make is that, unlike in civil law systems, there is indeed a formal doctrine of precedent in Jersey. The operation of this doctrine has, however, shown marked differences with that in the common law, and has thus contributed to a very dynamic approach to the development of case law. We will examine the specific rules, and then compare these with the civil law notion of *jurisprudence constante*.

The leading authority on the doctrine of precedent in Jersey is *The State of Qatar*.[151] In this case, the Jersey Royal Court rejected the English approach to *stare decisis*, considering that the rigours of the English rules of precedent did not apply in Jersey.[152] A series of reasons were given to explain the rejection of that conception of the doctrine. Accepting the attachment to civil law, it was emphasised that, as a corollary, Jersey as a *pays de droit coutumier* has in many ways 'more in common with France than with England'.[153] An interesting parallel was drawn by the judge in that case between the French ancient régime *parlements*,[154] and the Jersey Royal Court, notably the dual judicial and law-making functions, with the latter function abandoned in both jurisdictions, first in Jersey in 1771, and then as part of the revolutionary settlement in France.[155] Even though the well-known prohibition on *arrêts de règlements* in Article 5 of the French Civil Code[156] did not have an equivalent in Jersey, the judge noted the importance in both jurisdictions of the primary sources of law (namely customary law or legislation), as well as the phenomenon of *jurisprudence constante*/settled jurisprudence whereby 'a line of cases [decide] a point in a similar way'.[157] Other, more pragmatic reasons were also given. Unlike in England, there was not the requisite 'mass of case law' which was necessary for the proper functioning of the principle of precedent, and a perfected system of law reporting was only a relatively recent development; as a result 'there is no basis in this jurisdiction upon which a system of rigid precedent could be founded'.[158]

Despite the rejection of the English approach to precedent, and the greater proximity with the civil law notion of *jurisprudence constante*, the Court noted that, in common with other legal systems, Jersey 'acknowledge[s] the persuasive force of judicial precedent'.[159] The advent of reliable law reports in Jersey

[151] *The State of Qatar* 1999 JLR 118.

[152] Ibid, 122. See the discussion of the rules of precedent in Guernsey in G Dawes, *Laws of Guernsey* (Oxford, Hart Publishing, 2003) 13–16.

[153] Ibid, 125.

[154] See generally JWF Allison, *A Continental Distinction in the Common Law* (Oxford, OUP, 1996) 138–42.

[155] Ibid, 125.

[156] 'Judges are forbidden to decide cases submitted to them by way of general and regulatory provisions.'

[157] Ibid, 125.

[158] *The State of Qatar* 1999 JLR 118, 122, 124–25.

[159] Ibid, 123.

had assisted that process, as well as institutional developments, most notably the creation of the Jersey Court of Appeal in 1961. With that background in mind, the judge set out the rules as follows:

> [The Royal Court] is generally bound by the decisions of the Court of Appeal and of course, as it always has been by the decisions of the Judicial Committee of the Privy Council sitting on appeal from the courts of this jurisdiction. We qualify the proposition only because, in our judgment, it is open to the Royal Court, as it would be to a Scottish court, to decline to follow a decision which has been invalidated by subsequent legislation or some such compelling change of circumstance. … The court is not bound by the decisions of the Judicial Committee of the Privy Council sitting on appeal from some other jurisdiction.[160]

The approach to precedent is therefore different, and much more flexible, than the traditional English approach:[161] the Royal Court may depart from its previous decisions in case of 'compelling change of circumstance'.[162] The Jersey courts have considerably loosened the shackles of the traditional English approach to *stare decisis*. This is a feature of the law which has had an important impact on the general approach of Jersey lawyers.[163] Coupled with an open approach to sources, the less restrictive methodology as regards case law authority has created a dynamic and in many ways innovative approach to the development of the law, described in one case aptly as an 'organic'[164] evolution.

In this respect, contract law is no exception. There are myriad examples where the Jersey courts have developed contract law rules in a proactive manner. One striking example of this dynamic interpretation of the law was the advent and development of the doctrine of *vice cachés*/latent warranty defect in Jersey law—a civil notion par excellence as we shall see.[165] Other examples may be cited.[166]

This organic and dynamic development of the law has, however, entailed that case law stability, and to some extent legal certainty, has been sacrificed in favour of

[160] Ibid, 125.

[161] See though how continental *jurisprudence constante* reasoning is starting to filter through into English case law, particularly through the influence of the European Court of Human Rights. This can be detected in the judgment of Lord Slynn of Hadley in *R (Alconbury Developments Ltd) v Secretary of State for the Environment, Transport and the Regions* [2003] 2 AC 295 (HL) [26], as well as in more recent cases: see analysis in M Andenas, E Bjorge and D Fairgrieve, 'A Fair Price for Violations of Human Rights?' (2014) 130 *LQR* 47, 50. See also S Pattinson, 'The Human Rights Act and the doctrine of precedent' (2015) *Legal Studies* 142.

[162] *The State of Qatar* 1999 JLR 118, 125.

[163] Note also that until the 1950s, the Jersey courts adopted a style of judgment that was similar to the French approach. Known as *jugements motivés*, these were very concise decisions, commencing with a passage which usually began 'Considérant que par la loi et côutume de cette ile …' and then provided the procedural history and an overview of the facts, followed by a short summary of the reasons for the court decision. See further *Attorney General v Weston* (1979) JJ 141; *Fogarty v St Martin's Cottage Limited* [2015] JRC 068.

[164] *Grove v Baker* 2005 JLR 348, para 13.

[165] See pp 132–139 below.

[166] There are also other striking examples of interventionist approach of the courts in Jersey, such as the review of penalty clauses, or in an *action paulienne*. See pp 31–32 below.

innovation. There are indeed examples of some instability and lack of consistency in the contract law cases, as we shall see, and the examples of *dol par reticence*[167] or the remedy of *résolution*[168] spring to mind. In the future, one of the challenges for Jersey law will be to ensure that a more settled approach can be found, which reconciles the need for legal certainty in contract law, with the ability to adapt to new circumstances, or evolution in societal expectations of a modern contract law. We will examine this issue below.[169]

## B. Methods of Legal Reasoning

The methods and patterns of legal reasoning mark an important difference between the common law and civil law systems. Whilst this may be seen in a myriad different ways,[170] it is fair to say that civil law systems have traditionally illustrated an attachment to principle-based reasoning, whereby solutions are given by means of deductive reasoning from abstract principles to factual circumstances.[171] In France, this is typified by the application of the pithy principles found in the Civil Code by the judges to the facts of cases. This attachment to conceptualism[172] thus strikes one as very different to the typical pragmatic common law approach, famously described by Lord Goff as 'principles gradually emerging from concrete cases',[173] rather than the alternative approach in continental formulations of reasoning from external and abstract formulations. To take Lord Goff's characterisation, this is an example of common lawyers reasoning upwards and outwards from the facts of the cases, rather than the civil lawyer reasoning downwards and inwards from abstract principles.[174]

Whilst it is difficult to specify with precision the exact modes of reasoning in an individual system, it is submitted that there are indications in Jersey of patterns of thinking which reflect the civil law approach. Many Jersey cases illustrate a mode of reasoning which is strikingly principle-based. In that sense, it strikes a contrast with the casuistic method which typifies common law thinking, attached as it is to jurisprudential-based reasoning and thought-patterns. Two examples will be given. The first indication of this phenomenon is to be found in the prominence

[167] See pp 94–97 below.

[168] See pp 163–166 below.

[169] See Chapter 7 below.

[170] On this see A Garapon and I Papadopoulos, *Juger en Amérique et en France* (Paris, Odile Jacob, 2003).

[171] See generally ibid.

[172] For an elegant analysis of French conceptualism and English pragmatism, see D Harris and D Tallon, 'Conclusions' in *Contract Law Today: Anglo-French Comparisons* (Oxford, Clarendon Press, 1989) 386–90.

[173] R Goff, 'The Future of the Common Law' (1997) 46 *ICLQ* 745, 753.

[174] Ibid.

of maxims in Jersey. Whilst legal maxims play a role in most legal systems,[175] the ubiquity of these abstract principles in Jersey is striking. This is very much the case in Jersey contract law, and the superstructure of the law of contract is made up of a series of such maxims. These are not just convenient summaries of a legal rule, but are instead viewed as a basic premise upon which the law of contract rests. Indeed, such is the strength and importance of these principles that courts have on occasion referred to them as 'sacred' principles.[176]

The prime place of maxims in Jersey law has thus had a tangible effect on legal reasoning. There is a detectable preference for reasoning from such principles as a basic starting point of analysis of a legal problem. Many examples of this can be found in the case law, such as the recent judgments in *Incat Equatorial Guinee Ltd v Luba Freeport Ltd*[177] (concerning the maxim of *la convention fait la loi des parties*) or *Flynn v Reid*[178] (concerning *volonté or* 'true consent') or the burden of proof in showing that a non-competition clause in an employment contract goes no wider than reasonably necessary.[179] Principle-based reasoning is particularly apparent in cases raising novel problems.[180]

The second example is related to the previous one. Over and above the importance of these maxims, other features of the Jersey law of contract are also marked by the presence of underpinning precepts, or 'conceptual systemisation',[181] which are again illustrative of principle-based reasoning. There are thus frequent references to abstract concepts, or as one judge has labelled it, '[the] philosophical theory which underpins our law of contract'.[182] This can be seen in the fundamental concept of consent or *volonté*. As we shall see,[183] this broad concept underpins the entire law of contract, determining the main elements of a contract: how a contract is formed, how it is undermined, and the effects of a contract amongst others. *Consentement* or *volonté* also links to the discussion about the subjective or objective approach to the law of contract.[184] This is an essential dichotomy in

[175] Such as the maxims of equity in common law legal systems: see eg M Levenstein, *Maxims of Equity: A Juridical Critique of the Ethics of Chancery Law* (New York, Algora, 2014).

[176] Le Gros, *Traité du Droit Coutumier de L'Ile de Jersey* (1943), in his chapter entitled 'De la Clameur Révocatoire ou Déception D'Outre-Moitié du Juste Prix' described *la convention fait la loi des parties* as follows: 'C'est un principe en quelque sorte sacré que la convention fait la loi des parties' (350). However, note the word of caution uttered by the judiciary as concerns the weight of maxims: *Wood v Establishment Committee* 1989 JLR 213, 236.

[177] *Incat Equatorial Guinee Ltd v Luba Freeport Ltd* 2010 JLR 287, [22].

[178] *Flynn v Reid* [2012] JRC 100, [21].

[179] *CPA Limited v Keogh* [2015] JRC 09, at [22].

[180] Such as the case of *Cooke v Mold* 2010 JLR 193 in which, in the absence of any Jersey authority on the rules applying to a precontractual private tender, the Royal Court reasoned from the first principles, notably the maxim of *la convention fait la loi des parties.*

[181] G Teubner, 'Legal Irritants: Good Faith in British Law or How Unifying Law Ends Up in New Divergences' (1998) 61 *MLR* 11, 21.

[182] *Cronin and Luce v Gordon-Bennet* 2003 JLR N22, para 17.

[183] See pp 36–38 below.

[184] See pp 38–47 below.

determining the key characteristics of contract law, and shows an attachment to the abstract underpinning concepts of the law of contract in a way that would seem very unusual for a common lawyer. It is not of course the existence of principles that is surprising but rather the methodological approach of the Jersey courts in taking the principle or maxims as the *starting point* of the legal reasoning, which is then applied contextually to the specific issue in question. Recent cases have illustrated the way in which the consent of the parties—interpreted in a subjective manner—has had a crucial impact on the structure and content of specific contract rules.[185]

## C. An Outward-looking Mentality

A recent trend in many jurisdictions globally has been the growing use of comparative law during the forensic process. Judges now resort to comparative law as part of the reasoning process in a way that would have been impossible even a generation ago. In some jurisdictions, this use of foreign sources has been controversial,[186] and has brought with it certain methodological and practical challenges.[187] The practice and approach of the Channel Islands legal systems provide an interesting lesson for the forensic use of comparative law within the context of an extremely open legal system.

From the perspective of sources, we have already seen above the way in which the Jersey law of contract has been formed by resort to hybrid sources, predominantly Norman customary law, supplemented in recent times by French and English law. Over and above such an approach, there has also been a broader resort to comparative law in contract law cases. Examples are legion, with references made *in extenso* to foreign sources as a matter of course in many cases. One example may be found in the case of *Attorney General v Foster*,[188] which although a case concerned with *criminal fraud* has been influential in contract cases concerning the *vice de consentment* of *dol*. In that case, in a sophisticated comparative analysis, reference was made to a series of legal systems which derived from the common sources of Roman law, including Scottish and South African law.[189]

Another unusual, albeit not unique, feature of the Jersey system is the approach to doctrinal writers. As we have already seen, reference to local commentators is commonplace. More surprising, however, is the extent to which the courts

[185] *O'Brien v Marett* [2008] JCA 178. See pp 46–47 below.

[186] See in particular J Resnik, 'Constructing the "Foreign": American Law's Relationship to Non-Domestic Sources' in M Andenas and D Fairgrieve (eds), *Courts and Comparative Law* (Oxford, OUP, 2015).

[187] See generally T Kadner, 'Is it Legitimate and Beneficial for Judges to Use Comparative Law?' (2013) 3 *ERPL* 687.

[188] *Attorney General v Foster* 1989 JLR 70. Upheld by the Court of Appeal: 1992 JLR 6.

[189] *Attorney General v Foster* 1989 JLR 70, 83.

have resorted to civil law writers such as Pothier or Domat. Whilst it might seem unusual that commentators from a different era and from a different legal system should be relied upon so heavily, we have examined the intellectual and legal foundations for the use of such sources in Jersey above.[190] Moreover, this approach accords well with the civil law roots of the system, reflecting the traditional receptiveness of civil law cultures to *la doctrine*.[191] It is also illustrative of the porous and open-textured approach to both norms and sources of law in Jersey, so that even secondary sources have contributed to shape the law in this hybrid legal system.

This outward-looking mindset, combined with the 'organic' development of the law noted above, has meant that Jersey customary law has developed over time by making use of ideas, concepts or principles regardless of their provenance in a remarkably open-minded way. This feature is perhaps a product of the fact that Jersey is a small jurisdiction, and also reflects the open economic and recent history of the island.[192] Distinctive training also perhaps plays a role—with Guernsey lawyers attending as part of their training an academic stage provided by the University of Caen so as to acquire the Certificat d'Etudes Juridiques Françaises et Normandes;[193] as well as the more recent creation of an Institute of Law in Jersey which provides training for aspiring Jersey advocates followed by a series of exams on Jersey law topics.[194]

## D. The Appropriate Role of the Judge

Many of the issues of *mentalités* which we have broached so far have been general and transversal, but a final consideration is one which, to some extent, is specific to contract law. This issue concerns the appropriate role of the Jersey courts in reviewing the content of the contractual agreement, and this is perceived somewhat differently in Jersey to that in a common law context.

It is well known that the English courts are very reluctant to intervene to review the fairness of a contract between commercial parties. The approach in Jersey is somewhat different. It is established case law that the Jersey courts will intervene, in specific circumstances, to remedy the economic imbalance in a contractual bargain. We will thus see that, by means of the ancient customary law doctrine of *déception d'outre moitié de juste prix*, certain types of real estate transaction may be challenged where the price agreed is less than 50% of the real market value at

[190] See p 15 above.

[191] See eg J Bell, *French Legal Cultures* (Butterworths, London, 2001) 78.

[192] On this, see generally Bailhache (n 94).

[193] See the description by Gordon Dawes in his dedication to Terrien, *Commentaires du Droict Civil tant public que privé Observé au Pays & Duché de Normandie* (Guernsey Bar, 2010) 53.

[194] For further details, see the website of the Institute of Law: www.lawinstitute.ac.je/

the time of sale.[195] Under this doctrine, the courts are thus in effect authorised to unravel bad bargains. Another example of this phenomenon is the notion of *cause*. As we shall see,[196] the notion of *cause* in Jersey grants the courts a potential tool for evaluating, in specific circumstances, the adequacy of reciprocal arrangements between the contracting parties, and thus provides the courts with a potentially intrusive tool for scrutinising the contractual bargain between the parties. Other examples of judicial interventionism may be cited. In the sphere of penalty clauses, the recent decision of the Royal Court in *Doorstop Ltd v Gillman and Lepervier Holdings Ltd*[197] illustrates the high-water mark of judicial intervention in this sphere, where in the context of a *commercial* loan for the purpose of completion of a property development, various aspects of the interest level attached to the loan were considered by the court to be excessive and thus the level of interest in relation to the loans was capped.[198]

These examples illustrate how, in a number of spheres of contract law, the Jersey judiciary are prepared to undertake a more interventionist role than would be readily assumed in a common law context. Whilst it is difficult to assign specific reasons for this difference in approach, it may well be reflective of broader differences in philosophy in contract law,[199] with Jersey law allowing for a more paternalistic and interventionist role of the judge. It is also possible to point to contextual factors as supporting the more prominent role of the judge in reviewing contractual bargains—such as the need to take account of fairness within a small island jurisdiction.[200] It may also be linked to broader societal concerns, and interestingly, one commentator has identified the distinctive *esprit* of Norman customary law, including an attachment to family lineage and protection of family property or *patrimoine*.[201] Whilst this may be now of predominantly historical interest, it does set a counterpoint to the historical origins of English contract law. The language of the law is also revealing in this respect: it is striking how prominent the occurrences are in Jersey contract law to terms including a moral quotient, such as *dol*,[202] good faith,[203] *équité*[204] or *bonnes moeurs*.[205]

[195] See Chapter 5, pp 113–120.
[196] See Chapter 4 below, pp 73–82.
[197] *Doorstop Ltd v Gillman and Lepervier Holdings Ltd* [2012] JRC 199.
[198] The Royal Court held that it would be 'unconscionable to give judgment for interest rates which are not moderate or reasonable': *Doorstop Ltd v Gillman and Lepervier Holdings Ltd* [2012] JRC 199, [40].
[199] In one comparative law study, it has been argued that 'French contract law is both more "moral" and more dogmatic; English contract law is both more "economic" and more pragmatic' (D Harris and D Tallon, 'Conclusions' in *Contract Law Today: Anglo-French Comparisons* (Oxford, Clarendon Press, 1989) 386.
[200] From a comparative perspective, see the discussion in Harris and Tallon, ibid, 386.
[201] see eg S Poirey, 'L'Esprit of Norman Customary Law' in Bailhache (n 110) 17.
[202] See Chapter 5 below, pp 90–97.
[203] See Chapter 3 below, pp 49–58.
[204] See Chapter 7 below, pp 157–159.
[205] See pp 33 and 36 below.

# 3

# Basic Principles of Contract Law from a Comparative Perspective

## I. Introduction

In this chapter, we will examine a series of key characteristics of the Jersey law of contract, which make for the distinctive nature of this legal system. The scope of this chapter will cover basic principles such as the importance of consent/*volonté*, subjective and objective approaches to contract law, the overriding principle of *la convention fait la loi des parties*, the requirement of reciprocity and the role of good faith in a mixed system. We will commence by examining the key principle of *la convention fait la loi des parties*, before analysing how this links to the centrality of consent in this legal system.

## II. *La Convention Fait la Loi des Parties*

One of the cornerstones of the Jersey law of contract is the principle of *la convention fait la loi des parties*. It is cited in a myriad of different Jersey cases and can be traced back to Norman customary law.[1] The principle was set out in the case of *Wallis v Taylor*,[2] where the court held that:[3]

> It is an established principle of Jersey law that 'la convention fait la loi des parties' and the Court will enforce agreements provided that, in the words of Pothier, (Oeuvres de Pothier, Traité des Obligations, 1821 edition, at p.91) 'elles ne contiennent rien de contraire aux lois et aux moeurs, et qu'elles interviennent entre personnes capables de contracter'. Where an agreement is freely entered into between responsible persons, good cause must be shown why it should not be enforced.

As with many of the underpinning maxims of the Jersey law of contract,[4] this statement clearly owes much to the influence of Pothier. But Pothier is not the only

[1] *Donnelly v Randalls Vautier Ltd* 1991 JLR 49 at 57.
[2] *Wallis v Taylor* 1965 JJ 455.
[3] Ibid, 457. See also *Basden Hotels Ltd v Dormy Hotels Ltd* (1968) JJ 911, at 919.
[4] See Chapter 2 above, pp 28–29.

civil law source: Domat set great store by the principle,[5] and whilst he recognised that the principle did admit of some exceptions,[6] Domat saw it as underpinning the operation of the whole of society. It was thus one of the fundamental societal values and was anchored in public morality.[7] The Jersey Royal Court has more recently recognised that the principle is anchored in fundamental values: '[T]he strength of the maxim lies in the rationale that a man is the best judge of his own interests, and the best rules are those freely agreed by free men.'[8]

Unsurprisingly, given its prominence in civil law writings, a similar principle can be found in French law. One of the central provisions of the Code civil on contracts is Article 1134 of the original version of the Code which lays down that:[9] 'Les conventions légalement formées tiennent lieu de loi à ceux qui les ont faites. Elles ne peuvent être révoquées que de leur consentement mutuel, ou pour les causes que la loi autorise.'[10]

This is an iconic provision of the French Civil Code, and a symbolically important one,[11] which is seen as embodying the will-theory. As Nicholas notes, it is a natural extension of this Article that 'contracts are binding because they are an explanation of the free will of the parties'.[12] This provision also seems to place contractual obligations on a similar level—as between the parties—to that of Acts of Parliament ('la loi').[13] Whilst the principle still remains a cornerstone of French law, some academics nevertheless consider that the principle has, as Professor Aynès comments, 'lost much of its strength',[14] and it is certainly true that the interventionist tendencies of the French courts have often lead to valid contracts being undermined.[15] Indeed, there has been a shift away from the importance of party autonomy and the contract as an expression of the parties' intention. Account is increasingly taken of the social impact of contracts, as well as the influence of *dirigiste* economic thinking in France, and policy goals such as

[5] *Les Loix civiles dans leur ordre naturel; le droit public, et Legum delectus* 1735, 1re partie, livre premier, titre I, ss II, VII.

[6] Ibid, 35: 'les promesses et les conventions qui violent les lois ou les bonnes mœurs, n'obligent à rien, qu'aux peines que peuvent mériter ceux qui les ont faites'.

[7] 'Tout homme étant un membre du corps de la société doit y remplir ses devoirs, et ses fonctions, selon qu'il y est déterminé par le rang qu'il occupe, et par ses autres engagements. D'où il suit, que les engagements de chacun sont comme ses lois propres.' Ibid, 31.

[8] *Doorstop Ltd v Gillman* [2012] JRC 199, [18].

[9] Commentators have pointed out that this formulation was inspired by Domat's writings: see eg L Aynès, 'Le contrat, loi des parties' in Cahiers du Conseil constitutionnel no 17, 2005.

[10] 'Agreements which have been lawfully formed bind those who have entered into them. They may be revoked only by mutual consent, or on grounds authorised by law.' It is to be noted that this formulation has been maintained, despite some terminological changes, in the new version of the Civil Code (Art 1193).

[11] Aynès (n 9).

[12] B Nicholas, *The French Law of Contract* (2nd edn, Oxford, OUP, 2005) 32.

[13] S Rowan, *Remedies for Breach of Contract* (Oxford, OUP, 2012) 82–83.

[14] Aynès (n 9).

[15] J-P Chazal, 'De la signification du mot loi dans l'article 1134, alinéa 1er du code civil' [2001] *RTD civ* 265.

consumer protection.[16] This shift is illustrated by the recent changes in the French Civil Code. The original terminology in Article 1134 has become Article 1193 of the new Code civil, with the new wording as follows: 'Les contrats ne peuvent être modifiés ou révoqués que du consentement mutuel des parties, ou pour les causes que la loi autorise.'[17]

For a common lawyer, the notion of contracts as premised upon a requirement of mutual consent—a consensus ad idem—is familiar territory (albeit that the language of the autonomy of the will is not). This is not surprising given that, as Nicholas has noted, 'the philosophical, moral and economic pre-suppositions were the same on both sides of the channel' and mutual consent remains common to both French and English classical theories of contract.[18] Despite this element of commonality, there remain vast conceptual differences, in particular in terms of consent, concerning the subjective nature of the analysis in French law.[19]

In Jersey, local commentators have adopted the notion of *la convention fait la loi des parties*. Le Gros considered that the principle was so important that it had reached the status of a 'sacred'[20] principle of Jersey law. It has thus been mentioned in numerous cases,[21] and in the recent case of *Incat Equatorial Guinee Ltd v Luba Freeport Ltd*, the then Deputy Bailiff William Bailhache specifically pointed to the commonality with modern French law.[22]

The kernel of the principle of *la convention fait la loi des parties* in the law of Jersey is thus that if an agreement has been concluded between responsible adults, then only in exceptional circumstances will the courts interfere with the contract so formed.[23] In the case of *Cronin and Luce v Gordon-Bennet*,[24] the link between the maxim of *la convention fait la loi des parties* and the theory of the autonomy of the will was explicitly made.[25] In the aforementioned case of *Incat Equatorial Guinee Ltd v Luba Freeport Ltd*, the then Deputy Bailiff William Bailhache also examined the maxim, tracing back its historical origins as follows:

> At the heart of this provision in the French Code Civil, and behind the maxim to which we are so accustomed in Jersey, is the concept that the basis of the Law of Contract is that each of the contracting parties has a volonté, or will, which binds them together

[16] See generally J Bell, S Boyron and S Whittaker, *Principles of French Law* (2nd edn, OUP, Oxford, 2008) 296–301.

[17] 'Contracts can only be modified or revoked with the mutual consent of the parties, or for one of the reasons provided for by legislation.'

[18] Nicholas (n 12) 35.

[19] See W Barnes, 'The French Subjective Theory of Contract: Separating Rhetoric from Reality' (2008) 83 *Tulane Law Review* 359, 367.

[20] Le Gros, *Traité du Droit Coutumier de L'Ile de Jersey* (1943; reprinted St Helier, Jersey and Guernsey Law Review, 2007), in his chapter entitled 'De la Clameur Révocatoire ou Déception D'Outre-Moitié du Juste Prix': 'C'est un principe en quelque sorte sacré que la convention fait la loi des parties' (350).

[21] See eg the recent decision of *Cooke v Mold* [2010] JRC 093, [24].

[22] *Incat Equatorial Guinee Ltd v Luba Freeport Ltd* 2010 JLR 287, [21] et seq.

[23] See *Wallis v Taylor* (1965) JJ 455.

[24] *Cronin and Luce v Gordon-Bennet* 2003 JLR N22.

[25] Ibid, para 17.

and requires that the mutual obligations which they have agreed be given effect by the courts. The notion of volonté as the foundation of the contract is sometimes thought to result from the political liberalism of the age of reason and of the economic liberalism of the 19th century where obligations imposed from outside should be as few as possible. A man is bound only by his will, and because he is the best judge of his own interests, the best rules are those freely agreed by free men. However it is to be noted that rather earlier the same rationale appears in the commentaries of *Berault, Godefroy and d'Aviron on the Coutume Reformée du Pais Duché de Normandie Tome 1* p74, this edition being published in 1684, where the authors say this:

> 'Car la volonté est le principal fondement de tous contracts, laquelle doit avoir deux conditions, la puissance et la liberté ...'[26]

Before we turn to examine further the issue of consent in the law of Jersey, it should be noted that *la convention fait la loi des parties* admits of exceptions.[27] The principle of the sanctity of contracts enshrined in *la convention fait la loi des parties* is not set in stone. Indeed, Pothier had already noted that exceptions would arise where the agreements were 'contraire aux lois et aux bonnes mœurs'.[28] In Jersey, exceptions have been said to arise where a contract is contrary to public policy[29] or where a statute provides for a power to interfere with contracts[30] or where an agreement constitutes a restraint of trade,[31] or where public interest so requires.[32] The doctrine of *lesion* also represents circumstances in which the Jersey courts intervene to unravel a contract, potentially on the sole basis of the under-valuing of the property (real estate) which is the subject-matter of the contract.[33] This will be examined in more detail in a later chapter.[34]

## III. Centrality of Consent

As a corollary to the previous principle of *la convention fait la loi des parties*, the notion of contractual consent is a fundamental tenet of the law of contract. Along with capacity, *objet* and *cause*, consent is considered to be one of the four essential elements of a valid contract.[35] The Jersey courts have consistently referred to the centrality of consent in contract cases, and as a consequence have required proof

26 *Incat Equatorial Guinee Ltd v Luba Freeport Ltd* 2010 JLR 287, para 22.
27 *Basden Hotels Ltd v Dormy Hotels Ltd* (1968) JJ 911.
28 Pothier, *Traité des Obligations*, para 15.
29 *Basden Hotels Ltd v Dormy Hotels Ltd* (1968) JJ 911
30 *Macready v Amy* (1950) JJ 11 (Rent Control Tribunal given power by statute to intervene as regards parties' contractual arrangements on level of rent).
31 See the leading case of *Rossborough v Boon* 2001 JLR 416.
32 *CPA Limited v Keogh* [2015] JRC 09, when considering the burden of proof for showing that a non-competition clause in an employment contract goes no wider than reasonably necessary ([23]).
33 In *Incat Equatorial Guinee Ltd v Luba Freeport Ltd* 2010 JLR 287, Deputy Bailiff William Bailhache too makes this link to *lésion*, para 23.
34 See Chapter 5 below, pp 113–120.
35 See discussion in Chapter 4 below.

that there was a *meeting of minds* as to the agreement between the parties.[36] Thus in the case of *Cronin and Luce v Gordon-Bennet*,[37] which concerned a dispute about the payment of commission to estate agents, the Jersey Royal Court found that there was no evidence of a 'meeting of minds' that a commission would be paid in case of sale of the property in question. The claim was thus rejected: 'There being no meeting of minds, no *convention*, there can be no contract.'[38]

Jersey has thus wholeheartedly espoused a will-based approach to contract law, and the origin of that approach is clearly to be attributed to its civil law heritage. It is well-known that consent plays an important role in French law, in clear contradistinction to the approach of the common law.[39] According to French commentators, this position results from the philosophical movement developed in France during the eighteenth century, placing the notion of 'autonomy of the will' at the heart of the contractual process,[40] though the latter theory is not universally accepted.[41]

Indeed, in a number of recent Jersey cases, this civil law heritage has been explicitly acknowledged, with references made to the importance of the notion of *volonté*.[42] Whilst the temptation may be to think that the French terminology is more decorative than operative in some cases, the recent decision of *Flynn v Reid*[43] illustrates the concrete consequences that may flow from this terminology. In this case, a dispute arose about the status of an agreement signed by the parties (an unmarried couple) when they bought a house which was to be their family home. The agreement contained financial provisions concerning the property as well as outgoings connected to it. After the couple moved into the property, the agreement was in effect disregarded by the parties. Counsel for Mrs Flynn argued that there was an enforceable contract, which was subsequently varied in accordance with the behaviour of the parties,[44] or alternatively that Mr Reid had in effect waived the breaches of contract. In his judgment, the Deputy Bailiff rejected the argument that there was an enforceable contract, holding that it was a 'wholly artificial arrangement' and that 'as a contract setting out their mutual obligations, it was meaningless in the sense that the parties paid no attention to it from the

[36] As in French law, there is also a requirement that each party's consent be free from defect—ie that there is no *vice de consentement*. This issue will be examined further in Chapter 5 below.

[37] *Cronin and Luce v Gordon-Bennet* 2003 JLR N22.

[38] Ibid, [20].

[39] In French law 'consent remains the primordial element in the creation of obligations': Mazeaud, *Leçons de droit civil* (8th edn, Paris, Montchrestien, 1991) para 117.

[40] See generally E Gounot, *Le principe de l'autonomie de la volonté en droit privé, étude critique de l'individualisme juridique* (Paris, A Rousseau, 1912); V Ranouil, *L'Autonomie de la Volonté, Naissance et Evolution d'un concept* (Paris, PUF, 1980).

[41] In France, the predominance of the theory of 'autonomy of will' has been powerfully contested. For an account in English, see eg G Rouhette, 'The Obligatory Force of Contract in French Law' in D Harris and D Tallon, *Contract Law Today: Anglo-French comparisons* (Oxford, OUP, 1991) 38–44.

[42] See eg *Incat Equatorial Guinee Ltd v Luba Freeport Ltd* 2010 JLR 287, [21], [22]; *Classic Herd Limited v Milk Marketing Board* [2014] JRC 217, [13].

[43] *Flynn v Reid* [2012] JRC 100.

[44] As Mrs Flynn did not make the financial contributions to the loan as envisaged by the contract.

very beginning'.[45] The agreement had been drafted like a commercial agreement, but it 'is clear that it was a solution which did not reflect the reality of the parties' relationship'.[46]

The Deputy Bailiff suggested, therefore, that the requirement of consent in the formation of a contract was the absent element in this case:

> [I]n relation to the requirement for consent of the parties undertaking the obligations, there must be shown a true consent, a true desire, or, adopting the French word, 'volonté' that the arrangement become legally binding between them.[47]

On the facts of the case, the Deputy Bailiff held 'that the contract did not in fact govern the relationship between the parties, nor was it intended to do so'.[48]

A corollary of the centrality of consent is that a contract will be undermined if the consent is in some way deficient. Indeed, the doctrine of the autonomy of will entails that the agreement which forms the basis of a contract must have been given freely.[49] Otherwise, consent cannot be considered to have been validly given by the parties. In French law, a contract will thus be undermined by a series of *vices de consentement*.[50] Similarly, in the law of Jersey, a number of factors may negative consent to contract, and these are sometimes referred to as *defects in consent* as a direct translation of the French concept. According to this doctrine, the consent given to a contract will not be valid if it is given in *erreur*, due to *violence*, or through *dol*. We will examine this in more detail in a later chapter.[51] It should, however, be noted here that the scope and content of *vices de consentement* has proved to be a point of some controversy in Jersey, as we shall see. In some ways, this reflects the complex nature of legal transplants in Jersey, with many different and sometimes competing sources of the law of contract. The law relating to *vices de consentement* has been one of those areas where the tectonic plates of civil and common law have met, with not altogether harmonious results. This will be examined further below.

## IV. Subjective and Objective Approaches to Contract Law

As has already been noted, English and French law are traditionally contrasted from a comparative law perspective on the basis that English law adopts an

[45] *Flynn v Reid* [2012] JRC 100, [19].
[46] Ibid, [20].
[47] Ibid, [21].
[48] Ibid, [21].
[49] Pothier, *Traité Des Obligations*, part 1, ch 1, para 21: 'Le consentement qui forme les conventions doit être libre.'
[50] In the new Civil Code, see Arts 1130–44.
[51] See Chapter 5 below.

objective approach, whereas French law adopts a predominantly subjective viewpoint.[52] The respective approaches would thus seem to diverge greatly, with the French system looking to the actual intentions of the parties, whereas English law attaches greater relevance to an objective, external interpretation. However, it is important not to overemphasize the differences: appearances can, however, be deceptive. It will be argued that, on closer analysis, it actually transpires that these systems do not adopt an exclusively subjective or objective standpoint.

## A. French Contract Law: The Predominance of the 'Subjective Approach'

As we have seen, the notion of consent is at the centre of the law of contract in France.[53] French law is thus usually perceived as being a subjective-based system, given the centrality of consent, and the courts will look not to the *declared* consent of the parties but to their *real* intent.

This subjective approach, linked with the 'autonomy of the will' in France, has entailed a number of consequences. First, regarding the 'existence' of the contract, the subjective theory prompted and encouraged an approach whereby the rigidities of contractual formalism were rejected in French law with the effect that a contract is considered to be concluded by means of an abstract process of the 'meeting of the wills' (*la rencontre des volontés*). In concrete terms, this means that, under French law, the creation of a valid contract does not demand any specific formal requirement. Of course, this somewhat idealistic vision is not absolute, and it is right to note that 'more and more contracts must be reduced to writing in order to be found valid, such as real estate sales, leases, etc'.[54]

Second, the predominance of the subjective view is clear when considering French rules on interpretation of contracts.[55] In this context, Article 1188 of the Civil Code provides: '[T]he contract is interpreted according to the common intention of the contracting parties rather than merely the literal meaning of the terms.' This means that, *when faced with an ambiguous term*, judges are required to give effect to the meaning that best reflects the common intent of the parties rather than promoting an 'objective' approach to the term.[56] French commentators note that the courts will look not to the *declared* consent of the parties but to their *real* intent.[57]

[52] For a comparative account, see J Cartwight, 'Defects of Consent and Security of Contract: French and English law Compared' in P Birks and A Pretto (eds), *Themes in Comparative Law* (Oxford, OUP, 2002) 156–57; Barnes (n 19); Nicholas (n 12) 35.

[53] In French law '*consent remains the primordial element in the creation of obligations*': Mazeaud (n 39) para 117.

[54] P Malinvaud et D Fenouillet, *Droit des obligations* (13th edn, Paris, Litec, 2014) para 82.

[55] See Chapter 6 below, pp 125–126.

[56] J Bienvenu, 'De la volonté interne à la volonté déclarée' [1999] *Droits*, no 28, 3 et seq.

[57] C Larroumet, *Les obligations, Le contrat*, tome III, 1ère partie, *Conditions de formation* (6th edn, Paris, 2007) para 151, p 132.

Third, the subjective position of French law has also had an impact on evidential issues. The centrality of consent has meant that the focus of disputes sometimes shifts from an abstract legal analysis of the terms of a contract towards an evidential dispute aimed at shedding light on what the parties *really* intended. The impact of civil procedure in France will be analysed further below.

## B. English Law: Favouring an Objective Approach

English law is traditionally seen as preferring an objective approach to contract law.[58] Atiyah explains this as follows:

> It is one of the most fundamental features of the law of contract that the test of agreement is objective and not subjective. It matters not whether the parties have really agreed in their innermost minds. The question is not whether the parties have really agreed, or what they really intended, but whether their conduct and language are such as would lead reasonable people to assume that they have agreed.[59]

Across the Atlantic, Oliver Wendell Holmes affirmed that '[t]he law has nothing to do with the actual state of the parties' minds. In contract, as elsewhere, it must go by externals, and judge parties by their conduct.'[60] The common law preference for objectivity can be attributed to many factors. Two reasons seem, however, to predominate. On the one hand, it is seen to provide legal security for commercial transactions and, on the other hand, it avoids 'the evidential difficulties associated with an inquiry into the actual state of mind of a party to the contract'.[61] The pragmatic reasons underpinning this are explained by Lord Steyn extrajudicially in the following terms:

> It is a defensible position for a legal system to give predominance to the subjective intentions of the parties. Such a policy can claim to be committed to the ideal of perfect individualised justice. But that is not the English way. Our law is generally based on an objective theory of contract. This involves adopting an external standard given life by using the concept of the reasonable man. The commercial advantage of the English approach is that it promotes certainty and predictability in the resolution of contractual disputes. And, as a matter of principle, it is not unfair to impute to contracting parties the intention that in the event of a dispute a neutral judge should decide the case applying an objective standard of reasonableness.[62]

[58] From a comparative perspective, see eg J Cartwright, *Contract Law: An Introduction to English Law for the Civil Lawyer* (2nd edn, Oxford, Hart Publishing, 2013) 65; Barnes (n 19).

[59] P Atiyah, *An Introduction to the Law of Contract* (5th edn, Oxford, OUP, 2000) 9.

[60] O Wendell Holmes, *The Common Law* (New York, Little, Brown and Company, 1881) 242.

[61] E McKendrick, *Contract Law, Text, Cases and Materials* (2nd edn, Oxford, OUP, 2005) 24.

[62] Lord Steyn, 'Contract Law: Fulfilling the Reasonable Expectations of Honest Men' (1997) 113 *LQR* 433.

Consequently, the English and French systems seem to adopt starkly different approaches to the importance of consent within the contractual process. Cartwright encapsulates this point well in the following extract:

> [W]hat a French lawyer here understands by 'agreement' is not the same as the English lawyer. At least in its starting point, the French understanding is more subjective: something closer to the meeting of minds of the parties, their actual agreements. A contract is a convention; and one of the four essential conditions of a valid convention is le consentement de la partie qui s'oblige. Commonly, therefore, French writers speak of an accord de volontés. But this agreement is tested by reference to the internal, subjective intentions of the parties and in particular of the party whose obligation is in issue. … English law starts from a different point. A contract is also commonly referred to as an agreement, but beyond this even the language diverges. The English lawyer does not generally speak of the parties' 'consent', and so the vitiating factors are not united, as in French law, by the principle that they involve a vitiation of the claimant's consent. In analysing the 'agreement', the question becomes what the parties intended by way of the content of their obligation, what each has promised the other in the contract. But the 'agreement', a party's 'intention', or what he promised are tested not subjectively, as in the French conception of the accord de volontés, but by objective criteria.[63]

## C. Convergence of English and French Law?

A closer analysis reveals, however, that both systems do not adopt an *exclusively* subjective or objective standpoint. In France, the predominance of the 'autonomy of will' theory has been contested[64] and the desire for legal certainty has on occasion required the subjective position to be modified toward a mixture of objective and subjective approaches. Some concrete examples may be given of the French compromise between real intentions of the parties and contractual security. First, the notion of 'free will', though predominant within the French contractual system, is by no means absolute. Indeed, it was the initial conception of the drafters of the French Civil Code that the law would only give effect to the parties' common intent provided that their intentions were in full conformity with public policy.[65] Thus, a contractual system where a subjective approach prevails is by no means a system where the parties are free to depart from statutory requirements. Rather, a contract will only be enforced if it meets such requirements. The legislator's tendency to create compulsory rules is particularly prominent where the contracting parties do not enjoy the same 'negotiating powers', as in consumer law,

[63] Cartwight (n 52) 156–57.

[64] Professor Aynès (n 9) thus comments that it has 'lost much of its strength'.

[65] This is clearly stated in the old Art 1134 of the French Civil Code, which emphasises that contracts are binding only if they are 'lawfully entered into'.

employment law, insurance law, etc. In these areas, specific rules about the formation and the interpretation of contracts have been devised and often depart from an assessment of the parties' actual intent.[66]

Second, French law illustrates the occasional compromise between the desire to enforce the parties' real intentions and the need for contractual security.[67] Although consent itself is largely determined subjectively in the process of assessing the content of the contract, the *characterisation* of consent as such is the result of an objective determination.[68] In concrete terms, this means that the existence of mutual consent is assessed from an objective standpoint.[69] For example, the fact that the contracting parties put their signatures on a document is considered evidence of the parties' agreement to its content and its effect, irrespective of the parties 'real' understanding of the terms. This is particularly true when the contract takes place between professionals acting in the scope of their field of activity.

Similarly, it is an exaggeration to present the rules of contractual interpretation as imposing a purely subjective approach.[70] Whilst Article 1156 of the French Civil Code (now Article 1188 of the new Code) may invite judges to seek the parties' common intent, other provisions alongside it have a definitely objective end.[71] For example, Article 1135 of the Civil Code (now Article 1194 of the new Code) proposes a broad conception of the contractual agreement, incorporating not only the express provisions, but also matters of equity, usage and the nature of the obligation.

Third, objective elements have been injected into the French law notion of *erreur* within the context of *vice de consentement*. Whilst, as we shall see, the French approach to *erreur* is very much a subjective one, elements of objectivity may nonetheless be detected in the case law, for instance where the importance of the subject-matter (in respect of which the mistake was made) was known to the other party (or that he ought to have known it), or whether the erreur in question was 'excusable' or not.[72] The French commentator Professor Fabre-Magnan has thus observed that whilst the approach is in essence a subjective one, elements of objectivity may also be detected: 'An objective interpretation is also an instrument of judicial policy which allows for the avoidance [of the contract] to be denied where the error invoked by the contracting party does not appear to be legitimate.'[73] Indeed, Whittaker notes that the exercise of judicial discretion allows for judges

[66] A perfect example of this legislative 'interventionism' can be found in Art L 133-2 of the Code of Consumer Law (concerning consumer contracts whereby in case of ambiguity, such contracts must be interpreted in favour of the consumer).

[67] See, for instance, F Terré, P Simler and Y Lequette, *Droit civil: Les Obligations* (8th edn, Paris, Dalloz, 2002) paras 207 and 208.

[68] A Benabent, *Droit civil, Les obligation* (14th edn, Paris, Montchrestien, 2014) 41.

[69] F Limbach, *Le consentement contractuel à l'épreuve des conditions générales* (Paris, LGDJ, 2004).

[70] B Gelot, *Finalités et méthodes objectives d'interprétation des actes juridiques* (Paris, LGDJ 2003).

[71] See eg Art 1188(2) of the new Civil Code.

[72] See Chapter 5, p 100.

[73] M.Fabre-Magnan, *Droit des Obligations* (Paris, PUF, 2008) 305.

to inject objective considerations so as to 'put into effect their perception of the appropriateness of annulment, in particular being swayed by the prejudicial effect of the mistake on the party suffering from it'.[74]

Fourth, in understanding the impact of the subjective approach in France, it is important also to take account of the surrounding evidential context. One specific feature of French civil procedure should be noted here. French procedure is characterised by a predominantly written procedure with, at its centre, the judicial dossier composed of the parties' respective written pleadings, supplemented by documentary evidence.[75] Whilst the civil courts may hear witnesses, this in practice rarely actually occurs. Unlike the common law trial, the French civil justice system is characterised by a distrust of testimonial over documentary evidence.[76] This has a corresponding impact on the evidence that can realistically be presented during litigation to elucidate the parties' actual intentions in contracting. In practice, contemporaneous written documentation will be required to support what that intention really was. This therefore illustrates a very different approach to civil procedural patterns in the common law, and in effect also entails an inbuilt limitation on the subjective approach in the sense that the proof of the parties' intentions must be apparent from written documentary evidence. This may not always be possible to adduce. Linked to this issue is the potential impact of the transplant of a subjective approach within a legal system with a very different civil procedural environment, and thus where the limitations, evidential and otherwise, are very different. This is an interesting conundrum that we will explore further below when we examine the potential consequences of a subjective approach to contract within the Jersey legal system.

The English law attachment to objectiveness is also tempered, in certain circumstances, by subjective elements. A concrete example of this is the exchange of an offer and acceptance. In this respect, Cartwright notes: '[T]he courts adopt an objective test which asks how a reasonable person, *placed in the position of the parties themselves*, would have interpreted their communications; but that the subjective understandings of the parties are not wholly excluded.'[77] Valcke has argued more broadly that the objective standard is an elusive one. Taking the example of contractual interpretation, she argues that there is an 'inherent conceptual looseness of objective intention',[78] in that the courts mix two different approaches:

> English courts indeed commonly appeal to the shady notion of 'the parties' *reasonable* intention', without specifying whether by that they mean 'what the parties reasonably

[74] Bell, Boyron and Whittaker (n 16) 318.

[75] See generally, ibid, 90.

[76] See generally J Beardsley, 'Proof of Fact in French Civil Procedure' (1986) 34 *American Journal of Comparative Law* 459, 483.

[77] J Cartwright, *Contract Law: An Introduction to English Law for the Civil Lawyer* (2nd edn, Oxford Hart Publishing, 2013) p 95 (emphasis in original).

[78] C Valcke, 'On Comparing French and English Contract Law: Insights from Social Contract Theory' (2009) IV *Journal of Comparative Law* 69, 99.

> *ought to have intended*' or 'what the parties reasonably *ought to be taken to have intended*'.[79]

She argues that the reluctance of the English courts to choose between these distinct conceptions is in reality because they have combined both:

> [T]he parties' 'reasonable intention' stands for the intention which it is reasonable for them to have *precisely because* that is the intention which it is reasonable for each of them to attribute to the other. In other words, it is because a particular intention reasonably can (factually) be attributed to the parties that the court will endorse that intention as that which reasonably can (legally) be attributed to them.[80]

Cartwright has also dissected the English test, and underlined that its operation in areas of contract law is by no means entirely objective,[81] so that 'the subjective understandings of the parties are not wholly excluded'.[82] This is perhaps not so surprising: as Vogenauer has pointed out, the French subjective theory has its roots in the ideals of liberty and individualism which are not so alien to classic English contract law.[83]

## D. The Legacy of the Civil Law: The Centrality of the Parties' Consent in Jersey

The approach of Jersey lawyers to this question has not always been of the utmost clarity. Indeed, the law of Jersey can be seen as having a tendency to straddle the divide between subjective and objective approaches. Certain decisions of the Jersey courts have illustrated a preference for an objective approach; others have tended towards a more subjective approach. However, in recent times, the latter subjective theory has seemed to attract the favour of the judiciary. If this continues to be so, then, as we shall see, this will have a more general impact on the fundaments of the law of contract.

Given the civil law influences in Jersey and the centrality of consent, as we have seen above, it might be supposed that the Jersey courts would naturally have adopted a subjective approach. Earlier Jersey cases indicated, however, a different attitude. One example suffices. The case of *Mobil Sales & Supply Corp v Transoil (Jersey) Ltd*[84] concerned a contract for the supply of oil. Drawing upon English authority, the Royal Court held that, even where a mistake had arisen as to the parties' real intentions, a contract will be deemed to arise where a *reasonable* man

[79] Ibid, 96 (emphasis in original).
[80] Ibid, 96 (emphasis in original).
[81] See Cartwright (n 77) 96–99.
[82] Ibid, 95.
[83] S Vogenauer, 'Interpretation of Contracts: Concluding Comparative Observations' in A Burrows and E Peel (eds), *Contract Terms* (Oxford, OUP, 2007) 129.
[84] *Mobil Sales & Supply Corp v Transoil (Jersey) Ltd* (1981) JJ 143, 159.

would have deemed the terms of the contract to have been accepted. Indeed, the Royal Court expressly declared that:

> The question which the Court has to determine is not what the parties had in their minds, but what reasonable third parties, 'disinterested spectators', would infer from their words or conduct.[85]

This therefore relates to an objective test.[86] The approach in other cases was similarly underpinned by what seemed to be an objective approach to the elements of a contract.[87]

In more recent times, however, there has been a marked reaffirmation of the subjective approach. The origins of this movement can be traced back to the seminal case of *Selby v Romeril*,[88] in which the court acknowledged the centrality of the element of consent within the law of Jersey. This can also be seen in the cases, already reviewed above,[89] which have underlined the necessity to show the parties have reached a 'meeting of minds'.[90]

More recent cases have been even more explicit as to the subjective nature of the Jersey law of contract. Indeed, in the case of *O'Brien v Marett*, the Court of Appeal held that 'the Jersey law of contract determines *consent* by use of the subjective theory of contract'.[91] This unambiguous statement from high authority would therefore seem to have settled the debate, and the lower courts have followed this lead.[92] In *Incat Equatorial Guinee Ltd v Luba Freeport Ltd*, it was noted, with approval, by the Royal Court that the Defendant in that case had accepted the 'subjective meeting of minds that is fundamental and necessary to the existence of a proper consent and the creation of a contract under Jersey law'.[93]

The importance of this restatement of the law in Jersey should be underlined. A reaffirming of the subjective approach represents a different emphasis from that found in some of the earlier cases (which were often influenced by English law reasoning), and one which is more consistent with the civil law heritage of the law of Jersey and its underpinning philosophy, premised upon the centrality of individual consent/*volonté*. It is all the more surprising therefore that in a recent decision, *Home Farm Developments Ltd v Le Sueur*,[94] the Court of Appeal expressed

[85] Ibid, 159 and 163.

[86] See also *La Motte Garages Ltd v Morgan* (1989) JJ 312, 316; *Leach v Leach* (1969) JJ 1107.

[87] See eg *La Motte Garages Ltd v Morgan* 1989 JLR 312 and *Daisy Hill Real Estates Limited v Rent Control Tribunal* 1995 JLR 176.

[88] *Selby v Romeril* 1996 JLR 210.

[89] See pp 36–38 above.

[90] eg *Cronin and Luce v Gordon-Bennet* 2003 JLR N22.

[91] *O'Brien v Marett* [2008] JCA 178, [55].

[92] See eg *Cunningham v Sinel* [2011] JRC 015, [18] (importance of the will or *volonté* of the parties in respect of implied terms); *Flynn v Reid* [2012] JRC 100 (an agreement signed by an unmarried couple when they bought a property did not in fact govern the relationship between the parties, nor was it intended to do so).

[93] *Incat Equatorial Guinee Ltd v Luba Freeport Ltd* [2010] JLR 287, para 25.

[94] *Home Farm Developments Ltd v Le Sueur* [2015] JCA 242.

some doubts about this topic. One of the issues in the case concerned an alleged unilateral *erreur* of one of the parties as to the meaning and scope of a settlement agreement. The Court of Appeal accepted 'for the purposes of this appeal' (concerning a strike-out decision) that in such circumstances, 'a unilateral *erreur* by one party to a contract may prevent the required meeting of minds or amount to a defect of consent'.[95] It also seems to have been accepted by the parties that, 'for the purposes of this appeal', the question of consent in Jersey was determined by a subjective test.[96] Despite this approach, the Court of Appeal went on, in a postscript to the judgment, to express some concerns about the adoption of a subjective test. Whilst it was not prepared to take a definitive view on the topic within the context of the present case, the Court indicated that it considered 'there are potentially powerful arguments against the adoption of a subjective test'.[97] Brushing aside the unambiguous statements in previous cases on the topic,[98] the Court stated baldly that 'the point has not yet been definitively resolved'. Whilst this judgment may be reflective of a different approach to the doctrine of precedent than in English law,[99] it is nevertheless submitted that the stance of the court is somewhat surprising given the clear strand of case law affirming the subjective approach in Jersey (and, as we shall see below, overturning the previous cases adopting an objective approach). It is evidently unfortunate that there should be some prevailing uncertainty as to such a fundamental aspect of Jersey contract law.

## E. Consequences of Adopting a Subjective Approach

A shift away from an objective approach in Jersey inevitably impacts on the substantive law of contract. In light of the statement in *O'Brien v Marett*,[100] it is strongly arguable that a number of earlier cases must be wrong. The judge's application of the reasonable man test as the litmus test for determining the acceptance of a contract in *Mobil Sales & Supply Corp v Transoil (Jersey) Ltd*,[101] as referred to above, is clearly at odds with the subjective approach. The position is similar in the case of *La Motte Garages Ltd v Morgan*,[102] involving a dispute as to the terms of the purchase of a car from a garage (with part exchange) where the court applied an objective text, namely what the reasonable man would have assumed 'the sense of the promise' to mean. It is difficult to see how such an

95 Ibid, [45].

96 Ibid, [43]–[44.]

97 Ibid, [59].

98 Most notably, *O'Brien v Marett* [2008] JCA 178. The Court of Appeal in *Home Farm Developments Ltd*, however, brushed aside that decision, holding that 'we would … observe that the question whether an objective or a subjective test should be adopted was not argued in Marett either' (ibid, [59]).

99 See Chapter 2 above, pp 25–28.

100 *O'Brien v Marett* [2008] JCA 178.

101 *Mobil Sales & Supply Corp v Transoil (Jersey) Ltd* (1981) JJ 143, 159.

102 *La Motte Garages Ltd v Morgan* 1989 JLR 312.

approach can coexist with the subjective analysis. It is unsurprising, then, that the Court of Appeal in *O'Brien v Marett* explicitly ruled that *Mobil Sales* and *La Motte Garages* 'must now be considered *per incuriam* on this specific point in the light of *Selby v Romeril*'.[103]

The effects of the reaffirmation of the subjective approach are likely to be felt more widely than these two cases, however. There are several areas where the reaffirming of the subjective approach will have an impact. The principles of the formation of a contract are likely to evolve differently, with a primary focus upon the *real* consent of the contractual parties. This will affect the analysis of whether an agreement has been reached by the parties, whether there was a 'true' meeting of minds, and whether there has been acceptance by the offeree of the offer made by the offeror.[104] An impact will be felt on those factors undermining a contract, namely in terms of *vice de consentement.* By placing the subjective intention of the parties at the forefront of the contractual analysis, then almost inevitably the doctrine of mistake takes a prominent role in defeating a contract. We will examine this further in Chapter 5.

## F. Importance of Context—Procedural Factors

The shift to the subjective approach also raises challenges beyond the domain of substantive law. There may also be an impact in procedural terms. In adopting the subjective approach, Jersey lawyers will have to adapt to the need to inquire into the state of mind of the contractual parties. It could clearly be an important factor in litigation if one party can bring forth credible evidence as to the understanding at the time of the contractual arrangements. As we have seen in French law,[105] the limited use of testimonial evidence and consequential reliance on documentary evidence provides an inbuilt limitation on the subjective approach in the sense that the proof of the parties' intentions must be apparent from written evidence. That limitation does not exist in the very different civil procedural environment in Jersey, which is inspired predominantly by adversarial traditions.[106] This shows that reinforcing the centrality of consent and the subjective approach to contracts will not only have wide repercussions throughout the substantive law, but will also make it necessary to take account of the impact of different procedural traditions.[107]

[103] *O'Brien v Marett* [2008] JCA 178, at [55].

[104] This will be explored in Chapter 4 below.

[105] See p 43 above.

[106] T Hanson, 'Reforming Jersey's Royal Court Rules: Lessons from the CPR' [2014] *Jersey and Guernsey Law Review* 278.

[107] An example of this may be found in the *Flynn v Reid* [2012] JRC 100 where it was considered that an agreement signed by the parties (an unmarried couple) when they bought a property did not in fact govern the relationship between the parties, nor was it intended to do so ([21]).

## V. Reciprocity in a Contractual Context

Any claim that Jersey contract law is simply, in legal terms, a variant of English common law spoken with a slightly French accent is undermined by the simple but striking feature that there is no doctrine of consideration in the law of Jersey. The absence of such a doctrine clearly provides a stark contrast with the common law. Instead, the functionally most similar notion in the law of Jersey is the requirement that a contract has a *cause*. Drawn from its Norman origins, this notion is probably one of the most visible influences of the civil law on substantive contract law in Jersey. And yet, paradoxically, the notion of *cause* has been excised from French law (ostensibly at least) in the recent reforms of the Civil Code. We will examine this somewhat mysterious and amorphous concept in further detail in Chapter 4 below. A short introduction about the notion of cause from a broader perspective will, however, be given here.[108]

The Jersey courts have been very clear about the centrality of the notion of *cause* within Jersey contract law. It is moreover clear that *cause* is not simply a civil law stalking horse for the doctrine of consideration: the Jersey courts have underlined that there are important differences between the two notions.[109] We will examine the intricacies of the notion of *cause* below, but it is clear that, in some respects, it is a very much broader concept that consideration. An example of this can be found within the French case law on gratuitous promises, where it is shown that these can be enforceable if supported by a valid *cause*, such as the desire to confer a gift as expressed in an *intention libérale* (intention to gift).[110] This example has particular resonance in Jersey, due to the absence of any formality or instrument which would allow such a gift to be rendered enforceable. We will examine this issue in detail below, but it does illustrate the importance of a contextual analysis of comparative law issues. Whilst in practice in the common law, parties can indeed make an enforceable promise of a gift if the donor undertakes the promise in a deed, such an option is not available in Jersey, where the concept of a deed does not exist. Whilst in English law, the exigencies of consideration can thus be offset by the use of the instrument of a deed, Jersey does not have such an option, and therefore any attempt to introduce such a concept of consideration per se would be problematic (without broader reform). From such a perspective, it is perhaps unsurprising that the gravitational pull of recent cases is towards the civil law.

[108] For a modern treatment of this topic from a comparative perspective, see H Beale, B Fauvarque-Cosson, J Rutgers, D Tallon and S Vogenauer, *Cases, Materials and Text on Contract Law* (Oxford, Hart Publishing, 2010) ch 5.

[109] See a particularly clear statement on this in *Granite Products Ltd v Renault* (1961) JJ 163, 169.

[110] See pp 81–82 below.

## VI. Good Faith: Preferring a Civil or Common Law Approach?

The importance of a contextual analysis is illustrated also by the doctrine of good faith. As is well known, the notion of good faith permeates civil law systems generally,[111] a feature that is often attributed to civil law's Roman heritage, which was centered around the societal notion of proper conduct, *fides*, and its analogous legal construct, the notion of *bona fides*.[112] In modern civil law systems, the concept may be found in many areas of the law, but it plays a particular role in the law of obligations: many continental civil codes refer to the need for contracts to be performed or interpreted in accordance with good faith.[113] The doctrine is particularly apparent in French law, in which good faith principles are present in property law,[114] restitution,[115] employment law,[116] consumer law[117] and elsewhere.[118] Within the law of obligations, good faith plays a particularly prominent role as encapsulated by the iconic statement in the original Article 1134(3) of the French Civil Code that: '[Agreements] must be performed in good faith.'[119] Whilst this Article refers only to the *performance* of contracts in good faith, reference was also made to the precontractual stage in earlier drafts, but it is said that Portalis asked for the removal of this reference as he considered it superfluous.[120] Articles 1104 and 1112 of the new Civil code now explicitly apply good faith during the negotiating stage, which we will examine below.

The approach to good faith in the English common law is very different, as is well known. As we shall see below, the English courts have not traditionally shown a great deal of enthusiasm for good faith obligations during the negotiating stage.[121] A similar attitude has prevailed in English law in respect of contract

[111] See generally from a comparative perspective, R Zimmermann and S. Whittaker, *Good Faith in European Contract Law* (Cambridge, CUP, 2008).

[112] This central role both within Roman law and society is illustrated by the Roman deity Fides, who was the goddess of trust, and whose temple on the Capitol was used for meetings of the Roman Senate: L Richardson, *A New Topographical Dictionary of Ancient Rome* (Baltimore, Johns Hopkins University Press, 1992) 151.

[113] The German Civil Code provides that a contractual 'debtor must perform his obligation in accordance with the requirements of good faith, taking into account the prevailing practice' (§ 242 BGB). See also Art 1258 of the Spanish Civil Code; and Arts 1366 and 1375 of the Italian Civil Code.

[114] See Arts 549, 550 and 2272 Civil Code.

[115] Arts 1377 and 1378 Civil Code.

[116] Art L1222-1 of the Employment Code.

[117] See eg Art L 330-1 of the Consumer code on protection against excessive debt.

[118] See generally S Tisseyre, *Le Rôle de la Bonne Foi en Droit des Contrats* (Aix en Provence, Presses universitaires d'Aix-Marseille, 2012) para 5 and references therein.

[119] In Art 1104 of the new Civil Code it is stated that 'contracts must be negotiated, concluded and executed in good faith'.

[120] See generally Tisseyre (n 118) para 7.

[121] See eg *Walford v Miles* [1992] AC 128. Nonetheless, the reality is more nuanced that might first appear—see pp 53–54 below.

performance.[122] In Jersey, the precise role of the doctrine of good faith still remains somewhat open. This is another example of an area where the Channel Islands are pulled between different competing influences. Common law aficionados continue to be reticent about a general principle of good faith in contract law. However, there are important underlying differences between Jersey and the English common law on this issue. Unlike the latter, the notion of good faith has been a feature of Jersey contract law for a long period of time (due partly to its Norman origins). The concept of good faith thus informs and shapes issues such as *vice de consentement* (factors vitiating consent)[123] and the action of *lesion* or *déception d'outre moitié*.[124] Statutory intervention in Jersey has also expressly introduced notions of good faith. In the Supply of Goods and Services (Jersey) Law 2009, one of the preliminary articles is given over to a definition of the notion,[125] and the substantive rules of the Law rely upon this notion extensively.[126]

From the perspective of the sources of law in Jersey, the ubiquity of good faith is not surprising. *Bonne foi* underpins the analysis of civil law writers such as Pothier and Domat who, as we have seen,[127] have played such an influential role in shaping Jersey contract law. Domat drew greatly upon the notion, stating in general terms that the principle underpinned all agreements,[128] and that there were standards of conduct to be respected in the pursuit of one's interest, underpinned by the rule of good faith and equity.[129] Pothier's works are also replete with references to good faith.[130]

Given that heritage in Jersey, one might naturally think that the traditional English common law approach is not best adapted to local circumstances. Indeed, in some cases, a very distinctive approach has been advocated. Whilst the case of *Sutton v Insurance Corporation of the Channel Islands Limited*[131] did concern an insurance contract (subject therefore to *uberrima fides*), the judge in that case did

[122] Although in recent cases there have been signs that mindsets might be changing: see below.

[123] Most notably, *dol.* Pothier linked *dolosive* conduct to a breach of good faith: Pothier, *Traité Des Obligations*, part 1, ch 1, para 30.

[124] See Chapter 5 below. The Privy Council held that the doctrine was 'based on the principle of good faith': *Snell v Beadle* [2001] UKPC 5, [46].

[125] Art 5: 'A thing is taken to be done in good faith for the purposes of this Law when it is in fact done honestly, whether it is done negligently or not.'

[126] See eg Arts 49, 50 and 51 et al.

[127] See Chapter 2 above, 14–15.

[128] 'Il n'y a pas aucune espèce de convention, où il ne soit sous entendu que l'un doit à l'autre la bonne foi…tant dans la manière de s'exprimer dans la convention, que pour l'exécution de ce qui est convenue, et de toutes suites' *(Les Loix civiles dans leur ordre naturel; le droit public, et Legum delectus* 1735, tome 1, 25).

[129] See Deputy Bailiff Bailhache's comments in the case of *Flynn v Reid* [2012] JRC 100 that Domat 'reflects on rules of equity which take the place of a Law'.

[130] One particularly striking reference can be found in the context of contracts for the sale of goods; Pothier stated that: 'La bonne foi oblige le vendeur, non seulement à ne rien dissimuler des vices intrinsèques de la chose, mais en général à ne rien dissimuler de tout ce qui concerne la chose, qui pourrait porter l'acheteur à ne pas acheter, ou à ne pas acheter si cher' (*Traité du Contrat de Vente*, para 237).

[131] *Sutton v Insurance Corporation of the Channel Islands Limited* 2011 JLR 80.

nonetheless opine that '[i]t may well be that an obligation of good faith on both sides is a common understanding in all contracts governed by Jersey law',[132] giving examples of references to the requirement for good faith in Domat and Le Gros.[133] Other judgments have, however, been rather less atuned to the specific history and context of Jersey law. In the recent case of *Minister for Treasury and Resources v Harcourt Developments Limited*, which concerned a property development dispute, the Court of Appeal took a rather Anglocentric approach to this issue.[134] We will examine that judgment in greater detail below but it is open to doubt how much authority can be placed upon a decision which has illustrated such a shaky approach to the sources of Jersey contract law and overlooked so many of the recent Jersey cases discussing the potential role of good faith in the law of Jersey (such as the aforementioned case of *Sutton*).

## A. Reconsidering the English Law Approach to Good Faith?

It should also be noted at this stage that the English law approach is not entirely set in stone. Despite the lack of enthusiasm for a general principle of good faith, there have been signs that mindsets might slowly be changing. In the recent English High Court decision in *Yam Seng PTE Ltd v International Trade Corporation Ltd*,[135] Leggatt J gave a detailed consideration of the role of good faith in the performance of contractual obligations under English law.[136] Whilst he recognised that English law had not reached the stage when a general requirement of good faith could be implied by law, 'even as a default rule, into all commercial contracts',[137] he nonetheless argued that it could be implied into an ordinary commercial contract based on the presumed intention of the parties.[138] He then expanded on what this would mean, and thus identified a series of 'general norms'[139] such as the expectation of honesty in performance of a contract (extending to observance of 'commercially acceptable' conduct) and fidelity to the parties' bargain. These represented 'standards of commercial dealing which are so generally accepted that the contracting parties would reasonably be understood to take them as read without explicitly stating them in their contractual document'.[140]

[132] Ibid, para 16.
[133] Ibid.
[134] *Minister for Treasury and Resources v Harcourt Developments Limited* 2014 (2) JLR 353.
[135] *Yam Seng PTE Ltd v International Trade Corporation Ltd* [2013] EWHC 111.
[136] From a comparative perspective, see Jan van Dunné, 'On a Clear Day, You Can See the Continent—The Shrouded Acceptance of Good Faith as a General Rule of Contract on the British Isles' (2015) 31 *Construction Law Journal* 3.
[137] *Yam Seng PTE Ltd v International Trade Corporation Ltd* [2013] EWHC 111, [131].
[138] Ibid, [131].
[139] Ibid, [135].
[140] Ibid, [138].

From a broader perspective, Leggatt J made a series of observations about the traditional reluctance of the English common law in this sphere, and concluded with a statement which clearly could extend beyond the facts of the case, that 'the traditional English hostility towards a doctrine of good faith in the performance of contracts, to the extent that it still persists, is misplaced'.[141] Another important point made by Leggatt J in his judgment is that the dichotomy of 'continental paternalism and Anglo-Saxon individualism' is inaccurate.[142] Just as civil law jurisdictions have taken a different view on this issue, so the common law jurisdictions were not at one either. As is well known, the US Uniform Commercial Code sets out in section 1-203 that 'every contract or duty within this Act imposes an obligation of good faith in its performance or enforcement', and the Canadian Supreme Court recognised in 2014 that 'good faith contractual performance is a general organizing principle of the common law of contract'.[143] Following the *Yam Seng PTE Ltd* case, a number of English decisions have, however, reasserted the more traditional approach.[144] English law therefore thus looks far from performing a substantive shift on this point.

We will now turn to examine the stage immediate preceding the formation of a contract, namely the period of contractual negotiations.

## B. Good Faith and Precontractual Relations

As an illustration of the role of good faith, we will say a word here about the issue of precontractual relations. The legal framework governing the conduct of parties during contractual negotiations is a familiar topic of comparative law research.[145] The starting point for most legal systems is that negotiating parties are under no obligation to reach a successful conclusion to their contractual negotiations: a corollary of the principle of freedom of contract is thus the freedom not to enter into a contract. Despite this basic principle, many systems do provide

[141] Ibid, [153.]

[142] Ibid, [125].

[143] *Bhasin v Hrynew* 2014 SCC 71, [33]. See C Hunt, 'Good Faith Performance in Canadian Contract Law' (2015) 74 *Cambridge Law Journal* 4. In terms of civil law influences, it is to be observed that in this decision, Cromwell J noted that we may 'take comfort' from the Quebec experience which has not 'impeded contractual activity or contractual stability' ([82] and [85]). See further R Jukier, 'The Legacy of Justice Louis LeBel: The Civilian Tradition and Procedural law' (2015) 70 *Supreme Court Law Review* (2d) 27.

[144] See eg *Mid Essex Hospital Services NHS Trust v Compass Group UK and Ireland Ltd* [2013] EWCA Civ 200 (CA); *Myers v Kestrel Acquisitions* [2015] EWHC 916. Leggatt J's approach was endorsed though in *Bristol Groundschool Ltd v Intelligent Data Capture Limited* [2014] EWHC 2145.

[145] See eg J Cartwright and M Hesselink, *Precontractual Liability in European Private Law* (Cambridge, CUP, 2009); P Giliker, *Pre-Contractual Liability in English and French Law* (The Hague, Kluwer, 2002).

for circumstances in which wrongful conduct during negotiations can give rise to liability, or affect the validity of the contract, with the obvious example being, of course, precontractual misrepresentation.[146]

More generally, civil law countries have recognised a series of different scenarios in which precontractual behaviour will give rise to liability.[147] As we have seen above, in many civil law jurisdictions, the civil codes contain explicit provisions establishing a general duty of good faith in a precontractual scenario.[148] In France, even though the Code civil did not (until recently) contain any explicit provisions on precontractual liability,[149] the French Cour de cassation recognised as long as forty years ago a precontractual liability sounding in tort.[150] This line of case law is premised upon principles of fair dealing and good faith, and liability may now arise in a variety of circumstances, including the wrongful breaking-off of negotiations, the commencement of negotiations without a real interest in contracting, the prolonging of negotiations while knowing that the contract will not be concluded,[151] and the sudden breaking off of negotiations (particularly when the latter are well advanced).[152]

The different French reform projects have all incorporated these case law developments, and Articles 1104 and 1112 of the new Civil Code now explicitly apply good faith during the negotiating stage. Almost all the European or international projects of codifications include provisions on this issue.[153]

## C. Comparing English and French Law

The English courts have taken a different approach to this question, as famously enshrined in the case of *Walford v Miles*,[154] according to which a party is free to

[146] See generally Beale et al (n 108) 371.

[147] Some systems have developed broader rules concerning liability during the negotiating period. In 1861, the German writer von Jhering developed the sui generis doctrine of *culpa in contrahendo*, which was subsequently adopted by the German legislator (§311 BGB) and the German case law. On this theme, see B Markesinis, H Unberath and A Johnston, *The German Law of Contract: A Comparative Treatise* (2nd edn, Oxford, Hart Publishing, 2006) 91.

[148] See eg Art 1337 of Italian Civil Code: '*Pre-contractual negotiations and liability.* During the course of the negotiations and in the formation of the contract, the parties must act in good faith.' See generally Beale et al (n 108) 372.

[149] Art 1134 Code civil refers solely to good faith during the contractual performance.

[150] eg Cass com, 20 mars 1972, *Bull civ* IV, no 93; *RTD civ* 1972, 779 obs G Durry; *Cass civ*, 3ème, 3 oct 1972, *Bull civ* III, no 491; Cass com, 22 fév 1994, *Bull civ* IV, no 79.

[151] Cass civ, 1ère, 6 jan 1998, no 95-19199.

[152] Ibid.

[153] eg Art 2:301 PECL, Art 2.1.15 UNIDROIT Principles of International Commercial Contracts (2004) or Art 6 of the Gandolfi Project. See also the DCFR which lays down the rules in an article entitled 'Negotiations contrary to good faith and fair dealing' (Art II-3:301).

[154] *Walford v Miles* [1992] AC 128.

enter and break off negotiations at any time. From this perspective, the English common law[155] thus does not characterise the negotiations as a 'legally protected relationship'.[156] The commentaries therefore have generally asserted that under English law there is no principle to negotiate in good faith.[157]

Nonetheless, the reality is perhaps more nuanced than might first appear, and the stark contrast between the common law and civil law on this issue may be deceptive.[158] English law does sanction precontractual behaviour under different concepts such as the tort of deceit, negligence, unjust enrichment, undue influence, collateral contracts or equitable estoppel.[159] Mummery LJ has thus held that:

> Under English law there is no general duty to negotiate in good faith. ... [Nevertheless, there are] plenty of other ways of dealing with particular problems of unacceptable conduct occurring in the course of negotiations without unduly hampering the ability of the parties to negotiate their own bargains without the intervention of the Courts.[160]

In French law, the remedy available during the precontractual stage sounds in tort. The case law lays down that the aggrieved party is entitled to damages for the loss he or she sustained, covering all the expenses engaged during the negotiations (including those which occurred before the breach).[161] Furthermore, the injured party can claim damages for the loss of a chance to conclude the same type of contract with a third party as long as the chance was real and serious. The aggrieved party cannot, however, obtain damages for the expected profits.[162] The new version of the French Civil Code does not provide much more enlightenment on this remedial question. In Article 1112(2) of the new French Civil Code, it is stated simply that: 'In case of fault committed during negotiations, the compensation for loss which thereby results cannot compensate the loss of the benefits expected from the contract which was not concluded.'[163]

[155] It should be noted that the common law systems themselves vary somewhat on this issue: see 52 above.

[156] For a detailed approach, see J Cartwright, *Contract Law: An Introduction to English Law for the Civil Lawyer* (Oxford, Hart Publishing, 2007) 65.

[157] This is the approach in the standard texts. For a nuanced approach, see Cartwright (n 58) 72.

[158] See Lord Bingham's famous dictum in *Interfoto Library Ltd v Stiletto Ltd* [1989] 1 QB 433, 439, paras D–H.

[159] For a detailed approach, see Cartwright (n 58) 82–90.

[160] *Cobbe v Yeomans Row Management Ltd* [2006] EWCA Civ 1139.

[161] See M Fabre-Magnan, *Droit des Obligations: Contrat et Engagement Unilatéral* (3rd edn, Paris, PUF, 2012) 249–251.

[162] Cass com, 26 nov 2003, nos 00-10243 and 00-10949, *Bull civ* IV, no 186; *RTD civ* 2004, 80 note J Mestre and B Fages; Cass civ, 3ème, 28 juin 2006, no 04-20040. On this question, see O Deshayes, 'Le dommage précontractuel' [2004] *RTD com* 187.

[163] Art 1112.

## D. Drawn between Two Contrasting Approaches: The Jersey Law Position

For many years, there was no Jersey authority dealing directly with the question of precontractual duties or remedies for breach thereof. The position was therefore somewhat open, and the comparative law sources demonstrated different attitudes to the question, as we have seen.[164] There are many reasons why Jersey might adopt a different approach to that of the English common law on this issue. First, there are substantive reasons which would support a different approach in Jersey to this issue. As we have already seen,[165] the notion of good faith is a familiar one in the Jersey law of contract, informing and shaping issues such as *vice de consentement*, and *déception d'outre moitié*.[166]

Second, over and above the substantive law differences, there are some fundamental reasons of *mentalité* which illustrate the divide between the English and Jersey approaches. One of the traditional reasons cited for English lawyers' distrust of good faith is its open-textured or abstract nature. Cartwright has argued that one of the reasons for the reluctance of English law to impose a general duty on each party during negotiations is 'the reluctance of English law to work from general principles'.[167] Interestingly, on this point, Jersey law again illustrates a hybrid approach. We have already remarked that maxims are a particular feature of the law of Jersey, and the presence of overarching principles, from which concrete rules are drawn in individual cases, is a striking feature of the Jersey law of contract, in contradistinction to the casuistic common law methodology.[168] For this reason, amongst others, it may perhaps be argued that the introduction of a principle of good faith in a precontractual scenario in Jersey would not become a 'legal irritant' as Teubner predicted would be the case with the English common law.[169]

However, a more recent case has dealt directly with the issue of good faith in the law of Jersey. In the case of *Minister for Treasury and Resources v Harcourt Developments Limited*, the claimants were companies involved in a property development project known as Esplanade Quarter. The State of Jersey Development Company (formerly known as Water Enterprise Board Ltd or 'WEB')

[164] See, however, the decision of *Cooke v Mold* [2010] JRC 093 concerning the discharge of an injunction restraining the sale of property, in which the rules applying to a precontractual private tender were discussed, and the attachment to *la convention fait la loi des parties* was expressed.

[165] See p 50 above.

[166] In relation to which the Privy Council has held that: 'the remedy is based on the principle of good faith' (*Snell v Beadle* [2001] UKPC [5], para 46).

[167] Cartwright (n 58) 72.

[168] See Chapter 2 above, pp 28–30.

[169] G Teubner, 'Legal Irritants: Good Faith in British Law or How Unifying Law Ends up in New Divergences' (1998) 61 *MLR* 11.

the public company charged with the promotion of the waterfront area in [elier. Following a tender process, Harcourt Developments (the first claim-) was selected as the preferred developer for the project and heads of terms re signed in 2007. Under the heads of terms, the parties agreed inter alia 'to t in good faith and with all due diligence' to negotiate a broader development greement. A claim was brought against the Minister on the basis that the lat-er had committed the tort of inducing breach of contract by WEB, who, it was lleged, had failed to negotiate the terms of the development agreement in good faith and with all due diligence.[170] Substantial damages of circa £100 million were claimed.

The Minister brought a strike-out application, arguing that there was no reasonable cause of action. It was argued that the tort was not made out as there was no valid contract which WEB had breached: the heads of terms were simply an agreement to agree or an agreement to negotiate and that under Jersey law, such an agreement did not amount to an enforceable contract because it was too uncertain.

Harcourt countered that the key terms of the agreement had been reached in the heads of terms, as the core terms to be incorporated in the ultimate development agreement were set out in the heads of terms. Harcourt argued that the good-faith obligations were simply to flesh out the necessary detail required for the project. Thus the duty to negotiate in good faith required negotiations which would not effectively negate the key terms (unless this were mutually agreed), and required the parties to seek to negotiate to implement the key terms by fleshing them out and negotiating such other details as might be necessary for a full agreement. The factual situation in this case (so it was argued) was therefore very different from an open-ended agreement to negotiate and it followed that there was sufficient certainty for the heads of terms to be legally enforceable.

At first instance, the Bailiff[171] dismissed the strike-out application, holding that it was arguable that the heads of terms document was not merely simply an agreement to agree and that it was capable of being construed as an enforceable contract, the breach of which might found a claim for breach of contract.[172] In so doing, the Bailiff underlined that this was a developing field of law.

The Court of Appeal, however, took a different view, allowing the Minister's strike-out application.[173] On the question of sources, the Court made only very brief references to a handful of Jersey authorities, and instead based its decision

170 Due to delays in progressing the draft developments agreement, and alleged attempts by WEB to include clauses in the Development Agreement which were contrary to the Heads of Terms.

171 In Jersey, the Bailiff is President of the Royal Court in Jersey and is also civic head of the Island with responsibility for official communication with the UK authorities. The bailiff is also the President of the States Assembly.

172 *Minister for Treasury and Resources v Harcourt Developments Limited* [2014] JCA 179.

173 *Minister for Treasury and Resources v Harcourt Developments Limited* 2014 (2) JLR 353.

predominantly on English law, citing the well-known English case law, such as *Walford v Miles*.[174] It is very surprising to see such an approach to sources, given the continued, and recent Jersey case law warnings, against reliance purely on English sources.[175] Surprisingly, no mention was made of the rich civil law sources, or of Pothier or Domat, despite the fact that these had featured in the Bailiff's judgment at first instance. Over and above that point, the Court of Appeal completely failed to analyse the recent Jersey cases discussing the potential role of good faith in the law of Jersey.[176] From the perspective of sources, the Court of Appeal's decision in *Harcourt* is a very disappointing one indeed.[177]

On the substantive issues, the judgment of the Court of Appeal is unfortunately not a model of clarity. The Court overturned the Bailiff's decision, allowing the strike-out application. The essence of the decision seems to be that the clause of the agreement to negotiate in good faith was simply an agreement to agree or an agreement to negotiate,[178] and it was 'incontrovertible that in Jersey law an agreement, properly characterised as an agreement to agree or an agreement to negotiate, is not one which can create a contractual obligation and therefore is incapable of enforcement'.[179] The Court of Appeal held that if the position was otherwise, there would not be sufficient certainty of contract obligations: 'The reason such agreements fail is that there is no sufficiently certain "objet" for there to be a Jersey contract.'

The Court of Appeal then analysed whether the position would be different, if the other provisions of the heads of terms were taken into account and whether it could thus be argued that the duty to negotiate in good faith required negotiations that did not negate the key terms and required the parties to implement the key terms by fleshing them out, and thus an attempt to repudiate or negate a key term would amount to a breach of an enforceable contract. The Court accepted that there were clauses in the head of terms which set out important matters which the parties wished to be included in the development agreement. However, the judges considered it determinative that 'there is no clause in the Heads of Terms to the effect that those matters are key terms which the parties agree must be included in the Development Agreement in any event, unless they are to be excluded by mutual consent'.[180] They considered that in fact the 'most significant clause' was the good-faith clause, as it was that clause on which the claimants founded their claim.

[174] *Walford v Miles* [1992] AC 128.

[175] See eg *Incat Equatorial Guinee Ltd v Luba Freeport Ltd* 2010 JLR 287. See further Chapter 2 above.

[176] See eg *Sutton v Insurance Corporation of the Channel Islands Limited* 2011 JLR 80, [16].

[177] In this respect, it is to be noted that the claimant was not represented by legal counsel before the Court of Appeal.

[178] *Minister for Treasury and Resources v Harcourt Developments Limited* 2014 (2) JLR 353, paras 52–82.

[179] Para 53.

[180] See para 69.

On the strength of the decision of the Court of Appeal in this decision, the potential for liability during the precontractual stage in Jersey would thus seem to be somewhat limited. It might, however, be justifiably asked how strong a decision is which premises its analysis almost solely on English law, despite recent judicial warnings to the contrary,[181] overlooks almost entirely the relevant Jersey case law, and engages with almost none of the relevant older writers and contextual arguments. From that perspective, doubts do remain about the authentic Jersey approach to the doctrine of good faith in contract law.

[181] eg *Incat Equatorial Guinee Ltd v Luba Freeport Ltd* 2010 JLR 287.

# 4

# The Formation of a Contract

## I. Introduction

The language and concepts of the law pertaining to the formation of contracts differs greatly across the different legal systems,[1] reflecting underlying differences in philosophy. Despite such differences, there are, however, many common themes, and the study of a mixed jurisdiction such as Jersey illustrates how the issues are addressed using concepts and vocabulary which draw upon both common law and civil law influences.

The leading case in Jersey on the formation of a contract is *Selby v Romeril*[2] in which the Royal Court held that the four essential requirements for a valid contract were:[3] capacity; consent; *objet*; and *cause*. In establishing these requirements, the Court noted that Pothier referred to three elements of a valid contract, but then went on to look at Article 1108 of the French Civil Code, which provides for an additional requirement:

> It is true that Pothier has often been treated by this court as the surest guide to the Jersey law of contract. It is also, however, true that Pothier was writing two centuries ago and that our law cannot be regarded as set in the aspic of the 18th century. Pothier was one of those authors upon whom the draftsman of the French Code Civil relied and it is therefore helpful to look at the relevant article of that Code. Article 1108 of the Code provides:
>
> 'Quatre conditions sont essentielles pour la validité d'une convention:
>
> Le consentement de la partie qui s'oblige;
> Sa capacité de contracter;
> Un objet certain qui forme la matière de l'engagement;
> Une cause licite dans l'obligation.'
>
> In our judgment it may now be asserted that by the law of Jersey, there are four requirements for the creation of a valid contract, namely, (a) consent, (b) capacity, (c) objet and (d) cause.[4]

[1] See generally T Kadner-Graziano, *Comparative Contract Law: Cases, Materials and Exercises* (London, Palgrave Macmillan, 2009); H Beale, B Fauvarque-Cosson, J Rutgers, D Tallon and S Vogenauer, *Cases, Materials and Text on Contract Law* (Oxford, Hart Publishing, 2010).

[2] *Selby v Romeril* 1996 JLR 210.

[3] See also the Court of Appeal decision in *O'Brien v Marett* [2008] JCA 178, [55].

[4] *Selby v Romeril* 1996 JLR 210, 217.

This approach, approved in subsequent decisions,[5] means therefore that Jersey replicates the traditional approach of French law on this point, whereby the existence of a valid contract at French law is classically determined by the presence of four criteria listed in Article 1108 of the original Civil Code: *échange de consentements* (offer and acceptance), the *capacité de contracter* (capacity to contract) of the parties, a valid *cause* and finally 'a determinate objet forming the subject matter of the agreement'.[6] This is therefore an example of the Jersey courts directly drawing from *modern* French law in respect of one of the core aspects of the law of contract.

We will therefore look in turn at the four constituent elements of the formation of a contract in Jersey law, analysing the way in which, from a comparative law perspective, common law and civil influences have played a part in defining the distinctive Jersey law approach.

## II. Capacity

All legal systems have rules governing the capacity that the parties must have in order to contract.[7] Jersey is no exception. The Jersey law rules are relatively orthodox so we will not dwell on these in great detail. There are specific rules applying to minors, those acting whilst subject to mental incapacity,[8] as well as for corporations.

In terms of minors, the general principle is that those under 18 are not able to contract.[9] From this perspective, a contract entered into by a minor is void ab initio.[10] Reference is invariably thus made to Pothier who wrote that:[11]

> Il est clair que les fous, les insensés, les enfants ne sont pas capables de contracter les obligations qui naissent des délits ou des quasi délits, ni de contracter par eux mêmes celles qui naissent des contrats puisqu'ils ne sont pas capables de consentement sans lequel il ne peut y avoir ni conventions ni délit ou quasi délit.[12]

[5] See eg *O'Brien v Marett* [2008] JCA 178.

[6] It is to be noted, however, that the new Civil Code has now reduced the criteria to three, namely 'the consent of the parties', 'their capacity to contract', and a 'content which is lawful and certain' (Art 1128 of the new Civil Code).

[7] See generally J Smits, *Contract Law: A Comparative Introduction* (Cheltenham, Edward Elgar 2014) ch 5.

[8] Although in the absence of much authority, the position in respect of those with mental incapacity is not by all means clear.

[9] Anyone younger than 18 is a minor: Age of Majority (Jersey) Law 1999.

[10] See *Deacon v Bower* (1978) JJ 39. The question of nullity is discussed in more detail in Chapter 7 below.

[11] Pothier, *Traité des Obligations*, part 1, ch 1, para 128.

[12] 'It is clear that the mentally incapacitated, insane persons and children are not capable of contracting obligations arising from torts or restitution (quasi délits), nor to contract by themselves

As in most legal systems, an exception is made to this rule that a minor is not bound by contracts, so as to allow for contracting in respect of everyday transactions. In the absence of any case law, a practice has developed whereby, as expressed in the Civil Commissioners' Report 1861 that contracts for 'necessaries'[13] and beneficial employment can be enforced against a minor.[14] This was moreover explicitly provided for in the Supply of Goods and Services (Jersey) Law 2009.[15]

In terms of legal persons, legislative intervention has also allowed for companies to contract.[16] One continuing area of uncertainty is that of unincorporated associations,[17] though it has generally been assumed that rules of agency would apply to such an entity,[18] and in reality many such associations are in fact incorporated under the Loi (1862) sur les teneures en fidéicommis et l'incorporation d'associations which thereby accords legal personality and capacity to contract.[19]

## III. Consent: The Requirement of a Fundamental Meeting of Minds

Perhaps unsurprisingly given the civil law influences, the primacy of consent in the formation of contracts is ever present in the Jersey case law. It is striking how repeated reference is made in the cases to the need to show a 'meeting of minds' between the parties.[20] Moreover, contracts will be undermined where there has been a *defect* in consent: in the Jersey case of *Steelux Holdings Ltd v Edmonstone*, the court found that there had been a *vice de consentement*, and thus 'there will have been no consent, no meeting of minds, between the parties'.[21]

[obligations] that arise from contracts because they are not capable of giving their consent, without which there cannot be any agreement, torts or restitution (quasi délits).'

[13] On this, see Supply of Goods and Services (Jersey) Law 2009, Art 12, which defines necessaries as 'goods suitable to the condition in life of the minor or other person concerned and to his or her actual requirements at the time of the sale and delivery'.

[14] See *Report of the Commissioners appointed to inquire into the Civil, Municipal, and Ecclesiastical Laws of the Island of Jersey* (London, HMSO, 1861) xxx.

[15] In Art 12(2) of the Law, it is provided that: 'If necessaries are sold and delivered to a minor, and there was a duty so to sell and deliver them, the minor shall pay a reasonable price for them.'

[16] A company has legal personality and may thus enter into contracts in that capacity, as recognised by Arts 20(1) and 21(1) of the Companies (Jersey) Law 1991.

[17] Which do not have legal personality (unless incorporated).

[18] So that if the representatives of the association had actual or implied authority to enter into a contract, then the members of the association would be bound by the contract in question.

[19] See eg the incorporation of the Jersey Society for the Deaf and Hard of Hearing as pronounced by the Samedi Division of the Royal Court on 27 January 2006.

[20] See eg *Bennett v Lincoln* 2005 JLR 125; *Cronin and Luce v Gordon-Bennet* 2003 JLR N22.

[21] *Steelux Holdings Ltd v Edmonstone* 2005 JLR 152, 156.

We have already analysed above the centrality of consent in contract law cases.[22] The notion of *consentement* is in many ways the central, defining concept of Jersey contract law from which much else flows, including the principles guiding formation, the undermining and the effects of contracts.

In terms of the formation of contracts, the Jersey courts have consistently required proof that there was a *meeting of minds* as to the agreement between the parties. As was held in one case, '[t]here being no meeting of minds, no convention, there can be no contract'.[23] Various illustrations of the application of the litmus test of consent can be found in different Jersey cases, such as in respect of the formation of partnership agreements.[24]

The process of that meeting of minds has in many cases been examined through the Anglo-American prism of offer and acceptance. But such linguistic assumptions may be controversial given the distinctiveness of Jersey contract law, and the specificities of the sources.[25] Indeed, in one recent case, *Incat Equatorial Guinee Ltd v Luba Freeport Ltd,*[26] some reluctance was expressed in respect of the resort to common law terminology in this area. The Deputy Bailiff thus commented as follows:

> [B]oth parties agreed that the proper law of the alleged contract was Jersey law, and it is therefore Jersey law which we have applied. It follows that expressions such 'offer and acceptance' or 'invitation to treat' are not particularly helpful in considering the issue before us.[27]

However, this may simply be expressive of the inappropriateness of relying upon English law or commentaries such as *Chitty* in developing the law of Jersey in this sphere.[28] In any case, the use of common law terminology has continued in recent Jersey judgments.[29] From a comparative perspective, it should be noted that in the new French Civil Code, the terminology of 'offer' and 'acceptance' is deployed.[30]

In Jersey law, contractual consent is deemed to have been formed by way of an offer made by one party which is accepted by another. However, two additional elements are also required, namely the certainty of terms and the necessary contractual intention. We will examine in turn these various notions: offer and acceptance, certainty of contractual terms and the notion of a contractual intention.

[22] See pp 36–38 above.

[23] *Cronin and Luce v Gordon-Bennet* 2003 JLR N22, para 20.

[24] Contrast the findings of the courts as to whether there was meeting of minds as to the formation of a partnership agreement in: *Bennett v Lincoln* 2005 JLR 125 and *Cannon v Nicol* 2006 JLR 299.

[25] See generally Chapter 2 above.

[26] *Incat Equatorial Guinee Ltd v Luba Freeport Ltd* 2010 JLR 287.

[27] Ibid, 294.

[28] As was noted earlier in the judgment: ibid, 294.

[29] See eg *Minister for Treasury and Resources v Harcourt Developments Limited* 2014 (2) JLR 353.

[30] See eg Art 1113: 'A contract is formed by the meeting of an offer and an acceptance by which the parties demonstrate their will to be bound.' This subsection of the new Civil Code is entitled 'offer and acceptance'.

# IV. Offer and Acceptance

## A. Defining an Offer

The Jersey law on offer and acceptance is primarily derived from the case law of the Jersey courts. We will therefore review these decisions in some detail. It should be noted that there has been some legislation of relevance on this topic. In the recent legislation on the sale of goods and services, it is provided that 'a contract of sale of goods may be made in writing (either with or without seal), or by word of mouth'.[31] The reference to 'seal' is, however, erroneous given that no such instrument exists in Jersey, and this illustrates the dangers of direct transplants of texts,[32] without sufficient account being taken of specific context and surrounding instruments.

### *(i) Distinguishing Offer and Invitation to Treat: Display of Goods*

All legal systems require a concept for dividing between, on the one hand, firm offers to contract, which are thus susceptible of acceptance by the other party and, on the other hand, mere discussions falling short of a formal offer.[33]

As is well known, a distinction is made in English law between the making of an offer and a mere invitation to treat. Vast swathes of contract law textbooks are thus made up of an analysis of the case law on this topic,[34] and all English law students are familiar with the factual matrices of cases such as *Carlill v Carbolic Smoke Ball Co*,[35] *Pharmaceutical Society of Great Britain v Boots Cash Chemists Ltd*[36] and *Fisher v Bell*.[37] In terms of the display of goods in retail premises, the position is relatively clear, namely that, as held by Lord Parker in *Fisher v Bell*,

> according to the ordinary law of contract, the display of an article with a price on it in a shop window is merely an invitation to treat. It is in no sense an offer for sale the acceptance of which constitutes a contract.[38]

A number of Jersey cases have similarly examined this distinction, and the relevant English case law has been much cited. The two leading cases have focused upon the issue of the position of the display of goods.

[31] Art 13(1), Supply of Goods and Services (Jersey) Law 2009.

[32] In this case from the UK Sale of Goods Act. The Electronic Communications (Jersey) Law 2000 also provides that in the formation of a contract, unless the parties have otherwise agreed, the offer and the acceptance of the offer may be expressed by means of an electronic communication (Art 4(1)).

[33] See from a comparative law perspective Kadner-Graziano (n 1) ch I.

[34] See eg N Andrews, *Contract Law* (2nd edn, Cambridge, CUP, 2015) ch 3. For a pithy summary of the law, see A Burrows (ed), *Principles of the English Law of Obligations* (Oxford, OUP, 2015) paras 1.05–1.06.

[35] *Carlill v Carbolic Smoke Ball Co* (1892) 2 QB 484.

[36] *Pharmaceutical Society of Great Britain v Boots Cash Chemists Ltd* (1952) 2 QB 795.

[37] *Fisher v Bell* (1961) 1 QB 394.

[38] Ibid.

One early decision was interpreted by commentators as suggesting that the display of goods may amount to an offer, rather than an invitation to treat. In *AG v Galore Wholesale Limited*,[39] which concerned the alleged breach of the Sunday trading laws by a shop proposing to customers that they leave their shopping orders on a Sunday in writing for collection the next day, the Court had to decide whether the display of goods amounted to an offer capable of being accepted by the completion of an order form or a mere invitation to treat such that the completion of the order form amounted only to an offer. The decision of the Court is not entirely clear. Indeed, some statements[40] of the Royal Court seem to suggest that the display of goods can amount to an offer.[41] However, on closer analysis, the better view is that the Court accepted the argument of the appellant shop that it was the *customer's* actions which constituted an offer and thus the contract was not completed until the next day.[42] If that is right, then the display of goods amounted merely to an invitation to treat, rather than an offer.

In the later case of *Gilbraith v Attorney General*,[43] Gilbraith had placed a second-hand car for sale on the forecourt of his garage premises. It subsequently transpired that the car in question had been involved in an accident and declared a write-off. Gilbraith was thus charged in the Police Court with offering to sell a vehicle in such a condition that it could not lawfully be used. He was acquitted because the offence required an 'offer for sale' to have been made and not an invitation to treat. It was held that placing a car on the forecourt of a garage did not constitute an offer to sell, but rather an invitation to treat. Gilbraith was not therefore liable for the offence as the car had not in fact been 'offered' for sale. In reaching its decision, the Court referred to *Cheshire and Fifoot* and also relied upon the English case of *Fisher v Bell*.[44]

[39] *AG v Galore Wholesale Limited* [1983] JJ 67.

[40] Confusion stems from the fact that earlier in the judgment, the Royal Court held that: 'Now, it is accepted by the appellant company, that that action of a customer, by signing the order form and placing it in the particular receptacle, was part of a contract, that is to say it was the offer on behalf of the customer which could be completed on the following day. It appears to us that the learned Relief Magistrate took the view that there had been a completed contract, and with respect to his finding we cannot uphold him on that particular point' (ibid, 67–68). The Court would thus seem to be saying that it did not accept that a completed contract had actually occurred and is indicating a preference for the appellant company's argument that the customer's actions constituted an offer and that the contract was not completed until the next day. This runs contrary to the other statements in the judgment.

[41] eg '[T]here was ... at least an offer of a contract, made as the price was already affixed to the goods' (ibid, 69). Albeit that this statement was made in the context of the interpretation of the criminal offence in the relevant Sunday trading legislation, and not on a point of contract stricto sensu.

[42] See in particular the passage at ibid, 67–68.

[43] *Gilbraith v Attorney General* 1992 JLR 190.

[44] *Fisher v Bell* (1961) 1 QB 394. In which it was held that displaying a flick knife in a shop window was merely an invitation to treat, not an offer, and thus criminal liability did not arise.

### (ii) Comparative Law Sources on Display of Goods

In France, the Code civil did not traditionally contain rules on the issue of offer and acceptance.[45] There was, however, much case law on the topic and though the issue was considered to be inherently fact-sensitive,[46] practices have developed. Unlike in English law, objects displayed in a shop window at a price are *generally* considered by the French courts to constitute an offer, which is capable of acceptance.[47] It remains to be seen how this case law will be affected by the new version of the Civil Code, which provides more details as to 'offer' and 'acceptance', most notably distinguishing the former from an 'invitation to enter into negotiations'.[48] Whatever that may be, the traditional approach was explained by the doctrine of consensus: the shop owner has a continuing intention to sell items displayed and the buyer intends to buy the items placed in his basket with the result that, when the buyer takes the items to the checkout, then the contract has been formed.[49] However, it should be underlined that this is not a definitive rule: variants may arise depending upon evidence as to the intention of the parties.

Such an approach may perhaps provide an explanation for the Jersey case law. If the meeting of minds between the parties is a question of fact to be determined by the Royal Court,[50] then the response to that may legitimately vary depending on the particular circumstances of the case. This is particularly the case given that the subjective approach to consent is adopted in Jersey, as examined above,[51] thus entailing that the exact intention of the parties takes precedence.

## B. The Concept of Acceptance

There has also been case law in Jersey concerning the notion of acceptance. Unsurprisingly, proof of an offer to enter into legal relations must be followed by the acceptance of that offer. In Jersey, the Court held in the case of *Osment v Constable of St Helier*[52] that it must be shown that the offeree had accepted the offer and had intended to be bound by it. In other cases, it has been held that the acceptance

[45] The position has evolved in the new drafting of the Civil Code, see Art 1113 onwards, in respect of which the sub-section is now entitled 'Offer and Acceptance'.

[46] And generally dealt with by the *juges de fonds* and thus cassation-proof due to the 'pouvoir souverain d'appréciation'.

[47] See eg P Le Tourneau, *Droit de la Responsabilité et des contrats* (9th edn, Paris, Dalloz, 2012) no 3713; J Bell, S Boyron and S Whittaker, *Principles of French Law* (2nd edn, Oxford, OUP, 2008) 303.

[48] See generally Art 1114.

[49] For discussion in English, see B Nicholas, *The French Law of Contract* (2nd edn, Oxford, OUP, 1982) 64; Kadner-Graziano (n 1) 49–93; Bell, Boyron and Whittaker (n 47) 303.

[50] On this, see *Bennett v Lincoln* 2005 JLR 125, [22].

[51] Pages 44–47.

[52] *Osment v Constable of St Helier* (1974) JJ 1.

of the offer may also be inferred from words or conduct.[53] However, it would seem that mere silence on the part of the offeree cannot be deemed to constitute an acceptance,[54] as is indeed the position in French law,[55] and in the various European projects.[56]

We have seen that the consensual approach underpins this area of Jersey law and thus informs the relevant case law, so that a 'meeting of minds' requirement applies equally to the offeree in accepting the offer as it does to the offeror in making it.[57] The courts have, however, on occasion diverged from the subjective approach suggested by the reliance upon consent. A stark example of this is provided by the case of *Mobil Sales & Supply Corp v Transoil (Jersey) Ltd*,[58] concerning a contract for the supply of oil. The Royal Court held that, even where a mistake had arisen as to the parties' real intentions concerning the elements of the contract, a contract will be deemed to arise where a reasonable man would have thought the terms of the contract to have been accepted. This rule, however, does not sit entirely happily with the Jersey court's preference for the subjective doctrine of consent. In *Mobil Sales*, the Royal Court indeed did not duck the issue, expressly declaring that: 'The question which the Court has to determine is not what the parties had in their minds, but what reasonable third parties, "disinterested spectators", would infer from their words or conduct.'[59] This therefore relates to an objective test,[60] rather than the traditional subjective[61] approach found under French law. This diverges from the subjective theory adopted by the Jersey law of contract in determining consent.[62]

As we have already seen, it is now strongly arguable that the decision in *Mobil Sales* is no longer good law. Indeed, the Court of Appeal in *O'Brien v Marett* explicitly ruled that *Mobil Sales* and *La Motte Garages* 'must now be considered *per incuriam* on this specific point in the light of *Selby v Romeril*'.[63] If that is right, then

[53] *Mobil Sales & Supply Corp v Transoil (Jersey) Ltd* (1981) JJ 143, 159 and 163.

[54] As to terms and conditions, see *Bradley v Bates* (1982) JJ 197, 201.

[55] Cass civ 3ème, 16 avr 1996, no 94-16528: 'le silence ne vaut pas, à lui seul, acceptation'. See B Fages, *Droit des Obligations* (4th edn, Paris, LGDJ 2013) para 77; P Le Tourneau, *Droit de la Responsabilité et des Contrats* (Paris, Dalloz Action, 2014/15), para 864. Exceptions do arise, however, in legislation (see eg Art. 1738 Civil Code on extension of tenancy by lessee remaining in possession; or Art L112-2(5) Code des assurances), or in general business practice (Fages, ibid), or in certain cases, where the offer was made in the 'intéret exclusif' of the offeror and by virtue of this is presumed to have been accepted by the offeree (eg Cass civ 1ere, 1 déc 1969—unconscious victim of road accident accepted offer to help by rescuer injured in the process, giving rise to a 'convention d'assistance').

[56] See eg Art 2:204 (2) PECL: 'Silence or inactivity does not in itself amount to acceptance.'

[57] See eg *Bennett v Lincoln* 2005 JLR 125; *Cronin and Luce v Gordon-Bennet* 2003 JLR N22.

[58] *Mobil Sales & Supply Corp v Transoil (Jersey) Ltd* (1981) JJ 143, 159.

[59] Ibid, 159 and 163. In other cases, the courts have referred to the notion of the 'sense of the promise' (see *La Motte Garages Ltd v Morgan* (1989) JJ 312, 316).

[60] See *La Motte Garages Ltd v Morgan* (1989) JJ 312, 316.

[61] Note, however, that this is referred to as *in concreto* in French law (rather than 'subjective' which means something different).

[62] See further discussion in Chapter 3 above, pp 44–47.

[63] *O'Brien v Marett* [2008] JCA 178, [55].

it should entail a different approach to that adopted in *Mobil Sales*. In particular, it should result in greater emphasis being placed upon the evidential requirements of proving the parties' actual intentions at the time of the purported acceptance which would, as we have already seen, have procedural ramifications.[64]

## C. Certainty of Terms

An additional aspect of the requirement of meeting of minds or consent is that of certainty. In many ways, this overlaps with the question of the certainty of the contractual objet, an issue which will be examined in more detail below.[65] The Jersey courts have held that there must be certainty as to the contractual arrangements to which consent is to be given, and thus the terms of a contract must be certain in order for a contract to be valid. The Royal Court in the case of *Osment v Constable of St Helier*[66] referred to *Chitty on Contracts*, as well as English case law[67] as authority for the principle that the parties must agree as to the contractual terms with sufficient certainty.[68] It should, however, be noted that the Jersey courts' approach to the question of the certainty of contractual terms is one of degree. There are other cases where the courts' position on this is much less demanding. In the case of *Louis v Le Liard*,[69] the court enforced a payment for construction services despite what were very imprecise terms as to the requisite work and reward.

## D. Contractual Intention

The issue of whether legal effect is intended to attach to agreements is a primordial one in legal systems, tracing as it does a line between the areas of a defined legal relationship, and the other areas beyond the reach of the law, such as social and informal arrangements. The issue has been examined in comparative law, and it has also been considered in Jersey. The Jersey courts have declined to extend the reach of the law to informal or social arrangements. The principle is that the intention of the parties must have been to create contractual relations. This is closely associated with the principle of autonomy of will and the need for exchange of consent to create a valid contract. The comparative law perspective on this question will first be analysed, prior to reviewing the Jersey law position.

[64] See Chapter 3 above, pp 46–47.
[65] See 71–72 below.
[66] *Osment v Constable of St Helier* (1974) JJ 1.
[67] *May and Butcher v The King* (1934) 2 KB 17.
[68] *Osment v Constable of St Helier* (1974) JJ 1, 26. See also the cases of *Griggs v Coutanche* 1975 JJ 219 and *Mirpuri v Bank of India* [2010] JRC 129.
[69] *Louis v Le Liard* 1990 JLR N13.

### (i) Comparative Law

In comparative law, this issue is a classic one, and has been examined on many occasions.[70] The French and English systems adopt ostensibly different approaches.

In the common law, even if an agreement is supported by consideration, it will not be binding if the judge considers that there was no contractual intentional to be legally bound. Presumptions often apply. In ordinary commercial transactions, it is not, in principle, necessary to prove that the parties to an express agreement in fact intended to create a legal relation.[71] In case of an implied agreement, the proof of the necessary intention will, however, be more demanding.[72] In deciding issues of contractual intention, the English courts normally apply an *objective* test. On this basis, it may be clear from the statements of the parties whether or not they intend to be contractually bound. As Aikens LJ said in *Barbudev v Eurocom Cable Management Bulgaria Food*:[73] 'On the issue of whether the parties intended to create legal relations … [t]he court has to consider the objective conduct of the parties as a whole.'[74] Moreover, context can be important. The courts tend to consider certain types of statements as lacking the necessary intention 'if they were not seriously meant and that this should have been obvious to the person to who it was made'.[75] Many domestic arrangements between spouses thus lack binding force.[76]

In France, there is no criterion per se of intention to enter legal relations. However, some textbooks have nonetheless referred to this notion,[77] as a proper one to delimit what belongs to contract and what belongs to, as Carbonnier famously described it, the '*non-droit*'.[78] Reference is thus sometimes made to the Latin tag of *animus contrahendi* ('an intention to contract').[79] An example of this may be found in the writing of Professor Fabre-Magnan, who observes that:

> In order for there to be a contract, the agreement of the parties must have as its objective to create *legal* obligations. It is thus necessary that the parties had an intention to be bound in legal terms, in other words that they accepted the possibility of being sued before the courts in case of failure to perform their obligations.[80]

[70] See eg Smits (n 7) ch 4; J Cartwright, *Contract Law: An Introduction to English Law for the Civil Lawyer* (2nd edn, Oxford, Hart Publishing, 2013) 149–50.

[71] *Edwards v Skyways Ltd* [1964] 1 WLR 349, 355.

[72] *Blackpool & Fylde Aero Club v Blackpool BC* [1990] 1 WLR 1195, 1202: 'contracts are not to be lightly implied' (per Bingham LJ).

[73] *Barbudev v Eurocom Cable Management Bulgaria Food* [2012] EWCA Civ 548.

[74] Ibid, [30.]

[75] *Chitty on Contracts, General Principles*, vol 1 (32nd edn, London, Sweet and Maxwell, 2015) para 2-173, 309.

[76] Atkin LJ *in Balfour v Balfour* [1919] 2 KB 571, 578.

[77] M Fabre-Magnan, *Droit des Obligations: Contrat et Engagement Unilatéral* (3rd edn, Paris, PUF, 2012) 177; P Malaurie, L Aynes and P Stoffel-Munck, *Les Obligations* (Paris, Defrénois, 2007) para 435.

[78] J Carbonnier, *Flexible droit: Textes pour une sociologie du droit sans rigueur* (Paris, LGDJ, 1969).

[79] Fabre-Magnan (n 77) 177.

[80] Ibid, 177.

It should also be noted that this issue is an interesting illustration of the bridging of the objective–subjective divide in French law.[81] Although consent itself is largely determined subjectively in French law through the process of assessing the content of the contract, the *characterisation* of consent as such can be seen as the result of an objective determination.[82] For example, the fact that the contracting parties put their signatures on an annexed document is considered evidence of the parties' agreement to its content and its effect, irrespective of the parties 'real' understanding of the terms. This is particularly true when the contract takes place between professionals acting in the scope of their field of activity.[83] In English law, despite the prevailing objective approach as described above, there have been indications of subjective influences. Andrews thus notes that 'in borderline cases, a more nuanced approach is adopted. The court will inquire closely into what the parties actually thought to be the case.'[84]

Simple courtesy or family arrangements are not generally considered in France to belong to the realm of contract law. In other contexts, however, the courts have on occasion been prepared to enforce arrangements where contractual intention was uncertain.[85] The issue has also been raised in the case of gratuitous services. In France, the gratuitous nature of an agreement does not preclude the conclusion of a contract, but from the case law, it is nonetheless relevant to whether the parties really intended to be legally bound or not. Nicholas argues this is a significant control factor: '[I]n this area, where the absence of a doctrine of consideration appears to produce a practical difference, the need for an intention to create legal relations, which is otherwise little discussed, plays an essential part.'[86]

### *(ii) Mid-Channel Approaches to Contractual Intention*

In Jersey law, an intention to contract is a necessary feature of the formation of a contract. The position of the Jersey courts on this issue has not been entirely consistent. In Jersey law, there is a line of case law which would suggest that the litmus test is an objective one, namely what an objective person would have interpreted from the parties' acts or behaviour. We have already touched on this point in the earlier analysis of the case of *Mobil Sales & Supply Corp v Transoil (Jersey) Ltd*.[87]

[81] See discussion on this in Beale et al (n 1) 58.

[82] F Limbach, *Le consentement contractuel à l'épreuve des conditions générales* (Paris, LGDJ, 2005) vol 1, 412.

[83] CA Pau, 29 October 2007, no 05/00114

[84] Andrews (n 34) 159.

[85] Such as merely 'moral' obligations: Cass com, 23 jan 2007, no 05-13189, *Bull civ* IV, no 12; *RDC* 200.693. This broad approach is also illustrated by the way that French courts have recognised the contractual nature of a wide range of documents including advertising documents (F Labarthe, *La notion de document contractuel*, (Paris, LGDJ, 1994) para 330) and invoices (J Mousseron, *Technique contractuelle* (4th edn, Paris, Francis Lefebvre, 2010) para 85).

[86] Nicholas (n 49) 149.

[87] *Mobil Sales & Supply Corp v Transoil (Jersey) Ltd* (1981) JJ 143, 159.

In a more recent decision, *Daisy Hill Real Estates Limited v Rent Control Tribunal*,[88] the Royal Court revisited the issue. The decision concerned whether a letter to or from the advocate of the Rent Control Tribunal to provide further and better particulars about how a rent assessment was reached could create a contractual relationship. The Court applied an objective test, holding that no reasonable person would infer that a letter agreeing to provide further and better particulars was intended to create a legally binding contract between the parties.[89]

However, this line of case law must now be read in light of the Court of Appeal decision of *O'Brien v Marett*,[90] in which the subjective approach was approved of and *Mobil Sales* seemingly overruled (as seen above).[91] It is therefore doubtful whether the statement in *Daisy Hill* is still good law. Certainly, the bald statement of the court in *Daisy Hill* that 'it matters not what the parties had in their minds' is of course very difficult to reconcile with the subjective approach as traditionally adopted by Jersey law.[92]

Illustrative of a more traditional approach is the case of Flynn v Reid.[93] In this case, a dispute arose about the status of an agreement which had been signed by the parties (an unmarried couple) when they bought a house which was to be their family home. We have already examined the facts in detail above.[94] The Deputy Bailiff suggested that the requirement of consent in the formation of a contract was the absent element in the instant case. He held that:

> [I]n relation to the requirement for consent of the parties undertaking the obligations, there must be shown a true consent, a true desire, or, adopting the French word, 'volonté' that the arrangement become legally binding between them.[95]

On the facts of the case, the Deputy Bailiff held 'that the contract did not in fact govern the relationship between the parties, nor was it intended to do so'.[96] One way to interpret the case is that the necessary contractual intention was missing. It may also be relevant that the agreement was between family members, and we will turn to review this issue now.

As in many other legal systems, in Jersey law, there seems to be a presumption that 'family arrangements', namely agreements between husbands and wives or parents and children, do not create legally binding contracts.[97] However, this presumption is rebuttable when the *seriousness* of the matter in contemplation, the *consequences* of one party acting upon it and the *intention* of the parties is

[88] *Daisy Hill Real Estates Limited v Rent Control Tribunal* 1995 JLR 176.

[89] Ibid, 179.

[90] *O'Brien v Marett* [2008] JCA 178.

[91] See discussion above in Chapter 3, pp 44–46.

[92] See, however, the recent decision of the Jersey Court of Appeal in *Home Farm Developments Ltd v Le Sueur* [2015] JCA 242, which has generated some uncertainty on this issue.

[93] *Flynn v Reid* [2012] JRC 100.

[94] See 37–38 above.

[95] *Flynn v Reid* [2012] JRC 100, [21].

[96] Ibid.

[97] *Ferchal v Ferchal* 1990 JLR 117.

such that a contract was intended.[98] In the case of *Louis v Le Liard*,[99] the court enforced a payment for building labouring services when the work undertaken by the claimant for his brother in law clearly went beyond the mutual assistance normally offered by one family member to another.

## V. Contractual *Objet*

The *objet* is the third essential ingredient of a binding Jersey contract as identified in the case of *Selby v Romeril*.[100] The *objet* of an obligation refers to the subject-matter or gist of the obligation, namely the content of what the party undertakes according to the contract.[101] There is typically a tripartite of requirements for a valid *objet*, namely that it is identifiable, possible and licit.[102]

### A. Objet Must be Identifiable

The first requirement of the *objet* of a contract is that it is identifiable. In *Selby v Romeril*, the Royal Court held that this meant that the content of the undertaking must be sufficiently certain.[103] The Court cited Pothier on this issue as follows:

> Pour qu'un fait puisse être l'objet d'une obligation, il faut aussi que ce que le débiteur s'est obligé de faire soit quelque chose de déterminé.[104]

In *Selby*, the Court held that the agreement in question did not make it sufficiently certain as to what works the landlord was to pay for. This approach was illustrated in another case. In *Groom v Stock*,[105] the plaintiff brought a claim for wrongful dismissal, seeking to recover arrears of salary and a bonus against the defendant licensee of a pub. It was held by the Royal Court, citing Pothier, that the bonus was not recoverable as its quantum was indeterminable and was at the defendant's discretion. Consequently, the *objet* of the contract was not sufficiently certain and no valid contractual entitlement had been created.

In Jersey law, the contractual *objet* is not restricted to present, identified objects or obligations.[106] Indeed, Pothier notes that not only something ascertained may

[98] Ibid.

[99] *Louis v Le Liard* 1990 JLR N13.

[100] *Selby v Romeril* 1996 JLR 210.

[101] Note that the new version of the French Civil Code refers expressly to 'a licit and certain *content*' (Art 1128).

[102] See *O'Brien v Marett* [2008] JCA 178.

[103] *Selby v Romeril* 1996 JLR 210, 219.

[104] Pothier, *Traité des Obligations*, part 1, ch 1, para 137: 'In order for something to be the objet of an obligation, it is necessary too that that which the debtor has promised to do be identifiable.'

[105] *Groom v Stock* [1965] JJ 429. See also *Maçon v Quérée* [2001] JLR 80.

[106] Note, for instance, that under the Supply of Goods and Services (Jersey) Law 2009, the transfer of property in a contract for the sale of goods may take place 'at a future time' (Art 11(5)). See also *Golder v Société des Magasins Concorde Limited* (1967) JJ 721, 730.

be the subject-matter of an obligation, but also something *ascertainable*. Therefore, it is not necessary that the quantity of goods should actually be determined when the obligation is contracted, provided it is determinable.[107] In the recent case of *O'Brien v Marett*,[108] the Court of Appeal summarised the notion of certainty of *objet* as follows:

> As to certainty, the promised performance must be sufficiently certain if this particular requirement is to be satisfied: *Selby v Romeril* (where the contract failed because the objet was not defined or was uncertain). Alternatively, objet must be capable of determination: *Groom v Stock* [1965] JJ 429 (employee's right to bonus unenforceable because no means provided for its determination).[109]

Indeed, the recent legislation on the sale of goods and services allows for contracting as to future or conditional goods.[110] This is reflected in the modern French Civil Code, which provides that the subject-matter of a contractual obligation may either be determined under the contract or be 'capable of being determined'.[111] It is also now explicitly provided in Article 1163 of the new Civil Code that '[a]n obligation has as its *objet* a present or future act of performance'. The *objet* may thus consist of 'future things', for instance manufactured goods yet to be produced.[112]

## B. Objet Must be Possible

It has also been said that in Jersey law, it must be shown that the *objet* is possible. There does not seem to be any case law directly relevant to this point. This requirement can be traced back to Pothier who notes that:

> In order for something to be the objet of an obligation, it is necessary for it to be possible because impossibilium nulla obligatio.[113]

Modern French law also contains a similar rule, so that the impossibility of the contractual *objet* undermines the validity of the contract.[114] As Fages has observed: '[i]n the same way that no one can be bound to achieve the impossible, it is considered traditionally in French law that no one can promise the impossible.'[115] However, in French law, the impossibility which undermines the objet must

[107] See Pothier, *Traité des Obligations*, part 1, ch 1, para. 131.
[108] *O'Brien v Marett* [2008] JCA 178.
[109] Ibid, [60].
[110] Supply of Goods and Services (Jersey) Law 2009, Art 14.
[111] Art 1163 of the new Civil Code.
[112] Cf Pothier, *Traité des Obligations*, part 1, ch 1, para 132: 'Things that do not exist yet but which are expected to come into existence may be the objet of an obligation but in such a way that the obligation shall be conditional upon their future existence.'
[113] Ibid, para 136.
[114] Art 1163 of the new Civil Code.
[115] Fages (n 55) para 155.

be *absolute* rather than relative: the reason for the impossibility should not be personal to the debtor.

A corollary of this rule in French law is that if the subject-matter of the contract has ceased to exist at the time when the contract is made, then the contract no longer has an *objet.*[116] Similarly, the original French Civil Code lays down that only items which can be legally sold can constitute a valid object.[117]

### C. Objet Must be Licit

In order for a contract to be valid, the *objet* of the contractual obligation must also be lawful. In the Jersey case of *Jameson Ltd v Cuming-Butler*,[118] the plaintiff company carried out building work which was in breach of the relevant by-laws. The plaintiff apparently sought payment for the work done,[119] and the defendant as part of his defence alleged that in view of the infringement of the by-laws, the contract could not be enforced. The Royal Court held that the plaintiff was not entitled to payment: the contract was invalid due to the fact that the building works infringed the relevant by-laws. The Court referred to English authority[120] to support this conclusion. However, it may be that the same conclusion could be reached on the basis of failure of a licit *objet:* the building work to be performed under the contract was contrary to the relevant by-laws.

## VI. Rejecting Consideration: The Notion of Cause

### A. Introduction

The concept of a contractual *cause* is unique to the French family of legal systems and is not found in other legal systems such as the common law or Germanic systems. Nicholas traces it back to both Roman and canon law texts.[121] A degree of mystery has traditionally shrouded this notion in French law. In sum, the position is that, whereas the *objet* of an obligation refers to the content of the parties' contractual obligations, the *cause* refers to the reason or motivation for which the

[116] Although, as we have already noted, future things can constitute the *objet* of the contractual obligation.

[117] See Art 1128 Civil Code: 'Only things which may be the subject matter of legal transactions between private individuals may be the object of agreements.'

[118] *Jameson Ltd v Cuming-Butler* (1981) JJ 17.

[119] The law report provides an excerpt only and is somewhat unclear.

[120] *Brightman & Co Ltd v Tate* [1919] 1 KB 463; *Langton v Hughes* (1813) 1 M & S 593.

[121] Nicholas (n 49) 118.

parties enter into a contract. The *cause* therefore explains *why* a debtor owes an obligation, whereas the *objet* describes *what* the debtor owes.[122]

In Jersey law, the authority for the proposition that *cause* is an essential element of Jersey contract law is said to derive from the *Ancienne Coutume*, from Poingdestre's *Les Lois et Coutumes de l'Ile de Jersey*[123] and from Le Geyt's manuscripts. The Royal Court thus held in the case of *Gallichan v Gallichan* that:

> Jersey law requires that there should be a 'cause' for a promise which is to be enforceable. Authority for this proposition may be found in various places, eg in the 'Ancienne Coutume', Mr WL de Gruchy's edition, page 90, 'De Convenants', at page 207, in Poingdestre's 'Loix and Coutumes', pages 330–332, and in Le Geyt's Manuscripts, Volume I, pages 146–148.[124]

Pothier argues that any agreement must have a 'cause honnête'.[125] An agreement will thus fail if there is no *cause*, or if there is a 'cause fausse'.[126] He notes also that a contract will be annulled 'where the cause for which the agreement has been made is contrary to justice, good faith or public morals'.[127]

In modern cases, the Jersey courts have confirmed that *cause* is an essential element of Jersey contract law.[128] In order to understand the role and place of *cause* in Jersey law, we will first examine this notion from a comparative law perspective.

## B. Evolving Approach under French Law

The notion of *cause* has long been a cornerstone of contract law in France, albeit a somewhat contested notion, and a good deal of debate has surrounded the concept. The recent reform of the Civil Code has had a radical impact on this aspect of French law, resulting in the ostensible removal of this notion. We will examine the traditional notion of the *cause*, followed by an analysis of the recent developments.

## C. Overview of the Notion of Cause

Until recently, the notion of a *cause* was the fourth requirement of a valid contract as laid down by Article 1108 of the original Code civil as 'a lawful cause

[122] See Bell, Boyron and Whittaker (n 47) 317. Nicholas (n 49) 118 puts this elegantly: '[W]hereas *objet* provides an answer to the question *quid debetur*? (what is owing?), cause answers the question why it is owing (*cur debetur*?).'

[123] Published in 1928 by the Jersey Law Society, and available at: www.jerseylaw.je/Publications/Library/JerseyLawTexts/poin02/default.aspx

[124] *Gallichan v Gallichan* (1954) JJ 57, 62–63.

[125] Pothier, *Traité des Obligations*, part 1, ch 1, para 42.

[126] Ibid.

[127] Ibid, para 43.

[128] See Court of Appeal decision in *O'Brien v Marett* [2008] JCA 178, [55].

within the obligation.'[129] Other provisions of the French Civil Code also referred to the notion of cause, albeit in a somewhat enigmatic way.[130] Whilst the *cause* or 'end pursued'[131] by parties in entering into a contract may vary widely, doctrinal commentators have distinguished between two distinct ways of viewing the *cause*.[132] First, a subjective approach may be adopted by looking at the 'determining motive'[133] for the debtor's undertaking an obligation. Second, the *cause* may be viewed from an objective perspective, which encapsulates the abstract reason for the obligation. This objective reason will be invariable for all those who enter into the same type of contract,[134] whereas the former subjective motive will of course differ depending on circumstances. Attempts have been made to reconcile the two approaches by applying a subjective analysis where it is asserted that there is an unlawful cause in respect of a contract, and an objective examination is applied in cases of absence of cause.[135] However, this distinction is by no means clear cut.

The concept of cause has been used in practical terms by the French courts in order to impose a minimum reciprocity in contractual terms. In this respect, the analogy, albeit imperfect, with the common law concept of consideration is often made. Whilst, as we have seen, different types of contract have in common the same type of abstract or objective *cause*, the courts will verify the reality of the cause on the facts of the case, and a contract may be annulled for want of *cause*. In this respect, a distinction must be drawn between *contrats réels*, gratuitous contracts and bilateral contracts. As Whittaker has argued in respect of the former:

> While 'absence of *cause*' may be and has been used to annul *contrats réels* and gratuitous contracts, in neither case does it add much to analysis in terms of *objet* or absence of consent and its practical importance there has not been significant in the modern law.[136]

It is in relation to the area of synallagmatic or bilateral contracts where the use of *cause* has been most significant. In bilateral contracts, the cause of each party's obligation is constituted by the obligation of the other contracting party. As Nicholas recounts, 'each obligation is the counterpart of the other'.[137] The classic example is a *contrat de vente*, where the buyer will pay the price of the goods in

[129] 'Une cause licite dans l'obligation.' ('A lawful cause within the obligation.')

[130] Art 1131: An obligation without cause or with a false cause, or with an unlawful cause, may not have any effect; Art 1132: An agreement is nevertheless valid, although its cause is not expressed; Art 1133: A cause is unlawful where it is prohibited by legislation, where it is contrary to public morals or to public policy.

[131] This is Nicholas's phrase: Nicholas (n 49) 118.

[132] See Bell, Boyron and Whittaker (n 47) 318. For a detailed analysis in French, see J Ghestin, *Cause de l'Engagement et Validité du Contrat* (Paris, LGDJ, 2006).

[133] See eg Cass civ 1ère, 3 juil 1996, no 94-14800.

[134] eg the sale of goods, this will be the transfer of property: Cass civ 1ère, 12 juil 1998, no 88-11443.

[135] See eg Fabre-Magnan (n 77) 426.

[136] See Bell, Boyron and Whittaker (n 47) 319.

[137] Nicholas (n 49) 119.

return for the obligation of the seller to deliver the items in question. In bilateral contracts, there is a fundamental interdependence between *objet* and *cause.* If one party's obligation lacks an *objet*, then the other party's obligation will lack a *cause.*[138] A classic example of this is where the goods sold have perished at the time of the agreement, in which case the seller's obligation has no object and the buyer's obligation has no *cause.*[139] Another example may be found in the French case law. The Cour de cassation held that a contract whereby a driving school purported to transfer its official certificate of approval was unenforceable, and the assignee was justified in refusing to pay the price agreed, as anyone who was qualified could obtain such a certification as of right, and the number of such certifications awarded was not finite. As the *Cour* held: '[T]he contract concerning the assignment of the certificate did not have an *objet* … therefore the obligation to pay … in return was null due to absence of *cause*.'[140]

More striking, however, have been the French cases in which sales contracts have been annulled, not for an *absence* of counterpart, but instead due to a 'derisory' sale price. As Fages has opined, 'in the sphere of sales law, [the courts] traditionally elide the lack of a real and serious price with the total absence of a quid pro quo, in others words in case of a derisory price'.[141] This would thus seem to allow for a control of the 'adequacy' of the *cause* in the contractual arrangement—anathema to an English lawyer! However, there are limits to the paternalism of the French courts, as judges will not interfere with transactions in case of merely 'low' prices,[142] and even peppercorn sales will be upheld where other are in reality provided.[143]

Another striking illustration of the interventionist tendency of the French courts in respect of the notion of *cause* is in respect of agency contracts. The French courts have traditionally been prepared to revisit agency arrangements, and notably the issue of remuneration, if it considers that the agent's remuneration is disproportionate or excessive. This approach has thus been controversially applied to contracts for legal services with lawyers,[144] and courts will thus be prepared to reduce the fees agreed between the lawyer and client if it is considered

[138] See Cass civ 1ère, 7 fév 1990, no 88-18441 (impossibility to transfer clientele of dentists as patients are always free to choose their doctor/dentist).

[139] Indeed, Art 1601 of the French Civil Code provided that: 'where, at the time of the sale, the thing sold has wholly perished, the sale is void'.

[140] See Cass civ 3ème, 4 mai 1983. See also Cass com, 5 jan 1966, no 63-11836.

[141] Fages (n 55) para 162.

[142] The classic example is: Cass civ 1ère, 4 juil 1995, no 93-16198 (following a pricing error, a Cartier ring sold for 100,000 francs when it was worth 460,419 francs; the court refused to avoid transaction for want of *cause*).

[143] See eg Cass civ 3ème, 3 mars 1993, no 91-15613 (sale of real estate for 1 franc justified by overall contractual arrangements).

[144] Cass civ 1ère, 3 mars 1998, no 95-15.799.

that these fees are disproportionate to the services undertaken.[145] Again, there are limitations to the courts' appetite for intervention.[146]

The variable geometry of the notion of *cause* does afford the courts a margin for manoeuvre. The attitude of the courts has thus ebbed and flowed. Examples of cases on this issue may be given. A contract with a video club franchise was annulled because the area where the claimant shop-owners were based had only 1,314 inhabitants and their obligation to pay hire charges 'lacked any real counterpart'.[147] In a number of cases, a challenge has been made to contracts between genealogists and beneficiaries of an intestacy for drawing the inheritance to their attention where an heir would have heard about it anyway.[148] In another case, a franchise agreement was annulled as no know-how was in fact transferred under the agreement.[149]

The case law has not attracted unanimous approval. Whittaker has summarised the criticism of the more liberal cases on the basis that the courts

> use *la cause de l'obligation* to assess the validity of a contract which is affected by a 'subjective rather than an objective imbalance', that is, whether the contract has no point for one of the parties. To a common lawyer, this looks very much like annulment on the ground of having made a foolish or bad bargain and the case law remains controversial in France, the majority of *la doctrine* regretting the way in which a party's 'subjective reasons' for contracting have become relevant to an aspect of *la cause* long seen as 'objective' and also warning against the concomitant risk to legal certainty which this entails.[150]

## D. Abandoning the Notion of Cause: Recent French Reforms

Despite its long heritage in French law, the notion of cause has, ostensibly, been abandoned in the recent reform of the French Civil Code. The new version of the Civil Code no longer contains explicit reference to *cause*—henceforth there are only three criteria for a valid contract: the consent of the parties, their capacity to contract, and 'a licit and certain content' (Article 1128 of the new Civil Code). This has been supported by certain doctrinal writers, who have considered that the *cause* concept is too amorphous, and that other devices can equally be deployed to remedy injustices.[151]

[145] See generally H Ader and A Damien, *Règles de la Profession d'Avocat* (Paris, Dalloz, 2010) para 46.68

[146] Notably where the fees have been accepted and settled without complaint after the services have been undertaken: see eg Cass civ 2ème, 5 juin 2003, no 01-15411.

[147] Cass civ 1ère, 3 juil 1996, no 94-14800.

[148] Cass civ 1ère, 18 avr 1953, no 53-06152.

[149] Cass civ 1ère, 10 mai 1994 no 92-15834.

[150] See Bell, Boyron and Whittaker (n 47) 321.

[151] See eg L Aynès, 'La cause, inutile et dangereuse', *Droit et Patrimoine* no 240.

It should not be thought, however, that the formal removal of the notion of *cause* from the Code will entail the total jettisoning of the rules referred to above. On the contrary, many of the pre-existing case law rules are adopted (or even amplified) within the corpus of the new Code.[152] It is particularly important to note that, in terms of the balance of the contractual bargain, it is stated in Article 1169 of the new Civil Code that 'an onerous contract is annulled when, at the time of its conclusion, the quid pro quo agreed in favour of the person who contracts is illusory or derisory'. Moreover, Article 1170 of the new Civil Code provides that: 'Any contract term which deprives a debtor's essential obligation of its substance is deemed not written.' One also finds the notion of *cause* floating like Banquo's ghost behind Article 1162 of the new Civil Code, which provides that: 'A contract cannot derogate from public policy either in its stipulations or by its purpose, whether or not the latter was known by all the parties.'[153] Indeed, some commentators has thus argued that, in many respects, the change will be less radical than might first be thought,[154] and that in many cases, similar issues will necessarily need to be broached by the courts. Other writers have thus expressed reserves as to the merits of trying to abandon the *cause*.[155]

## E. A Mid-Channel Cause

The notion of *cause* has been held to constitute an essential element of Jersey law in a number of important cases. The iconic Jersey case is that of *Osment v Constable of St Helier*,[156] which we have already touched upon above.[157] In this case, the plaintiff, Osment, had been employed for 30 years by the Parish of St Helier and was thus the beneficiary of a pension scheme. However, under the terms of the pension scheme, Mr Osment would forfeit his entitlement if he was to resign from his employment (or be dismissed) prior to reaching the age of 60. Mr Osment was considering taking a position with the Parish of St Lawrence, but wanted his 30 years' service with St Helier to be taken into account in determining his pension rights. Negotiations thus took place between the Constables of St Helier and St Lawrence, with the result that the Constable of St Helier wrote

[152] D Mazeud, 'Droit des contrats: réforme à l'horizon!' *Dalloz* 2014.291.

[153] On this, see C Cousin, H Guiziou, M Leveneur-Azémar, B Moron-Puech et A Stévignon, 'Regards comparatistes sur l'avant-projet de réforme du droit des obligations' *Recueil Dalloz* 2015.1115.

[154] G Wicker, 'La suppression de la cause par le projet d'ordonnance: la chose sans le mot?' Recueil Dalloz 2015.1557. For a very different view, see T Genicon, 'Défense et illustration de la cause en droit des contrats—a propos du projet de réforme du droit des contrats, du régime général et de la preuve des obligations' Recueil Dalloz 2015.1551.

[155] Mazeaud (n 152); O Tournafond, 'Pourquoi il faut conserver la théorie de la cause en droit civil français' Recueil Dalloz 2008.2607; R Boffa, 'Avant-projet d'ordonnance portant réforme du droit des contrats, du régime général et de la preuve des obligations' *Gazette du Palais*, 30 avril 2015, no 120, 18. For an elegant critique of the new notion of contractual 'content', see M Fabre-Magnan, 'Critique de la notion de contenu du contrat' *Revue des contrats*, 1 septembre 2015, no 3, 639.

[156] *Osment v Constable of St Helier* (1974) JJ 1.

[157] Pages 65–66, and 67 above.

to the Constable of St Lawrence stating that he would be prepared to consider a negotiated settlement on terms that a percentage of Mr Osment's pension rights would be paid by St Helier notwithstanding his resignation. On the strength of this letter, Mr Osment accepted the post with St Lawrence. Following an audit of the St Helier accounts, and the discovery of a discrepancy for the department for which Mr Osment was responsible, St Helier wrote to St Lawrence indicating that this would have resulted in the termination of Mr Osment's employment had he still been employed by the Parish, and that it was therefore no longer prepared to make any payment towards his pension. Mr Osment brought a claim against the Constable of St Helier to gain payment of the proportionate capital value of the pension rights.

In its judgment, the Royal Court reiterated that a *cause* was an essential element of Jersey law, and that it was very different to the English notion of consideration.[158] It was held that there was sufficient cause in the original pension agreement (which the plaintiff would have received had he remained in the employment of the Parish until retirement), that cause being the plaintiff remaining in employment after the pension was introduced. However, the right to the pension was conditional upon Mr Osment remaining in the employment of the Parish until retirement, and on leaving his job, the plaintiff lost his right to a pension unless he could show a new agreement had been created.

In the case of *Selby v Romeril*,[159] the Royal Court reiterated that a *cause* was one of the four requirements for the creation of a valid contract,[160] and found in that case, which concerned a dispute over whether the seller of a hotel had agreed to pay for certain repair work identified in a surveyor's report, that the agreement lacked *cause*. The Court held that the *objet* was 'insufficiently certain to give rise to a valid contract',[161] and that correspondingly the cause failed as well.

Finally, in the more recent case of *O'Brien v Marett*,[162] the Court of Appeal confirmed the importance of *cause* in Jersey law and analysed the issue as follows:

> Cause is the basis of or the reason for the contract. It is thus constituted by the interdependence of promises or the mutual performance of obligations. Hence, where the basis upon which a party enters an agreement (the cause) either fails or never comes to pass at all, the agreement is, according to Jersey law, null: Pothier, paras 42–46; Domat, paras 147 and 148; French Civil Code, art 1131.[163]

The concept of *cause* has thus been applied in a series of different cases. In *Wightman v Cathcart Properties Limited*,[164] it was held that the *variation*, as well as

[158] *Osment v Constable of St Helier* (1974) JJ 1, 11.
[159] *Selby v Romeril* 1996 JLR 210.
[160] Ibid, 218.
[161] Ibid, 219.
[162] *O'Brien v Marett* [2008] JCA 178.
[163] Ibid, [58].
[164] *Wightman v Cathcart Properties Limited* (1970) JJ 1433, 1441: '"[C]ause" is not the same thing as "consideration", an element necessary to the validity of a contract in the United Kingdom, but not so necessary to a contract in Jersey.'

the formation, of a contract requires proof of valid *cause*. In that case, a contract of employment had been varied and the Royal Court held that such variation would not be enforceable unless there was sufficient cause. On the facts of the case, the court found that *cause* was indeed present as the employee had received various additional benefits in return for the variation (ie additional paid leave). In *Gallichan v Gallichan*,[165] which concerned a dispute between two brothers regarding the ownership of a farm, the Royal Court indicated that the cause of an agreement could be constituted by the forbearance from taking (legal) action which could otherwise have been commenced.[166]

Another application of the rule of *cause* may be found in the *action paulienne* procedure, which allows for questionable transactions undertaken by an insolvent debtor to be challenged by the defrauded creditor.[167] If the transaction in question is an 'onerous' one (ie for value), then the creditor is required to show that the third party beneficiary was *complicit* in the fraud. That requirement is, however, dispensed with in case of a gratuitous transaction (complicity is thus presumed), and since the judgment in *Re Esteem Settlement*,[168] this has been expanded to include so-called 'lucrative' *causes*, where the transaction was at below market rate. Relying on Poingdestre, the court held in Re Esteem Settlement that:[169]

> [A] transaction only becomes 'onéreuse' if the 'cause' given by the recipient is commensurate and proportionate to the value of the thing alienated; if the price is not commensurate or proportionate in this way, it is a transaction 'lucrative'.

This case law thus further illustrates the Jersey law tendency of scrutinising the exact *cause* provided by contracting parties.

## F. *Cause* and Consideration: Reflecting Different Systemic Approaches[170]

A series of Jersey cases has underlined the differences between *cause* and consideration. In *Granite Products Ltd v Renault*,[171] the Royal Court held that *cause* was not the same thing as consideration and that whilst the latter was a necessary

165 *Gallichan v Gallichan* (1954) JJ 57.

166 The reasoning in this case is, however, not entirely easy to follow, and it is difficult to avoid the conclusion that the court was influenced by equitable considerations, as well as by the prevailing cultural attitudes to family property in Jersey at the time. In the case, it is not crystal clear what exactly the forebearance of the younger son related to given that he had no interest in the farm at the relevant time.

167 See further *Golder v Société des Magasins Concorde Limited* (1967) JJ 721.

168 Unreported, 17 January 2002 (reissued 11 March 2002).

169 Ibid, para 299.

170 The classic comparative law article is: B Markesinis, 'Cause & Consideration: A Study in Parallel' (1978) 37 *Cambridge Law Journal* 53. See also Beale et al (n 1) ch 5; J Smits, *Contract Law: A Comparative Introduction* (Cheltenham, Edward Elgar, 2014) ch 4; C Valcke, 'English Consideration and French Causa: The Best of Faux Amis' in O Kresin (ed), *Comparativistica Yearbook 2012* (Moscow, Infra M, 2013).

171 *Granite Products Ltd v Renault* (1961) JJ 163.

requirement for the validity of a contract under English law, the same was not true of Jersey law. Similar sentiments were expressed by the Royal Court in *Wightman v Cathcart Properties Limited*.[172]

The absence of a doctrine of consideration in the law of Jersey provides an important fault-line between the Jersey system and that of common law countries. It marks a strikingly different approach to one of the central elements of the law of contract and thus provides a stark, and very visible, contrast with the common law. This difference has practical effects. The notion of *cause* is both potentially more extensive than consideration and also provides the courts with a more intrusive tool for scrutinising the contractual bargain.

An example of the more extensive scope of *cause* may be found in respect of gratuitous promises. From a common law perspective, a promise unsupported by consideration would not be enforceable. However, if civil law reasoning is applied (premised upon the need to show a *cause* but not consideration), then such a gratuitous promise could be valid as long as it was supported by the relevant *cause*, such as the desire to confer a gift as expressed in an *intention libérale* (intention to gift).[173] Applying this approach to a Jersey setting, then in the case of *Osment v Constable of St Helier*[174] (discussed above), an alternative interpretation of the *cause* of the Constable's act[175] in conferring the pension advantage upon Mr Osment would have been the desire to reward a faithful employee for his service (which subsequently transpired, in this case, to be a mistaken belief).[176]

Would the courts in Jersey unflinchingly uphold gratuitous promises which were unsupported by any form of consideration? The question has yet to be answered by the courts. Whilst commentators who are influenced by common law notions of contract law may find this a challenging position to support, there are strong arguments in favour of upholding gratuitous promises.[177] The relevant case law is crystal clear on the centrality of the notion of *cause* within Jersey case law, as well as the fact that there are important differences between cause and consideration, thereby militating in favour of the broader civil law solution for gratuitous promises. It should also be underlined that, in practice in the common law,

[172] *Wightman v Cathcart Properties Limited* (1970) JJ 1433, 1441.

[173] Whittaker translates this as 'donative intention' (see Bell, Boyron and Whittaker (n 47) 319), and Fabre-Magnan describes it as 'une intention de gratifier l'autre sans contrepartie' (M Fabre-Magnan, *Droit des Obligations* (Paris, PUF, 2008) 174), which is similar to Nicholas's explanation: 'intention to confer a gratuitous benefit on the promisee' (Nicholas (n 49) 124). Although in certain circumstance *donations* in French law must be notarised: see Art 931 Civil Code.

[174] *Osment v Constable of St Helier* (1974) JJ 1.

[175] The characterisation given by the Royal Court of the contract could also be improved upon. Whilst the Constable's act would certainly seem to be a unilateral one, it seems wrong to have equated it with a contract where money is offered in exchange for an act. Properly analysed, the Constable's act would seem effectively to have been an agreement to make a gift to Mr Osment in the form of a contribution to his pension pot (ie *even if* he left the employment.)

[176] And would have allowed the Court to invalidate the contract on the basis of a false *cause*.

[177] Interestingly, it should be noted that the law of Scotland ascribed from an early period a binding effect to unilateral promises: K Reid and R Zimmermann (eds), *A History of Private Law in Scotland*, vol II: *Obligations* (Oxford, OUP, 2000) 43.

parties can indeed make an enforceable promise of a gift if the donor undertakes the promise in a deed. The gratuitous promise thereby becomes enforceable by virtue of the formality of the deed even if the promise would not be otherwise binding because it is not supported by consideration. This option, however, is not available in Jersey, where the instrument of a deed simply does not exist. Thus, whilst in English law, the exigencies of consideration can be offset by the use of a deed, Jersey does not have such an option, and therefore any attempt to introduce such a concept of consideration per se would be problematic (without broader reform). Given the absence of such a formality in Jersey, then it would seem desirable for the Jersey courts to recognise the enforceability of gratuitous promises, subject to the condition of course that the *cause* is made out.

The use of *cause* in Jersey is also perhaps illustrative of a different philosophy to the law of contract, one which is less defined by economic efficiency and legal certainty, and in respect of which judicial interventionism is more readily accepted.[178] Such an approach is not entirely alien to Jersey. Whilst the English courts are very reluctant to intervene to review the fairness of a contract between commercial parties, the approach in Jersey is somewhat different. Jersey courts have developed an interventionist role in certain scenarios. One example is that, as we will see, by means of the ancient customary law doctrine of *déception d'outre moitié de juste prix*, certain types of real estate transaction may be challenged where the price agreed is less than 50% of the real market value at the time of sale.[179] Judicial intervention (and departure from the principle of *la convention fait la loi des parties*) in such a case is justified by the disproportion that exists between the bargain made and the *juste prix*. We will examine the underpinning principles of *déception d'outre moitié de juste prix* in a later chapter,[180] but it is possible to see parallels with the French law example of a control of the 'adequacy' of the *cause* in contractual arrangements. Other examples of judicial interventionism may be cited.[181] This may well be reflective of broader differences in philosophy in contract law. It is also possible to point to contextual factors as supporting the more prominent role of the judge in reviewing contractual bargains—such as the need to take account of fairness within a small jurisdiction.[182]

[178] Albeit that this is somewhat paradoxically for a *droit écrit* system in which judicial interventionism has always been viewed with a healthy dose of distrust. See generally J Bell, *French Legal Cultures* (London, Butterworths, 2001). There have been evolution in the 'office' of the French judge; see for an excellent analysis, A Garapon, *La Prudence et l'Autorité: L'Office du Juge au 21ième siècle* (Paris, IHEJ, 2013).

[179] See Chapter 5 below, pp 113–120.

[180] Ibid.

[181] There are also other striking examples of interventionist approach of the courts in Jersey: such as the review of penalty clauses, or in *action paulienne*, referred to above, at pp 31–32, and 80.

[182] Note the prominent occurrence in Jersey law of terms including a moral dimension, such as 'fraud', 'dolus', bad faith, serious fault. From a comparative perspective, see the discussion in D Harris and D Tallon, 'Conclusions' in *Contract Law Today: Anglo-French Comparisons* (Oxford, Clarendon Press, 1989) 386.

# 5

# Undermining a Contract: *Vices de Consentement*

## I. Introduction

Given the centrality of the notion of consent in legal systems with a civil law heritage, it is perhaps unsurprising that the rules relating to the undermining of contracts are analysed from the perspective of 'defects of consent'.[1] The doctrine of autonomy of will entails that the agreement which forms the basis of a contract must have been given freely.[2] Otherwise, consent cannot be considered to have been validly given by the parties.[3]

The position of the common law is, however, very different. Although, as Whittaker points out, the language and concepts may superficially suggest similarities, the true picture is in reality in stark contrast:

> At first sight the 'defects in consent' which the Civil Code enumerates appear familiar to a common lawyer: dol appears to be like fraud, violence like duress and erreur sur les qualités substantielles like fundamental mistake. However, quite apart from the curious absence of a law of innocent misrepresentation, such ready parallels are misleading where not downright wrong, for it is here that French contract law's consensualism is most in evidence. This means both that its grounds of vitiation are broader than in English law and that the logic of a genuine concern for the quality of each parties' consent is followed through, so that, notably, its law of mistake is concerned with unilateral mistakes (unlike English law which has focused on 'common mistakes').[4]

It is perhaps unsurprising that a system which does not adhere to a subjectivist, consent-based approach also lacks an overarching theory bringing together the

[1] Given that these systems are based on subjectivist, will-centered contractual theories.

[2] See eg Art 1130 of the new French Civil Code; Pothier, *Traité des Obligations*, part 1, ch 1, para 21: 'Le consentement qui forme les conventions doit être libre.' For a general discussion of this theme from a comparative perspective, see H Beale, B Fauvarque-Cosson, J Rutgers, D Tallon and S Vogenauer, *Cases, Materials and Text on Contract Law* (Oxford, Hart Publishing, 2010) ch 10.

[3] As noted in the Jersey case of *Steelux Holdings Ltd v Edmonstone* 2005 JLR 152: where there has been a *vice de consentement*, then 'there will have been no consent, no meeting of minds, between the parties' (156).

[4] J Bell, S Boyron and S Whittaker, *Principles of French Law* (2nd edn, Oxford, OUP, 2008) 307.

various equivalent topics of duress, misrepresentation and mistake. And yet, as we shall see, it is nonetheless accepted in English law that conduct of the other contracting party entails that a contract should be undermined.

As with other contract law topics, Jersey has been drawn between the two parallel influences. As a jurisdiction in respect of which consent plays a central role, and one in which a subjectivist approach to contract law has thus been prominent, it is not surprising that the civil law notion of 'defects in consent' has also played an important role. Following the broader pattern of civil law systems,[5] where defects invariably derive from one party being mistaken, deceived or threatened by the other party, consent in Jersey law will not be valid if it is given in *erreur*, due to *violence*, or to *dol*. In keeping with its mid-channel position, the courts in Jersey have also accorded some importance to common law notions, particularly the doctrine of misrepresentation. The resultant mélange is alas not an extremely harmonious one, and as we shall see, there are inconsistencies in the case law that it would be opportune to iron out.

We will look at the different categories of *vices de consentement* in turn. As the modern French law is an essential reference point for understanding the position and structure of Jersey law in this sphere, the relevant provisions of the French Civil Code will first be provided, prior to an examination of the Jersey case law, which will include comparative law perspectives.

Over and above the issue of *vices de consentement*/defects in consent, we will also examine the intriguing and controversial doctrine of *Lésion* or *Déception d'outre moitié du juste prix*, including the case law which reached the Privy Council in 2001. Over and above the substantive issues in respect of *Lésion*, we will explore the way in which this doctrine illustrates and explains the role of the Jersey courts.

## II. *Vices de Consentement*—Defects in Consent

As we have already seen, a corollary of the centrality of consent is that a contract will be undermined if the consent is in some way deficient. The increasingly subjective approach to contract law in Jersey has also reinforced the importance of analysing whether the contracting parties did in fact give consent freely to the contractual bargain.

Traditionally, the Jersey courts have thus looked to whether there are factors which negative consent to contract. These factors have generally been referred to as 'defects in consent'[6] as a translation of the French concept of *vices de consentement*. Thus in the recent case of *O'Brien v Marett*, the Court of Appeal placed the notion of *vices de consentement* at the centre of the analysis on the undermining

[5] See eg Beale et al (n 2) 540.
[6] See eg *Grove v Baker* 2005 JLR 348, 352.

of contractual consent.[7] Pothier characterised the different 'vices' in contracts as follows: 'Les vices qui peuvent se rencontrer dans les contrats sont l'erreur, la violence, le dol, la lésion, le défaut de cause dans l'engagement, le défaut de lien.'[8] Many of these can be found in modern Jersey law, and the Jersey courts have adopted the tripartite analysis of French law according to which the consent given to a contract will not be valid if it is given in *erreur*, due to *violence*, or *dol*.

The law of Jersey on *vice de consentement* suffers, however, from serious defects in clarity. Whilst it is one of the most fascinating spheres to study from a comparative law perspective, this area is also one of the most confused, and where the inconsistencies as to sources have played out in the content of substantive law. The diverse sources of the Jersey law of contract have combined to produce a rich and varied state of the law in relation to *vice de consentement*. This has, however, produced correlative challenges in terms of the coherence of the corpus of the rules in this sphere, particularly as concerns the evident tensions between English and French law.

The doctrine of *vice de consentement* is premised upon solid authority as to the tripartite limbs of *erreur*, *violence* or *dol*.[9] But there is also a strand of case law in which the courts have seemed to blithely disregard such an approach, and instead proceed on the basis that English law concepts, particularly those of misrepresentation, should instead apply. These mixed approaches do not always sit comfortably together. The mid-channel cherry-picking approach has led to a degree of confusion, as we shall see.

## III. *Violence*/Physical or Psychological Threats

### A. Comparative Law Backdrop

In most legal systems, the question arises as to whether a contract can be avoided if a party has entered into it under the influence of a threat. Circumstances can be very varied. On one end of the scale, there may be threats of serious physical violence in respect of which most legal systems provide a remedy. On the other hand, there may be minor pressure of an economic nature to obtain a commercial advantage, which many would see as being part and parcel of the cut and thrust of commercial relations. How do legal systems deal with the scenarios between those two extremes? The question is by no means a new one: the older civil law writers broached just such issues. In his treatise on obligations, Pothier considered

[7] *O'Brien v Marett* [2008] JCA 178, [55]–[57].

[8] Pothier, *Traité Des Obligations*, part 1, ch 1, para 16: '[T]he vitiating factors which can occur in contracts are error, violence, fraud, lésion and a defect of *cause* in the obligation, and defect of relationship.'

[9] *O'Brien v Marett* [2008] JCA 178.

that if the consent of any of the contracting parties is extorted by violence, the contract is thus 'vicieux'.[10] He notes that all obligations contracted by violence may be avoided, irrespective of the person from whom the violence emanates (even where the violence is committed by a third party who is not a party to the contract).[11] As to the seriousness of the threat, Pothier indicates that regard should be had to the age, sex and condition of the parties.[12] The violence may be directed at the party to the contract, or at his family and it must be an evil which is threatened to take place immediately if the thing which is required is not done.[13] Pothier notes that the violence must also be unjust.[14] According to Pothier, the exercise of a legal right does not suffice to constitute 'violence' according to this description.[15]

Comparative law studies have shown that in continental systems a broad view has generally been taken of the means and object of the threat.[16] This is confirmed in French law,[17] where Article 1140 of the new Code civil states that *violence* occurs when 'one party contracts under the influence of a constraint which makes him fear that his person or his wealth, or those of his near relatives, might be exposed to significant harm'. The nature of the threatened harm is thus broadly conceived, covering physical and pecuniary harm. Psychological pressure can also suffice, as long as—similar to physical violence—it was causative, namely that 'the victim must show that in the absence [of the threat], he or she would not have concluded the contract'.[18] As noted by Fabre-Magnan, the standard applied by the courts has been predominantly an objective one, albeit that Article 1112(2) of the previous version of the Civil Code referred to fact that certain characteristics of the victim (age, sex etc)[19] could be taken into account, thereby applying a modulated objective standard.

Similarly to the view expressed by Pothier above, Article 1140 of the new Code civil provides that *violence* may nullify a contract where it is exercised against the spouse or family of the contracting party (and in some cases, a wider circle of persons). It should also be noted that the duress, as defined by Article 1142 of the

[10] Pothier, *Traité Des Obligations*, part 1, ch 1, para 21: 'The consent that forms agreements must be given freely; if the consent of one of the contracting parties has been obtained by violence, the Contract is defective.'

[11] Ibid, para 23: 'Civil law … rescinds all Obligations contracted through violence, no matter the origin of the violence.'

[12] Ibid, para 25.

[13] Ibid.

[14] Ibid, para 26.

[15] Ibid.

[16] See Beale et al (n 2) ch 11.

[17] See also the international projects, eg 4:108 PECL.

[18] M Fabre-Magnan, *Droit des Obligations: Contrat et Engagement Unilatéral* (3rd edn, Paris, PUF, 2012) 357.

[19] Ibid, 357–58.

new Code civil, can derive from the conduct of the defendant or of a third party,[20] which distinguishes this *vice de consentement* from that of *dol* (below).

We have already seen that Pothier considered that the *violence* must be shown to be unjust.[21] Under modern French law, the rule is that the threat must be illegitimate. Physical violence clearly is unjust, but more difficulties arise from the exercise of a lawful right (eg to bring legal proceedings) in an *unlawful* manner (eg a threat to bring *vexatious* proceedings).[22] As Whittaker has noted, the issue of the legitimacy of the threat is much litigated.[23] In some cases, economic duress has even been considered sufficient to vitiate a contract.[24] In this context, the new French Civil Code is innovative in that it extends the concept of duress to include the wrongful exploitation of a situation of weakness caused by a state of necessity or dependence.[25]

Under Jersey law, there is some case law on the issue of *violence*. The Jersey cases have seemed to follow the familiar common law conceptualisation in this sphere, distinguishing between cases of physical duress, on the one hand, and on the other more complex issues of undue influence.

## B. Physical Compulsion/Duress

Drawing upon the common law, the terminology of duress has been adopted in certain Jersey cases. The Jersey case of *Bisson v Bisson*[26] is a stark example of the way in which *violence* will negate consent, thereby undermining the contract. The matrimonial house had been held in the joint names of Mr and Mrs Bisson. After the filing of a petition for divorce by Mrs Bisson, the defendant husband had forced his wife, under physical duress, to assign a half share in the property for the nominal sum of £500. The plaintiff consequently brought an application to have the conveyance set aside. The Court considered the importance of the principle of *la convention fait la loi des parties*, and noted that at the time the contract was entered into, there was a factor which 'negatived the essential condition for the establishment of the valid legal relationship'.[27] In the instant case, the

[20] 'Duress is a ground of nullity regardless of whether it has been applied by the other party or by a third party.'

[21] Pothier, *Traité Des Obligations*, part 1, ch 1, para 26.

[22] On this, see Art 1141 of the new French Civil Code: 'A threat of legal action does not constitute duress. It is different, where the legal process is deflected from its proper aims or is invoked or exercised in order to obtain a manifestly excessive advantage.'

[23] Bell, Boyron and Whittaker (n 4) 314.

[24] See eg Cass civ 1ère, 3 avr 2002: '[O]nly the abusive exploitation of a situation of economical dependence, with the objective of deriving a benefit from the fear of harm in respect of the legitimate interests of the individual directly, can result in a defect of one's consent by violence.'

[25] See Art 1143: 'There is also duress where one party, exploiting the state of dependence in which the other contracting party find himself, obtains from him an undertaking to which the latter would not have agreed absent the constraint, and thus obtains a manifestly excessive advantage.'

[26] *Bisson v Bisson* (1981) JJ 103.

[27] Ibid, 108–09.

Court held that Mrs Bisson had acted under duress as 'she was acting from fear'.[28] The contract was therefore set aside.

## C. Undue Influence: Sources of Law

The Jersey law on undue influence is somewhat more complex. An interesting preliminary point relates to the sources of law. In Chapter 2, we looked at the general issue of sources of the Jersey law of contract. Given the centrality of notion of consent within this area, and the reliance on the civil law structures, as referred to above, one might have assumed that the obvious starting point in Jersey would have been Pothier, and civil law influences. However, a very different approach was adopted in the leading case, *Toothill v HSBC Bank plc.*[29] In this case, a bank brought proceedings against Mr and Mrs Toothill for the repayment of loans and an overdraft. The husband submitted to judgment but his wife claimed inter alia that she had entered into two of the loans and the overdraft under the undue influence of her husband. At first instance, the Master granted summary judgment for the Bank. Mrs Toothill appealed. The Royal Court examined the defence relied upon by Mrs Toothill that in undertaking the loans, she was acting under the undue influence of her husband, the first defendant.

On the issue of sources of law, counsel for the plaintiff conceded during the hearing that, as she was not aware of any Norman or French principles which might assist her as against the bank in case her husband had been guilty of undue influence, she would have to rely upon the English law principles laid down in the well-known English cases of *Barclays Bank PLC v O'Brien*[30] and *Royal Bank of Scotland plc v Etridge (No 2)*.[31] Counsel for both parties thus accepted that on this issue, the law of Jersey should be similar to that of English law as outlined in these two cases.[32]

The Royal Court therefore held on this issue of sources of law that: 'The law of undue influence in Jersey is similar to that of English law and we find that the principles underlying the decisions in O'Brien and Etridge are entirely consistent with those of Jersey law.'[33]

The Court explained that this position was consistent with the underlying policy factors:

> [T]here are strong policy grounds for thinking that the law in this jurisdiction should be the same as in England. The majority of banks who lend money on the security of immovable property in the Island are UK-owned. Their guidelines and procedures have

[28] Ibid, 110.
[29] *Toothill v HSBC Bank plc* 2008 JLR 77.
[30] *Barclays Bank PLC v O'Brien* [1994] 1 AC 180.
[31] *Royal Bank of Scotland plc v Etridge (No 2)* [2002] 2 AC 773.
[32] *Toothill v HSBC Bank plc* 2008 JLR 77, 89.
[33] Ibid.

> been established in accordance with the clear judicial guidance offered in Etridge and their personnel will have been trained accordingly. Furthermore, the competing policy considerations referred to by Lord Nicholls in the passage quoted in para 24 above are equally applicable in Jersey and a solution which addresses both considerations needs to be found. In our judgment, the position established in Etridge achieves a proper balance between these competing considerations and we hold the law of Jersey to be of like effect.[34]

We will examine further below the problems arising from such a cherry-picking approach to this area of the law. However, at this stage, a word should be said about the reasoning behind this statement. Clearly, policy factors are relevant for judges to take into account when determining the contours of legal principles.[35] It seems strange, however, that policy factors are to be used in determining what *the relevant sources of law* should be. That must surely be a broader, and in some ways objective, approach to determining what the relevant sources should be. This is illustrated by the current case. A central consideration in the analysis is the consideration that the banks operating in Jersey are UK-owned. It is open to question whether such economic considerations should have an impact on the sources of contract law. In any case, whatever attitude may be taken to that question, it seems problematic to proceed in this way by small touches of common law reasoning, when the basic principles of *vices de consentement* are grounded in a very different legal approach and *mentalité*.

## D. Undue Influence: Substantive Law

We will now examine the relevant case law on this topic. The case of *Ballard v Lumb*[36] concerned a claim based on undue influence. The plaintiff sold her business, which had financial difficulties, to the defendant at a substantially reduced price. After the sale, the defendant persuaded the creditors of the business to compromise their claims by fabricating stories about an impending liquidation. Instead, the position of the business actually improved. The plaintiff had been in ill-health and sought to argue that the defendant had exercised 'undue influence' over her when negotiating the price.

The Royal Court held that there was no evidence that the plaintiff was incapable of giving instructions in relation to the sale and there was no evidence of any undue influence on the plaintiff by the defendant. It was held that in order to prove undue influence it was necessary to show:[37] that undue influence was exercised; that undue influence was operative; and that without undue influence,

[34] Ibid.
[35] See generally J Bell, *Policy Arguments in Judicial Decisions* (Oxford, OUP, 1983).
[36] *Ballard v Lumb* (1968) JJ 923.
[37] Ibid, 936.

no contract would have been made at all or would have been made on quite different terms. On the facts of this case, it was held that although the defendant drove a hard bargain, the plaintiff's negotiating position had been very weak given the financial state of the company. The defendant had, in any event, conducted negotiations with the plaintiff's accountant.

There are also particular rules relating to the existence of undue influence in the context of a relationship of trust between the parties. Such a special relationship of trust or dependence between the parties may give rise to a presumption of undue influence. In the case of *Leigh v McLinton*,[38] the Court of Appeal held that if a donor and a donee had a certain relationship of confidence and trust, the law would presume that parting with property was the result of the undue influence of the donee, who would then be required to provide positive proof to the contrary in order to maintain the validity of the gift. The rule did not, however, apply to all fiduciary relationships and that in the current case, it was not made out.

In the aforementioned case of *Toothill v HSBC Bank plc*,[39] the Royal Court examined the issue of a spouse seeking to set aside security over a jointly owned matrimonial home. Following the House of Lords decision in *Royal Bank of Scotland plc v Etridge (No 2)*,[40] it was held that to succeed, the spouse had to prove that:[41] he or she was unduly influenced by the other spouse to agree to the joint loan or to provide security or was induced to do so by misrepresentation on his part; the bank was put on inquiry as to the existence of the undue influence or misrepresentation; and if it was, the bank had not taken reasonable steps to minimise the risk of the other party entering into the transaction as a result of undue influence and was therefore fixed with notice of the undue influence or misrepresentation. However, on the facts of the case, the Court held that there was no arguable case that the appellant entered into these transactions under the undue influence of her husband.[42]

## IV. *Dol*: Fraud as a Ground for Avoiding a Contract

### A. Introduction—Comparative Law Dimension

Most legal systems provide for a mechanism to avoid contracts where the latter have been entered into due to the fraudulent or dishonest behaviour of the other

[38] *Leigh v McLinton* 1991 JLR 274.
[39] *Toothill v HSBC Bank plc* 2008 JLR 77.
[40] *Royal Bank of Scotland plc v Etridge (No 2)* [2002] 2 AC 773.
[41] *Toothill v HSBC Bank plc* 2008 JLR 77, 88.
[42] Ibid, 101.

contracting party.[43] In such a scenario, the focus of the remedy naturally shifts to a conduct-based analysis of the wrongful acts/omissions of the perpetrator.

In modern French law, the notion of *dol* has been extended to encapsulate dishonest scheming, which goes beyond fraudulent misstatements.[44] As Whittaker notes, the notion of *dol* 'includes fraudulent misstatements, but is rather wider, extending to any chicanery intended to deceive as long as it was effected by the other party to the contract'.[45] The behaviour, however, must have *caused* a 'decisive mistake' in the other party to a contract. As set out in Article 1130 of the new French Civil Code, the *dolosive* scheming must have been such that it was obvious that, without them, the other party would not have entered into the contract.[46]

More diversity is found within different legal systems in respect of the acts/omissions distinction in terms of whether non-disclosure of relevant information can suffice.[47] The French law concept has been developed and extended over the years with the French courts extending it, inter alia, as we shall see below, from positive acts of chicanery to cover certain omissions, such as wrongful silence known as *reticence dolosive.*

## B. The Jersey Law Position: Pothier, Domat and the Older Authorities

The notion of *dol* has appeared in a good number of cases in Jersey. As with many Jersey law concepts, Pothier is one of the primary sources. Reference is often made to his definition of *dol* as 'every artifice made use of by one person for the purpose of deceiving another'.[48] As to the exact meaning of fraud, Pothier states that:

> [A] person cannot be allowed to complain of trifling deviations from good faith in the party with whom he has contracted. … Nothing but what is plainly ingenious to good faith ought to be considered as a fraud sufficient to impeach a contract, such as the criminal manoeuvres and artifices employed by one party to induce the other to contract.[49]

[43] See Beale et al (n 2) ch 10.

[44] See Art 1137 of the new French Civil Code: '*Dol* is an act of a party in obtaining the consent of the other by scheming or lies. A *dol* also is constituted by the deliberate concealing by one contracting party of information which he knows is determinative for the other party.'

[45] Bell, Boyron and Whittaker (n 4) 309.

[46] 'Mistake, fraud and duress vitiate consent where they are of such a nature that, without them, one of the parties would not have contracted or would have contracted on substantially different terms.'

[47] J Smits, *Contract Law: A Comparative Introduction* (Cheltenham, Edward Elgar, 2014) 172–76.

[48] Pothier, *Traité Des Obligations*, part 1, ch 1, para 28: 'On appelle *dol*, toute espèce d'artifice dont quelqu'un se sert pour en tromper un autre: *Labeo definit dolum, omnem calliditatem, fallaciam, machinationem, ad circumveniendum, fallendum, decipiendum alterum, adhibatam.*' In Jersey, see eg *Attorney General v Foster* 1989 JLR 70, 84 (case on criminal fraud).

[49] Pothier, *Traité Des Obligations*, part 1, ch 1, para 30.

Domat's views have also been influential.[50] Reference has thus been made to Domat's characterisation of *dol* as 'all surprise, fraud, sharpness, manoeuvre and all other bad technique used to deceive another person'.[51]

Reference has also been made to the older Jersey commentators in the relevant case law. Citations have thus been made in some cases[52] to the writings of Maître Houard in his *Dictionary on Norman Customary Law*,[53] and particularly the assertion by Houard that the litmus test of *dol* is, in most cases, the presence of bad faith.[54] Poingdestre devotes a long section on the notion of *dol*, and gives a series of examples of behaviour amounting to *dol*.[55] Le Geyt also gives a series of examples of archtype circumstances involving *dolosive* behaviour,[56] and refers to *dol* as a 'fourberie'[57] (deceit) or undertaken 'maliciously',[58] and underlines that it comes close to theft: 'Dol is similar to theft: it means taking and appropriating someone's property by surprise and deceit.'[59]

## C. Jersey Cases on *Dol*

There have been a number of older Jersey decisions examining the notion of criminal fraud[60] or within the context of fraudulent breach of trust.[61] Whilst these cases covered a variety of factual and legal issues, the common denominator of the decisions was the express reliance upon older authorities, and in particular Pothier's conceptualisation of *dol*, as referenced above.

The leading case is now *Steelux Holdings Ltd v Edmonstone*.[62] We will need to look at this case in some detail, as it raises more questions than it necessarily resolves. The facts were as follows. The owner of Steelux Holdings Ltd, Mr Hall, purchased a house for £200,000 in the name of his stepdaughter Mary Edmonstone.

[50] See eg *Attorney General v Foster* 1989 JLR 70, 83 (case on criminal fraud).

[51] *Les Loix civiles dans leur ordre naturel; le droit public, et Legum delectus* 1735, vol 1, s III 'du dol et du stellionat', para 1.

[52] See eg *West v Lazard Brothers* 1993 JLR 165, 301, where the Dictionary is referred to as the 'surer guide to our customary law'.

[53] *Dictionnaire Analytique, Hystorique, Étymologique, Critique et Interprétif de la Coutume de Normandie* (Rouen, 1780).

[54] 'En effet, le dol personnel ou le réel ont, il est vrai, ordinairement pour principe la mauvaise foi' (549).

[55] Poingdestre, *Les Lois et Coutumes de Jersey* (reprinted 1953, St Helier) 206–07 (available at: www.jerseylaw.je/Publications/Library/JerseyLawTexts/legeyt02/default.aspx (last accessed 29 January 2016)).

[56] Le Geyt, *Manuscrits sur la Constitution, les Lois, & les Usages de Jersey*, vol 1 (reprinted 1846, St Helier) 297.

[57] Ibid.

[58] Ibid, 298.

[59] At 302–03: 'Le dol approche fort du larcin: c'est prendre et s'approprier le bien d'autruy par surprise et par subtilité.'

[60] *Attorney General v Foster* 1989 JLR 70 (Royal Court), 1992 JLR 6 (Court of Appeal).

[61] See eg *West v Lazard Brothers* 1993 JLR 165.

[62] *Steelux Holdings Ltd v Edmonstone* 2005 JLR 152.

However, prior to the purchase, a bond was executed by Ms Edmonstone (on the advice of Mr Hall) in favour of Steelux acknowledging a debt of £150,000. The parties subsequently fell out and Ms Edmonstone argued that she had not appreciated that she would have to repay the money and had assumed that she had been gifted the whole house. She also claimed inter alia that Mr Hall had told her the bond was not a real debt and that it would be better for her 'for tax reasons'. Ms Edmonstone also claimed that on the second execution of the bond (novating it to a different company) Mr Hall had not fully informed her of the implications and details of what she was signing.

The Royal Court examined the law relating to *dol* and fraud as follows:

> Fraudulent conduct, including the making of a fraudulent misrepresentation, can be a *moyen de nullité*, or a cause of the nullity of an agreement. The underlying principle of fraud, which we may say embraces both dol and *fraude*, is bad faith. Fraud is a *vice du consentement*, that is to say, a defect which nullifies the apparent consent between the parties and allows the defrauded party to treat the contract as void. If, therefore, a party knowingly makes a false statement which induces the other party to sign a document and thereby to enter a contract, there is a defect of consent which allows the other party to treat the contract as void.[63]

After giving this definition of a *vice du consentement* arising from a fraud, the Court went on to draw a parallel with the case of (innocent) misrepresentation:

> It may not be necessary that the statement is, at the time it is made, knowingly false; if the statement is in fact false, and the other party acts upon it, there is nonetheless a defect of consent (*vice du consentement*) because the other party enters the contract under the mistaken impression that the statement or representation is true. It may be seen, therefore, that the distinction between mistake (*erreur*) and fraud (*dol*) as defects of consent may sometimes be blurred. There is, in either event, a defect of consent which allows the injured party to treat the contract as void. The burden of proof lies upon the party who asserts that there is, in law, a defect of consent.[64]

The Royal Court thus seemed to elide the concept of false (innocent or negligent) and fraudulent statements, no doubt influenced by the English law position. This was a somewhat unfortunate statement. We will examine this issue in greater detail below, but suffice it to say that it is quite confusing to elide concepts as different as *erreur* and *dol*. As we have seen from French law, only a *fraudulent* misrepresentation is capable of amounting to *dol*. An innocent or negligent representation cannot therefore amount to *dol* (due to the absence of intention to deceive), but since the other contracting party will have contracted on the basis of a mistaken belief, this may result in the party's consent being vitiated on the separate ground of *erreur*. We will examine the consequences of the finding of lack of consent, in terms of nullity, in a later chapter.[65]

[63] Ibid, 156.
[64] Ibid, 156.
[65] See Chapter 7 below.

## D. Can *Dol* Result from Silence?

### *(i) Introduction: The Comparative Law Position*

Thus far, we have assumed that the fraudulent behaviour alleged to constitute a *dol* derives from a positive act of the contracting party: a positive and intentional misrepresentation, or scheming and assorted chicanery (under the French model). More complications arise where the alleged wrongdoing stems from an omission to provide information. The question thus arises as to whether fraud can derive from mere silence by the contracting party.[66]

In most legal systems, there are certain obligations to warn or inform a contracting party, with sanctions for non-compliance: even in the English common law, piecemeal solutions do exist.[67] However, the approach to general duties of disclosure is divided along lines mirroring the common law/civil law divide. This is amply illustrated by an Anglo-French comparison. As is well known, the general rule in English law is that mere silence cannot constitute misrepresentation.[68] Moreover, when a party knows that the other party is entering into a contact under some mistake, there is no need to alert the other party to the mistake.[69] As Lord Hoffmann has held, 'there is obviously room in the dealings of the market for legitimately taking advantage of the known ignorance of the other party'.[70] In stark contrast, the French courts—though initially reluctant[71]—now accept that a knowing and dishonest failure to disclose a matter which the other party has an interest in knowing, may result in *dol par reticence* and as such give rise to annulment (and potentially damages). This ties into the precontractual duty to disclose information which exists in French law.[72]

[66] From a comparative perspective, see the discussion in D Harris and D Tallon, 'Conclusions' in *Contract Law Today: Anglo-French Comparisons* (Oxford, Clarendon Press, 1989) 166–87.

[67] See generally N Andrews, *Contract Law* (2nd edn, Cambridge, CUP, 2015) 251–55. For instance, where a contract requires *uberrimae fides*, or where a fiduciary relation exists between the contracting parties. Moreover, there has been statutory intervention which has imposed duties of disclosure, such as in the case of distance contracts under which goods or services are supplied to consumers (Consumer Protection (Distance Selling) Regulations 2000 SI 2000/2334). On the issue of a contract subject to *uberrimae fides* in Jersey, see *Sutton v Insurance Corporation of the Channel Islands Limited* [2011] JRC 027.

[68] 'The failure to disclose a material fact which might influence the mind of a prudent contractor does not give the right to avoid the contract' (*Bell v Lever Bros Ltd* [1932] AC 161, 227 per Lord Atkin). See, however, the more nuanced view of Rix LJ in *ING Bank NV v Ros Roca SA* [2011] EWCA Civ 353, [92]–[95.] Tacit acquiescence in the self-deception of another creates no legal liability, unless it is due to active misrepresentation or to misleading conduct: M Furmston, *Cheshire, Fifoot & Furmston's Law of Contract* (16th edn, Oxford, OUP, 2012) 344–45.

[69] See eg *Smith v Hughes* (1871) LR 6 QB 596.

[70] *Bank of Credit and Commerce International SA v Munawar Ali* [2001] UKHL 8, [70].

[71] See discussion of earlier case law in Fabre-Magnan (n 18) 343.

[72] French courts have increasingly looked to whether such an *obligation d'information* existed, and in the *Baldus* case, the Cour de cassation indicated that *dol par reticence* was restricted to such cases (Cass civ 1ère, 3 mai 2000, no 98-11381, *Bull civ* I, no 131), but more recent cases indicate a more nuanced approach, eg Cass civ 3ème, 17 jan 2007, no 06-10442.

The notion of fraudulent behaviour deriving from an omission has been applied in the relevant French case law, and is known as *reticence dolosive.* To give rise to the avoidance of a contract, the *reticence dolosive* must meet different criteria:[73]

— a failure in the disclosure of information important for the other party;[74]
— an intention to mislead the other party;
— the error induced is decisive to the party's intention to contract;[75] and
— the misleading behaviour must come from the contracting party.

These case law developments have been integrated into the new French Civil Code, and it is thus provided in Article 1137(2) that 'intentionally concealing' information which the wrongdoer is under a legal duty to provide can constitute a *dol*, and thus lead to nullity.[76]

### (ii) *Controversy in the Channel Islands*

In Jersey, there has been recent judicial consideration of the issue of *dol par réticence* in a series of cases. Each of these decisions has taken a differing approach to this issue, illustrating a very different outlook regarding the extent to which disclosure obligations should be imposed upon contracting parties. This indicates not only differences of nuance as to substantive law, but more fundamentally reflects deeper arguments relating to the sources of law and underlying approaches to contract law.

The first decision to consider this issue was *Steelux Holdings Ltd v Edmonstone*,[77] a case we have already examined in detail above.[78] In this case, the court examined—albeit admittedly in an *obiter dicta* section of the judgment[79]—whether there was a dishonest silence by the defendant Mr Hall, in failing to explain the consequences of undertaking the second transaction in that case.[80]

[73] See also on this Cass com, 28 juin 2005, no 03-16794, *Bull civ* IV, no 140.
[74] That is, either that the contracting party was incapable of acquiring or that the party knew its importance for the other person.
[75] A distinction is usually made between *dol incident* and *dol principal*: the former being the one without which the contract would have been concluded but under other conditions, while the latter is the one without which no contract would have been concluded at all. The importance of the distinction lies in the fact that usually in case of *dol incident*, only damages could be granted, while in case of *dol principal* both damages and annulment of the contract could be obtained. However, recently the Cour de cassation seems to have abandoned this distinction: Cass civ 3ème, 22 juin 2005, no 04-10415, *Bull civ* III, no 137.
[76] Art 1137 (2): '*Dol* is an act of a party in obtaining the consent of the other by scheming or lies. A *dol* also is constituted by the deliberate concealing by one contracting party of information which he knows is decisive for the other party.'
[77] *Steelux Holdings Ltd v Edmonstone* 2005 JLR 152.
[78] See pp 92–93 above.
[79] As noted in the later case of *Toothill v HSBC Bank plc* 2008 JLR 77, 86.
[80] As the promissory note was interest-bearing, whereas the bond was expressed to be free of interest.

Was the failure of Mr Hall to draw attention to this difference wrongful? The Court examined the general question of whether a *dol* can result from silence:

> As a matter of general principle, under the law of Jersey the parties to a contract are expected to defend their own interests. The maxim is: *La convention fait la loi des parties.* But fraud is a flexible notion. Silence can, in certain circumstances, amount to fraud. If one party, particularly a party who is more experienced and worldly-wise than the other, is silent as to a material fact which, if it had become known to the other party, would have led to a refusal to enter into the contract, that may well amount to fraud which may lead to a setting aside of the contract. In French law, the concept is known as réticence dolosive. We would characterize it as dishonest or fraudulent silence.[81]

The Court held that it was unnecessary to decide this issue in the current case. However, it did indicate that a dishonest silence had occurred and that it would thus have set aside the obligation to pay interest encapsulated in the promissory note, if this had been necessary.[82]

In a more recent case, the Royal Court took a more nuanced approach to this question. In *Toothill v HSBC Bank plc*,[83] the Court—whilst ostensibly leaving the question open—seemed to indicate a preference for the English law approach. It noted that the discussion of this issue in *Steelux Holdings Ltd v Edmonstone* was 'clearly *obiter*',[84] and then cited a section of *Chitty on Contracts* expounding the general English law rule of non-disclosure.[85] The Court concluded on this issue that it

> would wish expressly to leave open the question of whether the law of Jersey should recognize a duty of positive disclosure in the wider circumstances envisaged by the Bailiff or whether a duty of positive disclosure should be confined to those circumstances where it exists under English law, even if, jurisprudentially, it is preferred in this jurisdiction to treat it as *dol par réticence*. Such a decision would be a matter of considerable practical importance to those who contract under Jersey law and should be the subject of full argument and consideration.[86]

The Royal Court nonetheless accepted in the instant case that, given the previous dictum in *Steelux Holdings Ltd v Edmonstone*, it was arguable that a defence for 'dishonest or fraudulent silence' was available.[87]

The issue has again been broached in another recent case, that of *Sutton v Insurance Corporation of the Channel Islands Limited*,[88] where it was held that

[81] *Steelux Holdings Ltd v Edmonstone* 2005 JLR 152, 156.
[82] Ibid, 156.
[83] *Toothill v HSBC Bank plc* 2008 JLR 77.
[84] Ibid, 85.
[85] Ibid.
[86] Ibid.
[87] Ibid, 86.
[88] *Sutton v Insurance Corporation of the Channel Islands Limited* 2011 JRL 80.

silence could result in a *dol*, in the context of an insurance contract subject to *uberrima fides*:

> We have considered the Court's hesitation in Toothill as to whether the doctrine of réticence dolosive is part of the law of Jersey. In our view the doctrine is useful in a case such as the present because it forms part of that package of principles which go to identify whether the parties to a contract of insurance, being a contract uberrima fides, have that common will or volonté to make it, and thus provide a proper basis for an assertion that la convention fait la loi des parties. Not all silences will have the effect of providing grounds for a claim in nullity. The party making that claim has to relate the alleged réticence dolosive to a material particular of the contract and its actual impact upon his will or volonté to make the contract in order to discharge the burden of showing that the claimed ground of nullity has been established.[89]

It is clear that the specific context of that case resulted in heightened obligations of the parties (as it would in most legal systems). The judge was careful thus to make reference to this context. Nonetheless, it is difficult not to conclude from the tone of the judgment in *Sutton* that the judge was more open to the doctrine of *réticence dolosive* than was the judge in the *Toothill* case.

The Jersey approach to *dol* resulting from silence thus remains unclear. Given the different approaches in the cases, there is a good deal of uncertainty on this issue. It remains to be seen what the definitive view of the Jersey courts will ultimately be. Different views have been expressed. The civil law heritage might be thought to indicate a broader approach to *dol* encompassing, in certain circumstances, omissions to disclose relevant information. On the other hand, those with a preference for orthodox common law thinking may instinctively recoil from the thought of a concept of 'fraud by silence', bolstered perhaps by the traditional reticence of the common law to impose liability for omissions to act.[90]

## V. *Erreur*

In a legal system which accords centrality to the notion of the subjective intention of the parties, the doctrine of mistake is, as remarked by Ruth Sefton-Green, one of the principal obstacles to a valid contract.[91] In contrast to English law, where the doctrine is rather restrictively defined, *erreur* is thus a major ground for vitiating contracts in French law.[92]

[89] Ibid, 98.

[90] See generally on the approach to omissions within civil liability: *Michael v Chief Constable of South Wales Police* [2015] UKSC 2 (tort law).

[91] See R Sefton-Green, *Mistake, Fraud and Duties to Inform in European Contract Law* (Cambridge, CUP, 2005) 72–73.

[92] See J Cartwright, 'Defects of Consent and Security of Contract: French and English law Compared' in P Birks and A Pretto, *Themes in Comparative Law* (Oxford, OUP, 2002) 153 et seq; Smits (n 47) ch 9; R Sefton-Green (n 91); Beale et al (n 2) ch 10.

The Jersey law on this question is somewhat complex. Indeed, the Jersey cases on *erreur* are an example of how a very different, local interpretation has been given of the French rule, which is infused with English law influences as well as those of a more local complexion. Whilst the French law concept of *erreur* generally relates to unilateral mistake, the Jersey courts have instead looked at this topic almost exclusively through the lens of misrepresentation but have also drawn on English concepts such as 'mutual mistake'.[93] We will thus preface the examination of Jersey law with a short summary of the relevant principles of both English and French law.

## A. French Law on *Erreur*

### *(i) Introduction*

We have already underlined that, in contrast to English law, the doctrine of *erreur* is a major ground for vitiating contracts in French law. Where the consent to contract is undermined by a misunderstanding—even a unilateral one—then the contract may be challenged due to the *vice de consentement*. It is recognised in French law that a balance, however, needs to be struck between the desire for full consent and the need for legal certainty in the undertaking of transactions.[94] Only certain types of error are operative in vitiating consent. Contracts may thus only be set aside where the contracting party's *erreur* fulfils a series of conditions. The French Civil Code thus makes it clear that a contract will be vitiated for *erreur* only where the mistake goes to the 'essential qualities' of the service promised or in respect of the contractor (see Article 1132 of the new French Civil Code). This means, therefore, that a mistake as to value[95] or reason for contracting[96] is not admitted in France unless, for the former example, it is a consequence of a *dol*.[97]

[93] See, however, the recent decision of the Jersey Court of Appeal in *Home Farm Developments Ltd v Le Sueur* [2015] JCA 242 in which an issue arose as to an alleged unilateral *erreur* of one of the parties as to the meaning and scope of a settlement agreement. The Court of Appeal accepted 'for the purposes of this appeal' that in such circumstances, 'a unilateral *erreur* by one party to a contract may prevent the required meeting of minds or amount to a defect of consent' ([45]). The Court, however, held that 'we do not agree that a misunderstanding as to the meaning of a contract can amount to such an *erreur*' (ibid).

[94] Fabre-Magnan (n 18) 340.

[95] Cass civ 3ème, 31 mar 2005, *Bull civ* III, no 81 on the mistaken appreciation of the economic profitability of an operation.

[96] Art 1135 of the new French Civil Code adopts a position which reflects the actual state of the case law: 'Mistake about mere motive, extraneous to the essential qualities of the act of performance owed or of the other contracting party is not a ground of nullity unless the parties have expressly made it a decisive element of their consent. However, mistake about the motive for an act of generosity is a ground of nullity where, but for the mistake, the donor would not have made it.'

[97] See Art 1137.

The notion of *erreur* under Article 1132 of the Civil Code leading to a *vice de consentement* should be distinguished from the concept of an *erreur obstacle*,[98] which provides an obstacle to the agreement arising.[99] In the case of an *erreur obstacle*, there clearly has been no meeting of minds. This type of error goes to the very *existence* of the contract. On the other hand, an *erreur* leading to a *vice de consentement* is somewhat different. As Ruth Sefton-Green has opined: 'This type of mistake does not destroy consent: it merely negatives consent, or to simplify again, the mistake concerns the validity of the contract.'[100] Under French law, the difference between these two types of *erreur* has an impact on the type of *nullité* that will arise.[101]

### *(ii) Mistake as to a Substantial Quality* (erreur sur la substance)

A mistake is traditionally defined as an incorrect appreciation of the reality, so that a party's mistake must relate as to a substantial quality, whether that be a mistake of law[102] or alternatively a mistake as to the characteristics of the item in question. According to the traditional case law, the claimant party must, however, show that the element in question (and in respect of which the mistake was made) was the *determining factor* in the conclusion of the contract—in other words if he or she had known the reality (and had not been mistaken), no contract would have been undertaken.[103]

In respect of a mistake as to the substantial quality, the term 'substance' can be understood as relating to the physical properties of the article bought or obtained. This notion, however, also extends further, known in French through the expression *qualités substantielles de la chose* which means the *essential qualities* of the thing such as the authenticity of a work of art, its age.

This approach regarding mistake as to the substantial quality typifies the subjective approach of the French courts[104] as the judge will analyse whether it was *essential* to the aggrieved party in question (and determinative of their consent to contract). The avoidance of a contract on the basis of such a unilateral error, which

[98] This categorisation has often been disputed considering the proximity of the concept with *erreur sur les qualités substantielles*: see, for instance, J Ghestin and Y-M Serinet, Rep civ Dalloz, V° Erreur, no 148, 38; Ch Larroumet, *Les obligations, Le Contrat* (Paris, Économica, 2007) nos 320, 346.

[99] eg a mistake as to the nature of the contract, one party thinking it a loan, the other a gift or a mistake as to the *objet* (see eg Cass com, 15 avr 2008, no 67-12645; Cass civ 3ème, 21 mai 2008, no 07-10772) where one party thinks a sale relates to one item, and the other party thinks it relates to another item, or mistake as to the *cause* of the contract.

[100] R Sefton-Green, 'General Introduction' (n 91) 6.

[101] See further analysis in Chapter 7 below.

[102] For instance, a person agrees to pay damages, when in fact it transpires that the person was not in fact liable.

[103] On this, see Fabre-Magnan (n 18) 328–29. See confirmation of this position in Art 1130 of the new Civil Code.

[104] See Fabre-Magnan (n 18) 328–29.

is analysed on a subjective basis, is both generous to the aggrieved party, and of course potentially harsh as to the other contracting party.

Nonetheless, some commentators on French law have indicated that objective elements may indeed have been introduced into the judicial equation. Whittaker notes that:

> [T]he issue as to whether a party's mistake was essential or determining is in principle within the discretion of the *juges du fond*, and this gives them considerable room to put into effect their perception of the appropriateness of annulment, in particular being swayed by the prejudicial effect of the mistake on the party suffering from it.[105]

Fabre-Magnan has conceded that whilst the approach is in essence a subjective one, elements of objectivity may also be introduced: 'An objective interpretation is also an instrument of judicial policy which allows for the avoidance [of the contract] to be denied where the error invoked by the contracting party does not appear to be legitimate.'[106] Bénabent has also accepted that objective elements are taken into account in the case law.[107]

One important limit to this approach regarding mistake as to the substantial quality is the notion of assumption of risk (*aléa*). This means that no remedy will be available if the parties have recognised the risk as part of the contractual bargain. For instance, the parties may contract on the sale of painting but are not sure of its authenticity, and thus no claim for mistake can follow.[108]

Two further constraints on the operation of the doctrine of *erreur* in French law should be mentioned. First, as Whittaker has pointed out, although a party's mistake does not need to be shared by the other contracting party, 'both must be aware of the factual circumstances which give rise to the essential quality of the mistake of the party applying for nullity'.[109] Whittaker thus gives the following example:

> [I]n one well-known case, buyers of a piece of land obtained the sale's annulment on the ground that, although aware of its physical extent, they were mistaken as to its hectarage, the latter being essential for them as they were intending to sell it off in parcels, a purpose which was known to their seller.[110]

Second, the mistake in question must be 'excusable', in other words a party cannot have a contract avoided where they should have known better.[111] This

[105] Bell, Boyron and Whittaker (n 4) 318.

[106] M Fabre-Magnan, *Droit des Obligations* (PUF, Paris, 2008) 305.

[107] Bénabent has thus indicated that the case law includes objective elements and has argued that if the essential quality or qualities in question were not obviously such (in objective terms), and was specific to the aggrieved party, then the latter will need to prove that this aspect had been included within the contract by showing that the other party was aware of its importance for the aggrieved party A Bénabent, *Droit civil. Les obligations* (11th edn, Montchrestien, Paris, 2007) no 78, 64–65.

[108] Cass civ 1ère, 24 mar 1987, *aff du Verrou de Fragonard*, *Bull civ* I, no 105; *D* 1987.489 note J-L Aubert; *RTD civ* 1987.743 obs J Mestre. This is confirmed in Art 1133 of the new Civil Code: 'Acceptance of a risk about a quality of the act of performance rules out mistake in relation to this quality.'

[109] Bell, Boyron and Whittaker (n 4) 319.

[110] Ibid, 319–20, referring to Cass civ, 23 nov 1931, DP 1932.1.129.

[111] See Art 1132 of the new Civil Code.

element introduces a control mechanism into the law of *erreur*, establishing a quasi-objective standard for reviewing the beliefs of the aggrieved party. Therefore, even in French law, the subjective approach has its limits.

### *(iii) Mistake as to Identity* (erreur sur la personne)

A mistake as to identity will only constitute a *vice de consentement* in French law where it relates to the 'essential qualities'[112] of the person, and where the contract has been concluded *intuitu personae* (due to the characteristics of the contracting party).[113] Such is the case for gratuitous promises (as the *intention libérale*, the intention to gift,[114] is intricately linked to the identity of the recipient), but also contracts for value where the identity of the other contracting party is important (eg qualities of the lessee/tenant for instance).

The notion of *erreur sur la personne* is potentially a broad one, so that not only questions related to the identity (eg name and age) are operative, but also other elements such as nationality, marital status and even (depending on the contract in question) issues relating to professional experience. The rules expounded above about the *erreur* being determinative of the consent, as well as it being excusable, similarly apply here.[115]

In contrast with the aforementioned types of mistake, two types of mistake are inoperative in French law, namely those relating to motive[116] and those relating to the value of the thing.[117]

### *(iv) Comparative Law Comments*

Earlier common law cases on mistake drew upon civil law writers, Pothier prominently amongst them.[118] As Beatson has explained:

> In the past, in reliance on the consensus theory of contract and influenced by the eighteenth century French jurist Pothier, the Courts were more readily disposed to hold that, where there was no 'true, full and free' consent, there was no valid contract.[119]

[112] See Art 1132 of the new Civil Code.

[113] See Art 1134 of the new Civil Code: 'Mistake about the essential qualities of the other contracting party is only a ground of nullity as regards contracts entered into on the basis of considerations personal to the party.'

[114] Whittaker translates this as 'donative intention' (see Bell, Boyron and Whittaker (n 4) 319), and Fabre-Magnan (n 18) 181 describes it as 'une intention de gratifier l'autre sans contrepartie', which is similar to Nicholas's explanation: 'intention to confer a gratuitous benefit on the promisee' (B Nicholas, *The French law of Contract* (2nd edn, Oxford, OUP, 2005) 124).

[115] See respectively Arts 1130 and 1132 of the new Civil Code.

[116] For instance, property is purchased in view of tax advantages, which eventually do not transpire. Note, however, that a mistake as to motive may be operative in French law if the parties have explicitly provided that it is a determining element of their consent: Art 1135 of the new Civil Code.

[117] See Art 1136 of the new Civil Code. See also Sefton-Green, 'General Introduction' (n 91) 20.

[118] See the excellent monograph on this issues, including a chapter devoted to Pothier's influence on the development of mistake in English contract law: C MacMillan, *Mistakes in Contract Law* (Oxford, Hart Publishing, 2010).

[119] J Beatson, *Anson's Law of Contract* (28th edn, Oxford, OUP, 2002) 308.

As such, Pothier was quoted in *Smith v Wheatcroft*,[120] *Gordon v Street*,[121] *Phillips v Brooks*,[122] *Lake v Simmons*,[123] *Sowler v Potter*[124] and *Lewis v Averay*.[125]

The current position is, however, more complex. The English concept of mistake is very different from its civil law counterparts. As Beatson has opined: 'Courts are very reluctant to intervene in this manner and the role of mistake is narrower than in many European legal systems.'[126] This is particularly the case in the commercial sphere, in respect of which, Andrews has observed, 'attempts to invoke the doctrine of mistake in the context of commercial agreements have been largely unsuccessful'.[127] As we have seen above,[128] one striking feature of the common law is that, contrary to French law, the perspective taken in English law is an objective one, an approach which is underpinned by the need to ensure legal certainty. A logical extension of reliance on the objective approach is therefore that the concept of mistake is a very narrow one. In practical terms, it is only really in the case of common mistake that a contract may be avoided.[129] Moreover, the test for such a mistake is a very strict one and has been restated in the *Great Peace*[130] case as follows:

> [T]he following elements must be present if common mistake is to avoid a contract: (i) there must be a common assumption as to the existence of a state of affairs; (ii) there must be no warranty by either party that that state of affairs exists; (iii) the non-existence of the state of affairs must not be attributable to the fault of either party; (iv) the non-existence of the state of affairs must render performance of the contract impossible; (v) the state of affairs may be the existence, or a vital attribute, of the consideration to be provided or circumstances which must subsist if performance of the contractual adventure is to be possible.[131]

Over and above common mistake, there is also the notion of rectification, where 'the parties' agreement is put in the form of a single written contract, and one or both parties misunderstand the document so that it fails accurately to record the terms which he or they agreed'.[132] The parties are thus said to be mistaken about

[120] *Smith v Wheatcroft* (1878) 9 Ch D 223, 230.
[121] *Gordon v Street* [1899] 2 QB 641, 647.
[122] *Phillips v Brooks* [1919] 2 KB 243, 248.
[123] *Lake v Simmons* [1927] AC 487, 501.
[124] *Sowler v Potter* [1940] 1 KB 271, 274.
[125] *Lewis v Averay* [1972] 1 QB 198, per Lord Denning at 206.
[126] Beatson (n 119) 308.
[127] Andrews (n 67) 262.
[128] See Chapter 3 above, at pp 40–41.
[129] There are scenarios in which the parties make different mistakes and are thus at such cross-purposes that they do not reach agreement at all but this has only been found in English law to impair the validity of the contract in exceptional circumstances. See generally A Burrows (ed), *Principles of the English Law of Obligations* (Oxford, OUP, 2015) paras 1.140–48.
[130] *The Great Peace Shipping Ltd v Tsavliris Salvage (International) Ltd (The Great Peace)* [2002] EWCA Civ 1407, [2003] QB 679.
[131] Ibid, [76].
[132] See Cartwright (n 92) 149.

the written document in so far as it fails to set out their intended terms. This possibility applies predominantly to a mistake shared by both parties.[133]

However, despite the restrictive common law approach to mistake, this does not mean, as Cartwright has pointed out, that a litigant is remediless in such circumstances:

> [T]here are [French] cases in which the courts have held that it can be a matter of substance for the buyer or seller of a work of art as to whether the work was an original; or for the buyer of a plot of land as to whether it can be built on for the particular purpose he intended; or for the hirer of a holiday villa as to whether the villa is of the high quality he expected; or for an employer as to whether an employee's previous employment history makes him suitable for employment. These are all situations in which it is doubtful whether the mistake would be sufficient in English law: certainly none of them would pass the restrictive common law test. This does not mean, however, that these situations in which French law gives a remedy for mistake would remain unremedied in English law. Very often they are situations in which English law would give remedies for misrepresentation: a buyer may make a mistake about the qualities of goods because he has been given false information by the seller. Indeed, in a sale contract there will often be an express or implied term that the goods will correspond with their description or fulfil the buyer's purposes where the buyer has made his purposes known to the seller.[134]

## B. Jersey Cases on Mistake

The general principles relating to this area of the law have been laid out in a recent Jersey Court of Appeal decision, *O'Brien v Marett*.[135] The Court examined the issue of *erreur* and distinguished clearly between *erreur obstacle* and *erreur vice du consentement* as follows:

> Consent is prevented, amongst other things, by erreur/error: Pothier, paras 17–20; Domat, paras 1224–1240; French Civil Code, art 1109 + 1110. In turn, erreur may be of two kinds: *erreur obstacle* (erreurs that prevent the meeting of minds necessary to constitute a contract's creation and cause a contract to be a nullity absolue) and *erreur vice du consentement* (a defect of consent where there is consent/meeting of minds but consent is impeachable for some other reason and which causes a contract to be a nullity relative: as to which see French Civil Code, art 1109 & 1118). *Steelux v Edmonstone* [2005] JLR 152 is recent Jersey authority for the proposition that a *vice du consentement* (and, *á fortiori,*

[133] If there is a unilateral mistake, it will be a harder task to obtain a rectification. In fact, since the document was written to accord with the non-mistaken party's intentions, it will be rectified only if the claimant can show not only his mistake, but also that the other party either knew of the mistake or at least wilfully failed to take proper steps to understand what the mistaken party intended (ie 'sharp practices' or 'unconscionable conduct').

[134] See Cartwright (n 92) 160.

[135] *O'Brien v Marett* [2008] JCA 178. See also *Home Farm Developments Ltd v Le Sueur* [2015] JCA 242 in which an issue arose as to an alleged unilateral *erreur* of one of the parties as to the meaning and scope of a settlement agreement.

> *erreur obstacle*) will render a contract *void ab initio*, that is to say, it never existed. *Erreur vice du consentement* is said to be relevant in this case.
>
> As to *erreurs obstacle*, such erreurs may, themselves, be of three kinds: *erreur sur la nature du contrat* (mistake as to nature of agreement eg gift for value); *erreur sur l'objet* (mistake as to subject of agreement); and *erreur sur l'existence de la cause* (mistake as to basis or purpose of agreement). Each of these *erreurs obstacle* will prevent the subjective meeting of minds that is fundamental and necessary to the existence of consent and the creation of a contract under Jersey law. Returning to erreurs vice du consentement, these erreurs are of two kinds: erreur sur la personne and erreur sur la substance.[136]

Whilst this summary of the civil law principles in the judgment of the Court of Appeal may seem straightforward, the translation of the concept into the broader Jersey case law on *erreur* has been less than clear. A variety of difficulties and misunderstandings has arisen, but the key problem has been that whilst the courts have ostensibly adhered to a consent-based *erreur* approach in theory, they have in reality applied English law concepts of a very different ilk. On closer analysis, therefore, the *erreur* cases that refer to this concept are not in fact an application of the French law of *erreur* (in the sense of *erreur sur la personne* and *erreur sur la substance* as outlined above), but rather appear closer to the English doctrine of misrepresentation.

We will initially look at two cases which most closely resemble the doctrine of *erreur* as described above. We will then go on to examine the further cases, which have been influenced by the English doctrine of misrepresentation.[137]

### *(i) Misunderstandings in the Jersey Cases on* Erreur

There were a number of older cases, in which references were made by the Jersey judges to the notion of 'mistake', but the analysis was generally very succinct and in any case the courts in reality adopted a predominantly English perspective with references made to 'mutual mistake',[138] reliance placed on English authorities,[139] and in many cases an objective approach to contract was applied.[140]

[136] Ibid, [56]–[57].

[137] Note also the recent decision of the Jersey Court of Appeal in *Home Farm Developments Ltd v Le Sueur* [2015] JCA 242 in which an issue arose as to an alleged unilateral *erreur* of one of the parties as to the meaning and scope of a settlement agreement. The Court of Appeal accepted 'for the purposes of this appeal' that in such circumstances, 'a unilateral *erreur* by one party to a contract may prevent the required meeting of minds or amount to a defect of consent' ([45]). The Court, however, held that 'we do not agree that a misunderstanding as to the meaning of a contract can amount to such an *erreur*' (ibid).

[138] See eg *Griggs v Coutanche* (1975) JJ 219, 231. This case concerned a dispute over the appropriate fees for work undertaken by an architect. The Court considered whether there may have been grounds for a 'mutual mistake' having arisen as to the agreement on fees, but ultimately dismissed this possibility. Frustratingly, very little was actually said about the scope and conditions of mistake in Jersey law, but the Court clearly placed much reliance however on *Cheshire and Fifoot*, and the English authorities laid down therein.

[139] See eg *Griggs v Coutanche* (1975) JJ 219, 231.

[140] See eg *Leach v Leach* (1969) JJ 1107, 1117.

The high-water mark of this approach can be found in the case of *La Motte Garages Ltd v Morgan*.[141] The plaintiff garage brought an action against the defendant to recover the balance allegedly due in respect of the latter's purchase of a car from them. The garage had advertised a car for £4,995. The defendant was interested in the car and the garage salesman offered her £2,000 for her existing car in part exchange. He undertook to discharge her existing hire-purchase debt of £2,270 but failed to include the value of the debt on the invoice, in consequence of which the defendant believed she was only liable to pay £2,995, rather than the £5,265 required to buy the new car and cover the outstanding hire-purchase in respect of the old car. When the salesman was told by the plaintiff's accounting department that the figures were incorrect, he gave the defendant the revised figures which showed that she still owed £2,270. Upon her refusal to pay the balance, the plaintiff brought the present proceedings.

The Royal Court examined the concept of *erreur* or mistake. The Court noted that 'mistake has long been accepted as negativing agreement'[142] in Jersey law, and referred to Pothier's writings on this topic. On the facts of the instant case, the Court held that a 'mutual mistake' had occurred. It laid down that the relevant test was an objective one, as to what the reasonable man would have assumed 'the sense of the promise' to mean. Applying this to the instant case, it was held that: 'There can be no doubt in our minds that a reasonable man would have seen at once that the plaintiff meant to ask for £5,265 even though at the time the defendant had not seen the mistake and assumed that the sale price was £2,995.'[143] On this basis, the Court held that a contract had been formed on the terms contended for by the plaintiff and thus gave judgment to the plaintiff for the balance owed of £2,270.

In this decision, the Royal Court seems to have applied an approach not as to what the parties had in their minds, but rather what *reasonable third parties* would infer from the words or conduct. Adopting this objective approach, the Royal Court thus came to the conclusion that an agreement had been formed on the terms contended for by the plaintiff. On the facts of the instant case, the decision in *La Motte Garages Ltd* does seem quite a harsh result for the defendant given that neither party was acting in bad faith and they were clearly at cross-purposes.

In sum, there is very limited case law on the issue of mistake *stricto sensu* under Jersey law, and when it has occurred, the predominant approach seems to adopt an English law analysis.

### *(ii) Jersey Cases on Misrepresentation*

In a separate line of cases, the Jersey courts have—whilst ostensibly applying the concept of *erreur*—introduced into Jersey law the English law of misrepresentation.

141 *La Motte Garages Ltd v Morgan* 1989 JLR 312.
142 Ibid, 316.
143 Ibid.

In many of these cases, the Jersey courts have purportedly analysed the issue as resulting from *erreur* whereas, on closer examination, it transpires that they instead concern misrepresentations made prior to the formation of a contract.

In an initial case of *Scarfe v Walton*,[144] which concerned an action by the plaintiff to set aside a contract for the sale of shares in a quarrying company on the ground of error as to the extent of the land owned by the company, it was alleged that the defendant vendor's legal adviser had made a material misrepresentation as to the ownership of the land and its boundaries. The court recognised that this case dealt with an error induced by misrepresentation.[145] In determining the law in this respect, the Court expressly looked to both 'the civil law and the law of England', and noted that 'it can be said that the principles enunciated by Domat, which cover not only error induced by misrepresentation but also error not so induced, have much in common with the law of England relating to misrepresentation and mistake'.[146] However, the excerpts cited by the Royal Court from Domat's *Les Loix Civiles* related to the circumstances in which an *action redhibitoire* (*vices cachés*) may be brought, rather than the issue of *vice de consentement*. Thus, the ancient sources referred to by the Royal Court had nothing to do with *erreur* at all![147] On the facts, the Court dismissed the claim, holding that the defect complained of[148] was a defect that the plaintiff buyers could have discovered had they carried out the appropriate investigations.

By erroneously eliding the rules enunciated by Domat with the English law of misrepresentation, the judgment in *Scarfe v Walton*[149] paved the way for the wholehearted adoption of the English law,[150] which occurred in the following case of *McIlroy v Hustler*.[151] There was a dispute over the sale of a café to the defendant, and it was subsequently alleged that false representations had been made about the takings of the establishment and that health inspection information had been withheld. The defendant decided to withhold the balance of the purchase price. The plaintiff seller sued for the remainder, and the defendant countered that there had been a misrepresentation and thus sought avoidance of the contract (or damages representing the alleged differential in value).

[144] *Scarfe v Walton* (1964) JJ 387.

[145] Ibid, 393.

[146] Ibid, 393.

[147] See ibid, 389–92. Indeed, the misinterpretation of the sources by the Royal Court was underlined by the Court of Appeal in the later case of *Kwanza Hotels Ltd v Sogeo Co Ltd* (1983) JJ 105, 122.

[148] Namely the fact that the southern boundary was in a different position to that which the buyer had thought and the area of land was therefore less extensive than anticipated.

[149] *Scarfe v Walton* (1964) JJ 387.

[150] Leeuwenburg has argued that it was only later that misrepresentation was truly adoped as a head of claim in Jersey, but the judgment in *Scarfe v Walton* clearly prepared the ground for such developments, and was the case law foundation for the latter developments. See further R Leeuwenburg, 'Une très Grosse Erreur: Jersey's Mistake over Misrepresentation' (2013) 17 *Jersey and Guernsey Law Review* 5, 11–13.

[151] *McIlroy v Hustler* (1969) JJ 1181.

The Court referred to *Scarfe v Walton*, and again repeated the (erroneous) conclusion that 'it can be said that the principles enunciated by Domat and Pothier have much in common with the law of England relating to misrepresentation and mistake'.[152] The Court accepted the definition of misrepresentation in *Cheshire & Fifoot*, and thus held that in misrepresentation cases, three questions were relevant:[153]

— Were factual representations made by the plaintiff (or agents) to the defendant (or agents)?
— If such were made, were they false?
— If false representations were made, did they constitute one or more of the causes that induced the other party to sign the agreement?

The Court held that, on the evidence, no misrepresentations had been made by the plaintiff, and many of the statements were merely statements of opinion and not fact. Moreover, the evidence showed that the plaintiff had not *relied* upon the representations as he had required the accounts to be verified by an accountant (but he had not awaited that response before signing the contract).

A series of cases then followed the case of *McIlroy v Hustler*,[154] in which misrepresentation was applied by the Jersey courts. In *Kwanza Hotels Ltd v Sogeo Co Ltd*,[155] a dispute concerned the sale of a guest house and an attendant chalet. The chalet had been described in the advertisement as the owner's accommodation but in reality there was no permission for the chalet to be used in such a way. The plaintiff purchased the property in the belief that he and his family could live in the chalet. Upon discovering the true position, the plaintiff brought an action in misrepresentation. At first instance, the Royal Court again asserted that English law was relevant as there was 'much in common' with the principles expressed by Pothier and Domat.[156] The Court, however, held that misrepresentation was not made out on the facts. The term 'owners' accommodation' was merely descriptive: merely advertising a house for sale is not to represent that all statutory consents had been complied with. There had been no misrepresentation and the plaintiff's case failed.

On appeal, the Court of Appeal[157] also agreed that there was no misrepresentation here. The references to 'owners' accommodation' in the advertisement and the particulars were merely descriptive. The Court went on to consider whether, if the statements had been a misrepresentation, the fact that the plaintiff had failed to carry out the searches and enquiries which would have revealed the existence

[152] Ibid, 1185.
[153] Ibid, 1186.
[154] Ibid.
[155] *Kwanza Hotels Ltd v Sogeo Co Ltd* (1981) JJ 59.
[156] Ibid, 65–66.
[157] *Kwanza Hotels Ltd v Sogeo Co Ltd* (1983) JJ 105.

of the defect precluded a remedy based upon the misrepresentation. On this issue, the Court considered that the decision in *Scarfe v Walton* was an 'unsatisfactory authority'. Referring to English case law, the Court indicated that it is no defence to an action for misrepresentation to show that the plaintiff could, by exercising reasonable diligence, have discovered the misrepresentation to be untrue.

The *Kwanza* case was followed by the picturesque *Newman v Marks*[158] in which certain representations had been made about the age of the horse, which subsequently transpired to be wrong, as the horse was older than stated. The Court dismissed the resultant claim as the representation about the age did not constitute one of the 'causes that induced the plaintiff to buy the horse'.[159] Age was not a 'material factor in the decision to purchase'.[160]

Despite the flurry of Jersey cases on misrepresentation, few such claims have ever succeeded. One exception was the case of *Channel Hotels & Properties Ltd v Rice*,[161] in which it was found that a misrepresentation had been made at the time of sale of a hotel that noise emanating from a nightclub would not affect a future licensing application.

### *(iii) Reasserting Customary Law*

We have seen therefore that, due to a judicial sleight-of-hand in the older cases, the English law doctrine of misrepresentation has been reintroduced into the Jersey law version of *vice de consentement.* Three more recent Jersey cases have, however illustrated a perceptible shift away from the gravitational pull of English law in this sphere.

The first case to examine is that of *Steelux Holdings Ltd v Edmonstone.* We have already presented the facts above in the context of *dol.*[162] The issue of a misrepresentation arose because the stepdaughter argued that she had been induced to execute the promissory note by the fraudulent misrepresentation of her stepfather. In examining the issues relating to *vice de consentement*, the Court anchored its analysis firmly within the sphere of civil law concepts, as was clear from the following excerpt:

> Fraudulent conduct, including the making of a fraudulent misrepresentation, can be a moyen de nullité, or a cause of the nullity of an agreement. The underlying principle of fraud, which we may say embraces both dol and fraude, is bad faith. Fraud is a vice du consentement, that is to say, a defect which nullifies the apparent consent between the parties and allows the defrauded party to treat the contract as void. If, therefore, a party knowingly makes a false statement which induces the other party to sign a document and

[158] *Newman v Marks* 1985–86 JLR 338.
[159] Ibid, 351.
[160] Ibid.
[161] *Channel Hotels & Properties Ltd v Rice* (1977) JJ 111.
[162] See pp 92–93 above.

thereby to enter a contract, there is a defect of consent which allows the other party to treat the contract as void.[163]

As we have seen, the Royal Court in this case explicitly—and somewhat unhelpfully—drew a parallel between *dol* and innocent misrepresentation:

> It may not be necessary that the statement is, at the time it is made, knowingly false; if the statement is in fact false, and the other party acts upon it, there is nonetheless a defect of consent (vice du consentement) because the other party enters the contract under the mistaken impression that the statement or representation is true. It may be seen, therefore, that the distinction between mistake (erreur) and fraud (dol) as defects of consent may sometimes be blurred. There is, in either event, a defect of consent which allows the injured party to treat the contract as void. The burden of proof lies upon the party who asserts that there is, in law, a defect of consent.[164]

We will examine the consequences of this approach below. It is submitted here that the concept of 'blurring' between *erreur* and *dol* was a somewhat unfortunate one. The concepts of *erreur* and *dol* are different ones in terms of constituent elements and approach. Perhaps what was meant by the court was that both concepts are united by the common overarching concept of *vices de consentement*, which necessarily entails that they share common consent-based approach, as well as a common remedy.[165] In any case, and despite the eliding of the various limbs of *vice de consentement*, the important point to note here is that the Royal Court in *Steelux* nonetheless reasserted civil law terminology and analysis in this sphere.[166] Other cases have shared this move back to the civil law roots.[167]

The subsequent case of *Sutton v Insurance Corporation of the Channel Islands Limited*[168] built upon this analysis, though is itself not entirely free of controversy. This case concerned an insurance contract subject to *uberrima fides*. The plaintiff had made a claim under an insurance policy for a Hublot Big Bang watch said to be worth £46,000. The defendant insurance company, with whom the watch was insured, queried the genuineness of the claim. Amongst the issues in play, the defendant alleged that a series of misrepresentations had been made by the plaintiff. The judge examined inter alia the notion of *vice de consentement*, and noted

[163] *Steelux Holdings Ltd v Edmonstone* 2005 JLR 152, 155.

[164] Ibid.

[165] See further Chapter 7.

[166] Note, though, the mixture of language and terminology in the concluding section of the judgment on this point: 'It is therefore for the defendant to prove, on a balance of probabilities, that (i) false or fraudulent misrepresentations were made by Mr Hall, and (ii) she was induced to enter into the contract of loan as a result of those false misrepresentations. If the court is satisfied on these two points, there will have been no consent, no meeting of minds, between the parties. The fraudulent misrepresentations will have given rise to a defect of consent, with the result that the contract is void *ab initio*' (*Steelux Holdings Ltd v Edmonstone* 2005 JLR 152, 155).

[167] See also *Incat Equatorial Guinee Ltd v Luba Freeport Ltd* 2010 JLR 287, 294–95: 'The doctrine of *erreur* is thus generally applied to vitiate a contract which has been made where the *erreur* goes to the heart of the *volonté* to make the contract; where one can genuinely say that there was a lack of true consent to make it.'

[168] *Sutton v Insurance Corporation of the Channel Islands Limited* 2011 JLR 80.

that in a number of cases, confusion had entered the case law due to the 'eliding of mistake, misrepresentation and the principles of *erreur*'. The judge identified the culprit as that of counsel relying upon the wrong sources of law: '[U]nfortunately the Court has been faced with citations of English authority by counsel, when a surer guide is the Law as enunciated by *Poingdestre* or *Pothier* or indeed even the Civil Law enunciated by Domat.'[169] The judge thus commented that: '[I]t appears to us that the Court should be cautious to declare the Law of Jersey by abstracting principles from the Law of England which have been drawn fundamentally from a different approach to the law of contract.'[170]

The judge then underlined that the proper approach is to resort to Jersey precedent or customary law. As far as the substantive law of *vice de consentement* is concerned, the judge then made the very cogent point that if the proper customary law analysis of *erreur* had been applied, the result would probably in many of the cases have been very similar:

> In our view, cases in Contract which have been brought before the Royal Court upon the basis of misrepresentation, where the claim is that an innocent misrepresentation did not become part of the contract terms but did induce the making of a contract which would otherwise not have been made, can sometimes be properly understood by reference to the Law on Erreur, the most recent exposition of which is to be found in the decision of the Court of Appeal in *Marett-v-O'Brien* [2008] JLR 384. It has to be recognised that whatever might have been the position in England or in France, the decisions of the Royal Court in reported contract cases since 1950 show that the Court has been prepared to investigate whether there has been an innocent misrepresentation which did not become incorporated in the contract terms as a warranty or condition but did induce the making of the contract. This must have been taken to have been upon the basis of a vice du consentement which goes to the issue as to whether there was any true common will or volonté to agree the terms of the contract.[171]

This part of the judgment thus seems clear as to the preference for the orthodox, civil law approach to *erreur* as premised upon the will/consent of the parties (rather than focused upon conduct, as in misrepresentation).[172] It thus seems consistent with the recent cases reasserting the customary law approach in Jersey. Within this context, a later part of the judgment adds a wrinkle to the analysis. In a final section on *vice de consentement*, the judge seems to conclude that the consent-based approach to *erreur* should, rather than supplanting the misrepresentation case law, be complemented by an additional head of … misrepresentation:

> A fraudulent misrepresentation clearly allows the contract to be avoided. But we go further and hold that Jersey's contract cases show that, depending on the facts, including, in

[169] Ibid, 96.

[170] Ibid.

[171] Ibid, 97.

[172] As a counterpoint, however, see also *Home Farm Developments Ltd v Le Sueur* [2015] JCA 242 in which an issue arose as to an alleged unilateral *erreur* of one of the parties as to the meaning and scope of a settlement agreement.

> particular, the *materiality* of the alleged misrepresentation to the contract and its *actual* impact on the party to whom it was made, an innocent misrepresentation which induces a contract can be another form of vice du consentement just as erreur or dol.[173]

Thus, on the strength of the Deputy Bailiff's statements in *Sutton v Insurance Corporation of the Channel Islands Limited*,[174] it would seem that he goes as far as suggesting that there should be an autonomous category of *vice de consentement* constituted by misrepresentation.

## VI. General Conclusion on *Vices de Consentement* and Reform Options

The diverse sources of Jersey law of contract have combined to produce a rich and varied state of the law in relation to *vices de consentement*. This has, however, produced correlative challenges in terms of the coherence of the corpus of the rules in this sphere, particularly as concerns the evident tensions between English and French law.

In terms of sources of law, the current position is complicated. As we have seen, within the law of undue influence, the Jersey courts in *Toothill v HSBC Bank plc* have indicated a preference for the approach of English law as encapsulated in the case law of *Barclays Bank PLC v O'Brien*[175] and *Royal Bank of Scotland plc v Etridge (No 2)*.[176] On the other hand, in respect of *dol*, reluctance was expressed in respect of adopting English law. Indeed, in the case of *Steelux Holdings Ltd*, the courts made an important distinction between English law and Jersey law. The cases on *erreur*/misrepresentation are, in many ways, even more confused on sources as noted above.

From one perspective, these differences can be seen as merely reflective of the broader debate on the sources of Jersey law of contract, which we have already analysed in Chapter 2 above. That may be true, but the interrelated nature of the heads of *vices de consentement* means that confusion over sources has spilled over into the substantive law. The interpretation of *erreur* by the Jersey courts as a form of misrepresentation may itself be a product of this phenomenon, as may the eliding of the concept of false and fraudulent statements in *Steelux Holdings Ltd*, which has broken down the distinction between *erreur* and *dol*.

There is thus a need to clarify the doctrine of *erreur*. As the case law has illustrated, some fundamental misunderstandings have crept into the analysis of *erreur*

[173] *Sutton v Insurance Corporation of the Channel Islands Limited* 2011 JLR 80, 97.
[174] *Sutton v Insurance Corporation of the Channel Islands Limited* [2011] JRC 027.
[175] *Barclays Bank PLC v O'Brien* [1994] 1 AC 180.
[176] *Royal Bank of Scotland plc v Etridge (No 2)* [2002] 2 AC 773.

in Jersey. The first point to underline is that it is not correct, as was suggested in cases such as *Scarfe*,[177] that civil law doctrines of *erreur* can be assimilated with the English law concept of misrepresentation. *Domat* and *Pothier* were not expounding doctrines which share many common features with misrepresentation. As we have seen, the older Jersey authorities which are relied upon for this proposition were not even analysing *vices de consentement* but in fact *vices cachés*[178] in the writings of *Domat*![179]

It is also very unfortunate that the English law doctrine of misrepresentation has been introduced into *vices de consentement.* This is for reasons both of practice and principle. From a perspective of principle, there is a coherence and cogency in the civil law approach to *vice de consentement*, as we have already seen above, where the rules defining the undermining of contracts are premised upon an overarching structure relating to the integrity of the consent given. Misrepresentation does not fit naturally into that matrix. The doctrine of misrepresentation is conduct based: the focus of the analysis is upon the *conduct of the representor.* The doctrine of *erreur* is very different: it is consent based, and the focus of the analysis is thus upon the state of mind of the person suffering from the misunderstanding. That misunderstanding may of course have been partly generated by a misstatement (made in good faith) of the other contracting party. It may, however, just as plausibly be derived from other circumstances where no representation or statement has been made by the other side—the victim was quite simply under a misapprehension. The focus of analysis and the raison d'être of the remedy of *erreur* is the vitiation of the consent of the party concerned. As the consent of one of the contracting parties has been vitiated, then the contract should thus be set aside. The analysis is thus, as we have already seen, based upon an essentially subjective approach, in contrast to the objective analysis encapsulated in the doctrine of misrepresentation.[180] The doctrine of *erreur* is thus both distinctive from, but complementary to, the notion of *dol.* In French law, the conduct and mental elements of *dol* are not required, but the doctrine of *erreur* is subject to different and nonetheless effective control mechanisms, as we have seen above. Additionally, there are also questions about how the doctrine of misrepresentation would interact with the pre-existing *vice de consentement* of *dol.* We have already seen above that this was the subject of not entirely convincing reasoning in the case of *Steelux Holdings Ltd.*

From a practical perspective, there is uncertainty as to whether it is actually necessary to maintain the concept of misrepresentation within this area of the law.

[177] See p 106 above.

[178] For further analysis of this notion, see Chapter 6 below, at pp 132–139.

[179] See p 106 above.

[180] See also Leeuwenburg (n 150) 22–23: '[T]here is no rationale for forming a contract using a subjective analysis of the meeting of minds of the parties, while attacking the same contract with an objective analysis of the parties' knowledge at the time of formation of the contract.'

In most cases, the standard approach to *erreur* would have sufficed. Indeed, Deputy Bailiff Bailhache (as he then was) explicitly pointed out in the case of *Sutton* that most of the earlier cases could have been resolved by using the traditional customary law doctrine of *erreur.*[181] Commentators have also made a similar point.[182]

It is thus submitted that Jersey law should revert to the classic tripartite analysis of *vice de consentement: erreur*, *dol* and violence. Misrepresentation is superfluous and ultimately confusing. Violence deals with the specific factual circumstance of unlawful *constraint* undermining free will. The tandem of *dol* and *erreur* are sufficient additional tools to allow the courts to deal with circumstances of fraudulently provoked misunderstanding or mere unilateral errors. The Jersey courts should have the confidence to state this. The law would be clearer and simpler to apply. As Leeuwenburg has elegantly pointed out in a critical appraisal of the current Jersey law, the concept of *erreur* is simpler, easier to explain to lay persons, and also more compatible with the sources of the Jersey law of contract.[183]

## VII. *Lésion or Déception d'Outre Moitié du Juste Prix*

Closely linked to the previous discussion of defects of consent is the intriguing civil law-inspired doctrine of *déception d'outre moitié de juste prix.*[184] Also known as *lésion,* the doctrine of *déception d'outre moitié* notion is an ancient one,[185] with roots in the Roman law of *laesio enormis.*[186] Despite its long heritage, the notion has somewhat uncertain contours, but generally entails that a contract can be unravelled where there is a serious imbalance between the mutual performances initially agreed by the parties.

The potential breadth of a remedy which allows contracts to be avoided for disparity in value alone has meant that the principle exists in few legal systems.[187]

[181] *Sutton v Insurance Corporation of the Channel Islands Limited* 2011 JLR 80, 97.

[182] Leeuwenburg (n 150) 23 notes that the earlier cases 'are all capable of having an analysis of *erreur* applied to them in lieu of the misrepresentation analysis and generating the same outcome'.

[183] Ibid.

[184] Another ancient name for the cause of action in Jersey is that of *la clameur révocatoire.* See comments in the Court of Appeal in *Snell v Beadle* 1999 JLR 1, 10.

[185] For the history of the doctrine of lésion in French law, see: E Chevreau, Y Mausen, and C Bouglé, *Introduction Historique au Droit des Obligations* (Paris, Litec, 2007) para 84.

[186] R Zimmermann, *The Law of Obligations* (Oxford, OUP, 1996) 259–70; M-J Schermaier, 'Mistake, Misrep and Pre-contractual duties' in Sefton-Green (n 91) 53–55.

[187] Neither Dutch, English nor German law recognise disparity in value per se as a ground of invalidity of a contract: Beale et al (n 2) 565.

The doctrine still, however, plays a role in French law, as a head of invalidity independent from that of *vice de consentement*.[188]

In Jersey, the origins of the doctrine stretch back to Norman customary law.[189] An action for *déception d'outre moitié* may be brought in respect of certain types of sales transaction where the price agreed is less than 50% of the real market value at the time of sale. Whilst the principle runs contrary to the rule of *la convention fait la loi des parties*,[190] the exception is said to be justified by the disproportion that exists between the bargain made and the *juste prix*.

The doctrine was for many years quasi-dormant but has in recent times experienced a resurgence due to case law which reached the highest level. There are some older decisions,[191] but the leading case is now *Snell v Beadle*,[192] which resulted in a decision of the Privy Council. Over and above the technicalities of the case law, the concept engages with important broader considerations concerning the role of the courts on the one hand, and the sanctity of agreements on the other: in the absence of any other vitiating factors, should a judge be able to intervene to review the *economic balance* of agreements entered into by consenting contractual parties? In many jurisdictions, the answer to that question would be in the negative, but faithful to its civilian origins, the Jersey courts have allowed judicial review of the economic balance of the bargain—albeit in restricted circumstances.

## A. The Case of *Snell v Beadle*

The main point at issue in this case was whether a mere shortfall in the sale price of real estate (namely *dol réel*) is enough *in and of itself* to found an action in *déception d'outre moitié*, or whether contrariwise other circumstances were in fact required, such as proof of fraud, or in civil law terminology, *dol personnel*. The case arose from a dispute between the plaintiff and the defendant who were neighbours owning adjacent properties. The plaintiff wanted to develop his property and a written agreement was reached between the parties to the effect that the defendant

[188] See eg Cass Civ 1ère, 19 oct 1960, *Bull civ* I no 366. It is thus not necessary to show that *dol*, *erreur* or *violence* was present—the disparity in value suffices: see discussion in Fabre-Magnan (n 18) 433. For the history of this action in French law, see Chevreau, Mausen, and Bouglé (n 185) para 84.

[189] The origins of the doctrine in the Channel Islands were discussed in the case of *Snell v Beadle*. The Court of Appeal noted that there was evidence of the cause of action to be found in the *ancienne coûtume* of Normandy: *Snell v Beadle* 1999 JLR 1, 7.

[190] *Snell v Beadle* [2001] UKPC [5], para 54.

[191] See *Le Bas v Richardson* (1896) 49 H 75 (action to annul a sale contract made between plaintiff's elderly mother and the defendant); *Bisson (née Ferbrache) v Bisson* (1981) JJ 103 (where contract was set aside when it was found that the plaintiff had acted under duress from her husband in agreeing to transfer a half share in property for the nominal sum of £500, the Royal Court indicated *obiter* that for an action based on *déception d'outre moitié* to succeed 'it is not just sufficient to show that the price of the contract was less than half the value of the property').

[192] *Snell v Beadle* [2001] UKPC 5.

would grant a right of way to the plaintiff for access over a strip of land in return for a payment of £100.

The defendant subsequently argued, however, that pressure had been brought to bear by the plaintiff to induce her to enter into the contract and that the sum that should have been paid was much higher—in the region of £10,000–15,000. Due to the dispute, the contract was therefore never passed before the Royal Court so as to put it into effect. The defendant asserted that a deception had been practised on her and that as a result of that, the price agreed was less than half of the actual value of the right of access. The plaintiff brought an action in damages for breach of contract and the defendant responded on the basis of *déception d'outre moitié*, arguing that as a consequence she was not bound by the agreement (or entitled to repudiate it).

At first instance, the Royal Court rejected the defence based upon *déception d'outre moitié.*[193] Quoting inter alia Le Gros, the Court said that they were unable to see what *dol* had been practised on Mrs Beadle. She was an astute business woman, who had bought and sold property before. Her family had, the court said, owned much of the land at Grève d'Azette, and even remarked that 'Her grandfather had been landlord to Victor Hugo'! The contract had thus been entered into without inducement between adults, and the court was not persuaded that there was a *déception d'outre moitié*. The effect of the judgment was thus that the defence based on the principle of *déception d'outre moitié* failed on the ground that this cause of action required something more than a finding that the price was less than half of the *juste prix*.

On appeal, the Court of Appeal examined a series of legal issues,[194] but the bulk of the analysis focused on whether this cause of action required proof of *dol* (in the sense of fraud or otherwise) going beyond the mere disparity in price. On the question of sources, the Court noted that as the cause of action formed a part of Jersey law and affected property rights, it was not legitimate to import into it concepts derived from the law of England.[195] The cause of action was thus to be 'derived from the custom of the people and from its earlier Norman sources'.[196]

On the issue of *dol*, the Court examined both the relevant case law, and accompanying commentaries in detail including Terrien, Le Rouillé, Houard, Basnage, Le Geyt, and, of course Le Gros.[197] An issue arose as to the correct interpretation of a passage on the doctrine in Le Gros's *Traité du Droit Coutumier de L'Ile de Jersey*. Le Gros had written that:

> Ce n'est pas à dire que le préjudice qu'éprouve le vendeur par suite de l'insuffisance du prix suffit pour rescinder le contrat. D'autres circonstances doivent concourir à

[193] In an unreported judgment dated 4 February 1998.
[194] *Snell v Beadle* 1999 JLR 1.
[195] Ibid, 7.
[196] Ibid, 8, quoting *Romeril v Davis* (1977) JJ 135, 138.
[197] *Snell v Beadle* 1999 JLR 1, 8–10.

l'annulation du contrat, tel que le dol. En l'absence de toute allégation, autre que celle de la déception, le défendeur peut être reçu a son offre de suppléer ce qui manque au juste prix.[198]

Whilst this seemed to suggest that something additional to the disparity in value was required—such as fraud *tel que le dol*—the Court of Appeal considered that Le Gros 'fell into error' in this respect.[199] The Court was emphatic in its view that the shortfall in the price amounts *in and of itself* to a *dol réel* (or *dolus ipsa*). It was not necessary for the claimant to show any further fraud or *dol* on the part of the other contracting party.[200] As Collins JA held:

> [S]uch a shortfall in the price amounts to a dol réel or, to use the oldest phrase used by the writers, dolus ipsa. Thus where such a shortfall is established, it is not necessary to establish a dol personnel, that is to say, some trick or fraud or conduct of that nature. The words 'dolus ipsa' are to be found in a later passage in Terrien and clearly import a situation in which the dolus is inherent in the nature of the transaction itself.[201]

The litigation continued onwards to the Privy Council.[202] A central issue was again whether, under Jersey law, the cause of action in question required an element of fraud, or *dol personnel*, over and above the shortfall in price. The Privy Council surveyed the case law, writers and commentators on the question. Much turned on the discussion of the work of Le Gros.[203] The majority in the Privy Council made the following interpretation of Le Gros' statement on this rule:

> Their Lordships consider that the critical passage in Le Gros's discussion, where the two sentences quoted in *Ferbrache v Bisson* [1981] JLR 103, 108 appear, is capable of another reading which is consistent with the treatment of the cause of action by the earlier writers. This is that he is concentrating at this point on the question of the appropriate remedy. Two different situations are distinguished in these sentences. The first is where the necessary shortfall is established so that there is a *dol réel*, but there are no other grounds for saying that the contract is defective because it was procured by fraud or deception. The second is where there is evidence of fraud or deception in the procuring of the contract such as to amount to *dol* in the sense of a *dol personnel*. In the first situation the primary remedy is to make good the shortfall in the price, so that the object of the transaction is achieved and the property passes from the vendor to the purchaser at the juste prix. The purchaser is entitled to maintain the bargain by offering to pay the amount of the shortfall. In the second situation the transaction is so infected by the dol personnel that the purchaser has no such right, and the vendor is entitled at once

[198] 'It is not to say that the loss suffered by the seller due to the insufficient price is enough for a rescinding of the contract. Other circumstances are required for the annulment of the contract, such as *dol*. In the absence of any allegation, other than that of deception, the defendant can be eligible for his offer to supplement the amount which is missing [to attain] a fair price.'

[199] Ibid, 13.

[200] Ibid, 9.

[201] Ibid, 8.

[202] *Snell v Beadle* [2001] UKPC 5.

[203] Ibid, see [33] onwards.

> to rescind the contract. It is clear from the context that the assertion by Le Gros that something more to bring about what he describes at p 35 as l'annulation du contrat was directed to the second situation and not to the first.[204]

The Privy Council then proceeded to apply the rule to the instant case. The reasoning given by the majority of the Privy Council was alas by no means crystal clear. Their Lordships ultimately dismissed the claim based on *déception d'outre moitié* for the following reason:

> [A]s this was not a contract for the sale of land and as it has not been shown that there was a juste prix for the servitude right which could be determined objectively by the parties transacting with each other in good faith, this is a case to which the remedy does not apply.[205]

From that perspective, it could thus be argued that the ratio of the judgment was limited to the issues raised in this aspect of the judgment, namely that the doctrine of *déception d'outre moitié* was inapplicable as the transaction in question was not a sale of land (it was simply a grant of servitude over land), as well as the inherent difficulty in attributing a market price to the asset in question. If this reasoning is right, then the portion of the judgment governing the other issues, most notably the role of *dol*, is strictly *obiter*. With that in mind, we will turn to examine the issue of the relevant mental element.

The majority indicated that the doctrine of *déception d'outre moitié* was based upon the principle of good faith[206] and thus *déception d'outre moitié* may only be found where 'something has occurred which is different from that which would have occurred if the parties had been transacting with each other in good faith'.[207] This would seem to suggest that it was necessary to prove behaviour indicating a departure from bad faith to make out *déception d'outre moitié*. Indeed, the generally restrictive attitude of the majority in the Privy Council to the doctrine was set out in a later section of the decision:

> [T]the fact is that Mrs Beadle is seeking to invoke an ancient doctrine which few legal systems of our time have accepted. It runs counter to the general principle that where parties of full age and capacity contract with each other freely and without any element of dol personnel they should be held to their contract. It is not generally recognised to be just, according to the notions of our time, that such a contract should be at risk of being reopened for thirty years simply because it occurred later to one of the parties that he or she would have been able, by asking for more, to obtain more than twice the price that was agreed to.[208]

[204] Ibid, [40].
[205] *Snell v Beadle* [2001] UKPC 5, [54].
[206] Ibid, [44].
[207] Ibid, [44].
[208] Ibid, [54].

However, other areas of the judgment suggest that the disparity in value is the crucial element. At one stage, the majority held that:

> [T]he dol réel owes its existence not to a desire on the part of the purchaser to outwit or harm the vendor but from a lack of knowledge on the part of the contracting parties of the value of the property.[209]

This, and other passages, suggests that a fraudulent motive is not essential. Indeed, the minority judgment of Lords Cooke and Hope was explicit on this issue:

> We are in agreement with the opinion of the majority that the Court of Appeal was right to differ from the Royal Court and to hold that the remedy for *déception d'outre moitié* is available where the vendor receives less than one half of the *juste prix* without the need to prove *dol personnel*.[210]

The kernel of the Privy Council's decision on the role of *dol* seems, however, to be encapsulated in its interpretation of the relevant passage of Le Gros, referred to above. The key aspect is the impact that *dol* has upon the remedy available for *déception d'outre moitié*. The Privy Council thus indicated that there were two different remedies applicable to *déception d'outre moitié*. In case of a mere *dol réel*, namely where there is merely a differential in price but no evidence of *dol* or fraud, then the primary remedy is for the purchaser to make good the shortfall in the price, and thus the transaction takes place. Indeed, in a later section of the decision, the Privy Council underlined that 'in a case of déception the primary remedy is to call on the purchaser to make good the shortfall in the price so that he can maintain the bargain'.[211] Presumably, however, if the purchaser fails to make good this shortfall, then the sales contract will be set aside. In case of *dol personnel*, where fraud or deception is made out, then the seller may have the contract annulled, and the purchaser cannot maintain the contract by virtue of paying the shortfall. This latter scenario is of course consistent with the *vice de consentement* of *dol*.[212]

## B. Concluding Remarks on *Déception d'outre Moitié*

The recent case law confirms that the doctrine of *déception d'outre moitié* is alive and well in Jersey. The doctrine is, however, subject to severe restrictions: first and foremost of which is that it only applies in case of sales of land or *heritage* and

[209] Ibid, [46].

[210] Ibid, [61]. However, the minority goes on to note that the majority placed the notion of good faith at the centre of their analysis (see [64] onwards). The minority nonetheless disapproved of the potential 'defence' based on good faith, holding that: 'We consider that this principle applies where a vendor claims that she has received less than one half of the *juste prix*, and that it is not open to Mr Snell to argue that Mrs Beadle is not entitled to annul the agreement because he and she were dealing with each other in good faith' ([67]).

[211] Ibid, [55].

[212] Ibid.

not movables.[213] Even in respect of sales of land, the doctrine will be inapplicable: in case of leases of short duration;[214] where land is sold at public auction;[215] where property is bought at a bargain price and both parties knew and intended to depart from the concept of *juste prix*;[216] and where land is gifted (as there is no *juste prix*).[217]

As to the remedial perspective, whilst the reasoning of the Privy Council could have been clearer, it has nonetheless been established that in case of mere *dol réel*, the primary remedy is for the purchaser to make good the shortfall in the price, thereby maintaining the transaction. This is consistent with the position in French law, where despite some initial indications to the contrary,[218] a so-called 'objective' approach to *lésion* has been adopted by the courts whereby the disparity in mutual performances of the contractual parties is enough per se.[219] From that perspective, and given the origins of Jersey contract law, it is perhaps unfortunate that the Privy Council considered that modern French law was not of any assistance at all.[220]

The doctrine of *déception d'outre moitié* does, however, run contrary to the prevailing position in most other legal systems,[221] as well as in the various European projects,[222] where 'qualified *lésion*' is in general a requirement, so that it must be shown *a minima* that one party took an excessive economic advantage by abusing the situation in which the other party found himself.[223] There has been academic consideration of this issue from comparative lawyers. Zwalve reviewed the doctrine and the case law and concluded that:

> The doctrine of laesio enormis has always been regarded as an oddity. There is no mention of it in the Digests and only twice in the Codex Justinianus (C 4,44,2 and 8). In the long course of its history after the reception of Roman law it has seen a considerable expansion, followed by a slow but steady decline. It has been abolished in most continental-European codes and even where it still obtains (as, for example, in France art 1118 & 1674 ff Cc), it has been much criticised. The rationale of the doctrine is better served

[213] The principle does not apply eg to shares in a property company, or to the grant of a servitude over land.

[214] *Snell v Beadle* [2001] UKPC 5, [43].

[215] See comments in the Court of Appeal in *Snell v Beadle* [1999] JLR 1, [11] (overturned on different grounds by the Privy Council).

[216] Ibid, [12] (overturned on different grounds by the Privy Council). See also *Snell v Beadle* [2001] UKPC 5, [44].

[217] Ibid, [12] (overturned on different grounds by the Privy Council).

[218] '[A] portion of the doctrinal writers and the case law considered that, in these contracts, the serious disproportion in the [mutual] performances was not enough and that it was necessary to to show additionally that a *vice de consentement* was at the basis of the *lésion*. The *travaux préparatoires* of the Civil Code seemed to indicate in that direction as well' (Fabre-Magnan (n 18) 433).

[219] See eg Cass civ 1ère, 19 oct 1960, *Bull civ* I, no 366. It is thus not necessary to show that *dol*, *erreur* or *violence* was present—the disparity in value suffices: see discussion in Fabre-Magnan (n 18) 433.

[220] 'French law as it exists today in the French Codes or the current jurisprudence is unlikely to be of direct assistance here' (*Snell v Beadle* [2001] UKPC 5, [21]).

[221] Although it does seem also to be present in Austrian law: see Schermaier (n 186) 54.

[222] See eg Art 4:109 PECL relating to 'Excessive benefit or unfair advantage'.

[223] Beale et al (n 2) 570.

> by incorporating it in the general doctrines of mistake, innocent misrepresentation and (economic) duress. As it seems to me, the law of Jersey is going that way. It is thus joining the general trend of the continental-European ius commune, a tradition which the legal profession of that island so proudly adheres.'[224]

It remains to be seen what the future holds for this doctrine in Jersey law. In light of the Privy Council decision, one does wonder of how much utility the doctrine of *déception d'outre moitié* will actually be in practice. Standing back from the detail of the discussion, it is submitted, however, that the continuing operation of the doctrine of *déception d'outre moitié* in its broader sense is consistent with the general approach of Jersey law. Not only does the doctrine correspond with the Norman/civil law sources, but it is also consonant with underlying principles in Jersey contract law. We have already noted that in a number of spheres of contract law, the Jersey judiciary are prepared to undertake a more interventionist role than would be readily assumed in a common law context.[225] One striking example of this is the notion of cause, which is a more malleable tool than its common law equivalent of consideration. The notion of a contractual cause provides the courts with a more intrusive tool for scrutinising the contractual bargain between the parties; a phenomenon which is also reflected in other recent cases, such as the *Doorstops* case where the Royal Court was prepared, under the cover of the control of penalty clauses, to rewrite the level of contractual interest rates which is considered to be appropriate.[226] It is thus possible to see parallels with the civil law cases of a control of the 'adequacy' of the *cause* in contractual arrangements, as examined above.[227] From this perspective, the ability of parties to petition the court by means of the doctrine of *déception d'outre moitié* where there is a disparity in value in real estate no longer seems such an unusual cause of action. On the contrary, it corresponds with a conception of the role of the judge in respect of reappraising contractual bargains which is consistent with the broader approach in the Jersey law of contract.[228] It is also possible to point to contextual factors as supporting the more prominent role of the judge in reviewing contractual bargains—and particularly so in the case of real estate transactions, where the role of the courts has always been prominent in Jersey.[229]

224 WJ Zwalve, 'Snell v Beadle: the Privy Council on Roman Law, Norman Customary and the Ius Commune' in L Ligt and J de Ruiter (eds), Viva Vox Iuris Romani (Amsterdam, Gieben, 2002) 379, 385–86.

225 See pp 31–32.

226 The Royal Court held that it would be 'unconscionable to give judgment for interest rates which are not moderate or reasonable': *Doorstop Ltd v Gillman and Lepervier Holdings Ltd* [2012] JRC 199, [40].

227 See pp 76–77 and 82.

228 See pp 31–32 above.

229 Note that one commentator has identified the distinctive *esprit* of Norman customary law as including an attachment to family lineage and protection of family property: S Poirey, 'L'Esprit of Norman Customary Law' in P Bailhache (ed), *A Celebration of Autonomy: 1204–2004, 800 Years of Channel Islands' Law* (St Helier, Jersey Law Review, 2005) 17.

# 6

# Effects of Contracts

In this chapter, we will examine from a comparative perspective a selection of important issues which arise during the life of a contract. A number of issues are grouped together under the heading of 'Effects of a Contract', many of which are not often examined in comparative perspective, such as contractual interpretation, and the circumstances in which terms can be implied into contracts. For the purposes of analysis, we will divide this into separate sections. In the first section, we will examine the nature of obligations between the parties, deriving from the fundamental principle of the *convention fait la loi des parties* and including the binding force of the contractual obligation. Closely related to that, the effect of the contract beyond the parties will be scrutinised in a second section, in particular the application of the doctrine of privity of contract in Jersey. In a third section, we then analyse the approach to the interpretation of contracts, as well as the implication of implied terms. We will then examine the various warranties, including the latent defect warranty and the statutory warranties. In a final section, the scenarios in which the Jersey courts will defeat the principle of *convention fait la loi des parties* will be presented, namely in case of penalty clauses and exemption clauses.

## I. Nature of Obligations between the Parties

As we have already seen, the principle of *la convention fait la loi des parties* is one of the cornerstones of the Jersey law of contract. It has been cited and applied in many Jersey cases,[1] and is referred to as of a 'sacred'[2] principle of Jersey law. The application of the principle in Jersey owes much to the influence of civil law

[1] *Donnelly v Randalls Vautier Ltd* 1991 JLR 49; *Wallis v Taylor* (1965) JJ 455; *Cooke v Mold* [2010] JRC 093.

[2] Le Gros, *Traité du Droit Coutumier de L'Ile de Jersey* (1943), in his chapter entitled 'De la Clameur Révocatoire ou Déception D'Outre-Moitié du Juste Prix': 'C'est un principe en quelque sorte sacré que la convention fait la loi des parties' (350).

writers such as Pothier and Domat.[3] The kernel of the principle of *la convention fait la loi des parties* in the law of Jersey is thus that if an agreement has been concluded between responsible adults, then only in exceptional circumstances will the courts interfere with the contract so formed,[4] and the Jersey Royal Court has recognised that the principle is anchored in fundamental values underpinning Jersey law.[5]

It should be noted that the principle of *la convention fait la loi des parties* admits of exceptions.[6] Pothier had already noted that the principle would not apply where the agreements were 'contraire aux lois et aux bonnes mœurs',[7] and in Jersey, exceptions have been said to arise when a contract is contrary to public policy,[8] where a statute provides for a power to interfere with contracts,[9] or where an agreement constitutes a restraint of trade.[10] We will examine below the position concerning penalty clauses and exemptions clauses.

Closely linked to the aforementioned principle of *la convention fait la loi des parties* is the notion that by entering into a contract, the parties are entering a binding agreement. The contract is thus accorded 'obligatory force', and unless there are any vitiating factors, the contracts will not in general intervene to change that which has been decided by the parties as consistent with the principle of *la convention fait la loi des parties*. On the other hand, the personal, contractual nature of the obligations represents both the extent and the limits of the principle of binding obligations. As Whittaker has pointed out:

> [T]he nature of contractual obligations also explains the main exception to its binding force: as the often-quoted maxim puts it, *impossibilium nulla obligation*—one cannot be bound to do the impossible—and so *force majeure (supervening impossibility)* is a general ground of excuse for contractual non-perfomance.'[11]

In Jersey, the doctrine of *force majeure* has thus been applied in such a way.[12] There are other limits to the binding nature of the contract. We have already noted that the courts will interfere with contractual relationships in certain circumstances. The scope of the parties bound by the contract is also restricted, with the general rule being that contracts will not bind third parties. We will turn to examine this issue in greater detail now.

[3] See pp 33–36 above.
[4] See *Wallis v Taylor* (1965) JJ 455.
[5] See *Doorstop Ltd v Gillman* [2012] JRC 199, [18].
[6] *Basden Hotels Ltd v Dormy Hotels Ltd* (1968) JJ 911.
[7] Pothier, *Traité des Obligations*, para 15.
[8] *Basden Hotels Ltd v Dormy Hotels Ltd* (1968) JJ 911
[9] *Macready v Amy* (1950) JJ 11 (Rent Control Tribunal given power by statute to intervene as regards parties contractual arrangements on level of rent).
[10] See the leading case of *Rossborough v Boon* 2001 JLR 416.
[11] J Bell, S Boyron and S Whittaker, *Principles of French Law* (2nd edn, Oxford, OUP, 2008) 327.
[12] See *Hotel de France Ltd v Chartered Institute of Bankers* (unreported, 21 December 1995).

## II. The Effects of Contracts beyond the Parties

We will first say a word about the notion of privity of contract and the effect of contracts beyond the parties. There are of course limits to the binding nature of the contract. We have already noted that the courts will in certain circumstances interfere with contractual relationships. The scope of the parties bound by the contract is also restricted. Whilst most European legal systems now allow, in certain circumstances,[13] for a contract to create enforceable rights in third parties, this has been the product of a slow evolution over time.[14] In many systems, the contrary was, for a long time, true. It is well known that in Roman law the principle of *alteri stipulari nemo potest* applied, namely that no one could validly contract for the benefit of another person who had not been party to the original contract.[15]

In French law, the general rule was also that contracts could not bind third parties. Article 1165 Code civil thus provided that: 'Agreements have effect only between the contracting parties; they do not impose burdens on third parties, and they benefit him only in [specific cases].' The formulation in the new Code civil is as follows: 'A contract creates obligations only as between the parties. Third parties may neither claim performance of the contract nor be constrained to perform it, subject to the provisions of this section.'[16] The starting point in French law is therefore clear: contracts create obligations only in respect of those who are contracting parties. Flowing from the personal nature of an agreement, this is referred to in French law as the principle of the 'relative effect of contracts'.

There are, however, exceptions to the principle of the relative effect of contracts,[17] as is indicated in the latter part of Article 1199 of the new Civil Code. These exceptions initially derived from the courts interpreting the previous provisions in a broad manner,[18] so as to allow third parties to gain rights in contracts in specific situations. The new version of the Civil Code thus enshrines those case law developments in new articles, as exceptions to the 'relative effect' principle, including the notions of *porte-fort* (where a contracting party undertakes that a third party will undertake an act—Article 1204 of the new Code civil) and *stipulation pour autrui* (an agreement creating rights in third parties) found in

[13] The initial historical developments were prompted by the advent of life insurance contracts. In the UK, this was dealt with by piecemeal statutory reform: Married Women's Property Act 1182, s 11.

[14] See H Beale, B Fauvarque-Cosson, J Rutgers, D Tallon and S Vogenauer, *Cases, Materials and Text on Contract Law* (Oxford, Hart Publishing, 2010) 1173.

[15] R Zimmermann, *The Law of Obligations: Roman Foundations of the Civilian Tradition* (Oxford, OUP, 1996) 34.

[16] Art 1199 Code civil.

[17] See generally B Nicholas, *The French Law of Contract* (2nd edn, Oxford, OUP, 2005) 177–99.

[18] See Beale et al (n 14) 1174–75.

Articles 1205–09 of the new Code civil. There are also other ways in which French law allows the benefit of a contract to be enjoyed by a third party.[19]

The position in English law is well known.[20] Until relatively recently, English law took the position that a person who was not a party to a contract could not acquire directly enforceable rights under it.[21] Only parties that were 'privy' to the contract acquired rights under it. Coupled with the doctrine of consideration, the doctrine of privity was relatively rigidly applied in the English common law,[22] despite growing criticism from commentators, the judiciary[23] and law reformers.[24] The enactment of the Contracts (Rights of Third Parties) Act 1999 changed that, however, and there are now substantial exceptions to the privity of contract doctrine in English law.[25]

The mid-channel position is not, however, entirely clear. It has generally been assumed amongst Jersey practitioners that the privity of contract principle was applicable in Jersey, and that third parties could not acquire directly enforceable rights under it. There is very little authority for such a position, though the case law that there is would seem to provide some support.[26] It might nevertheless be questioned whether such an approach is entirely compatible with Jersey's civil law origins. We have noted above that many legal systems have evolved from an initially restrictive position as to third party rights regarding contracts, though in contradistinction with the common law, that occurred more quickly in civil law countries such as France, and through case law developments, rather than legislative reform.[27]

It might be thought that in a system such as Jersey which places a great deal of importance on the subjective intention of the parties, that the law should recognise the ability of parties to extend the benefit of contracts to third parties. If the parties so desire to extend the contract, then their expectations should be respected, in line with the principle of *la convention fait la loi des parties*. Other mixed systems have allowed for third-party beneficiary contracts, such as the *jus quaesitum tertio* in Scotland.[28] Moreover, Jersey does not have the doctrine

[19] Such as the ability to bring contractual claims as against all those in a distribution chain in certain circumstances (eg for a product liability claim). A consumer can thus sue the manufacturer directly for latent defects in products sold to him by a retailer. Bell, Boyron and Whittaker (n 11) 337–38.

[20] N Andrews, *Contract Law* (2nd edition, Cambridge, CUP, 2015) ch 7.

[21] See generally R Merkin (ed), *Privy of Contract: The Impact of the Contracts (Rights of Third Parties) Act 1999* (Informa Law, 2000).

[22] *Dunlop Pneumatic Tyre Co Ltd v Selfridge & Co Ltd* [1915] AC 847, 853.

[23] See eg comments of Steyn LJ in *Darlington BC v Wiltshier Northern Ltd* [1995] 1 WLR 68, 76–77; and comments of Lord Diplock in *Swain v Law Society* [1983] 1 AC 598, 611.

[24] Law Revision Committee, Sixth Interim Report, 1937, para 61.

[25] See generally Andrews (n 20) ch 7.

[26] *Huet v Lewis* (1976) JJ 435.

[27] See *Darlington BC v Wiltshier Northern Ltd* [1995] 1 WLR 68, 77 per Steyn LJ: '[D]o well to remember that the civil law legal systems of other members of the European Union recognise such contracts'

[28] See generally H MacQueen, 'Third Party Rights in Contract: Jus Quaesitum Tertio' in K Reid and R Zimmermann (eds), *A History of Private Law in Scotland*, vol 2: *Obligations* (Oxford, OUP, 2000).

of consideration to provide conceptual objections to the loosening of the privity doctrine. It does not have the benefit of the legislative amendment afforded in the common law by the enactment of the Contracts (Rights of Third Parties) Act 1999. It is submitted that Jersey customary law could thus fill the gap.

## III. Terms and Interpretation

### A. Comparative Perspectives

It is well known that the approach to contractual interpretation is very different in common and civil law jurisdictions.[29] In textbooks on English law, the notion of contractual construction/interpretation features prominently in the tables of contents of the main textbooks, as well as in the relevant case law.[30] Interpretation under French law is perceived as a very different exercise. As we have seen, the binding effect of a contract derives from the obligatory force attributed to each contract pursuant to the original Article 1134 of the French Civil Code.[31] In concrete terms, the judges will assess the content of the contractual terms based on the contractual documentation. In this context, even though French law is traditionally perceived as a 'subjective' system, the judges are under a strict duty to enforce 'clear and precise' terms. The French Cour de cassation has supervisory powers to make sure that the judges do not modify the content of clear agreements and distort the principles of contractual interpretation.[32] This is a traditional and undisputed position of case law,[33] and is now enshrined in Article 1192 of the new Civil Code,[34] whereby '[c]lear and unambiguous terms are not subject to

[29] See generally Nicholas (n 17) 47–58; C Valcke, 'Contractual Interpretation at Common Law and Civil Law: An Exercise in Comparative Legal Rhetoric' in J Neyers (ed) *Exploring Contract Law* (Oxford, Hart Publishing, 2008) 77; A. Vey, 'Assessing the Content of Contracts: Implied Terms from a Comparative Perspective' [2011] *EBLR* 501.

[30] For Lord Hoffmann's famous 'restatements', see *Investors Compensation Scheme Ltd v West Bromwich Building Society* [1997] UKHL 28. The accompanying literature is very varied: see e.g. A Burrows and E Peel (eds), *Contract Terms* (Oxford, OUP, 2010); G McMeel, *The Construction of Contracts* (Oxford, OUP, 2007). From a comparative perspective, see Beale et al (n 14) ch 13.

[31] 'Agreements which have been lawfully formed bind those who have entered into them. They may be revoked only by mutual consent, or on grounds authorised by law.' It is to be noted that this formulation has been maintained, despite some terminological changes in the new version of the Civil Code (new Art 1193).

[32] C Marraud, *La notion de dénaturation* (thesis, University of Nancy, 1974); J Voulet, 'Le grief de dénaturation devant la Cour de cassation' [1971] *Jurisclasseur Périodique* 1.2410

[33] Civ, 15 avr 1872, DP 1872, 1.176; Civ 1ère, 6 mar 1979, *Bull civ* I, no 81; Com, 19 jan 1981, *Bull civ* IV, no 34; Soc, 3 juin 1981, *Bull civ* V, no 490; Civ 1ère, 19 déc 1995, *Bull civ* I, no 466.

[34] 'On ne peut interpréter les clauses claires et précises à peine de dénaturation.'

interpretation as doing so risks distorting them'. Consequently, the 'declared' intent of the parties, expressed in an unequivocal way, will prevail over the 'real intent', unless the party is able to demonstrate, through the production of valid evidence, the existence of an ambiguity as to the meaning of the terms.[35] Being a matter of fact[36] falling within the scope of the 'sovereign power' (*pouvoir souverain*) of lower-level judges,[37] the determination whether a clause is 'clear and precise' will of course depend on the judges' understanding of the term.

If any ambiguity is found to be present in the contract, then the issue will become an 'interpretative' one,[38] and may thus lead to a judicial interpretation of the contract. Here French law does suggest a judicial search of the 'parties' common intent' at the time they contracted. In this context, Article 1188 of the new Civil Code provides: '[T]he contract is interpreted according to the common intention of the contracting parties rather than merely the literal meaning of the terms.' This means that, *when faced with an ambiguous term*, judges are required to give effect to the meaning that best reflects the common intent of the parties rather than promoting an 'objective' approach to the term.[39] In practice, however, such a judicial introspection will only be conducted either on the basis of written documents produced by the parties or by reference to more 'objective' standards, such as the existing 'trades and usages' in the relevant sector.[40] It should be noted that the new version of the Civil Code, provides that, where the 'parties' common intention' cannot be discerned, 'a contract is to be interpreted in the sense which a reasonable person placed in the same situation would give to it' (Article 1188(2) of the new Civil Code).[41]

The importance of contractual interpretation is broached by Pothier, who noted that:

> Usage is of so much authority in the interpretation of agreements, that a contract is understood to contain the customary clauses although they are not expressed; in *contractibus tacite veniunt ea qua sunt moris et consuetudinis.*
>
> For instance, in a contract for the lease of a house, though it is not expressed that the rent shall be paid half-yearly at the two usual feasts, and that the tenant shall do such repairs as are usually done by tenants; these clauses are understood.

[35] P Malaurie, L Aynes and P Stoffel-Munck, *Les obligations* (6th edn, Paris, LGDJ, 2014) para 772.

[36] JL Aubert, 'La distinction du fait et du droit dans le pourvoi en cassation en matière civile', D 2005.1115.

[37] C Atias, 'La fonction d'appréciation souveraine des faits', D 2009, Chron 744.

[38] MH Maleville, *Pratique de l'interprétation des contrats* (Université de Rouen, 1991) no 164; B Fauvarque-Cosson, 'L'interprétation du contrat: observation comparatives', RDC 2007, 481; C Grimaldi, 'Paradoxes autour de l'interprétation des contrats', RDC 2008, no 2, 207.

[39] J Bienvenu, 'De la volonté interne à la volonté déclarée', Droits, 1999, no 28, 3 et seq.

[40] Cass com, 22 mar 2011, no 09-72426.

[41] Note also that Art 1135 of the Civil Code (now Art 1194 of the new Code) gives a broad conception of the contractual agreement, incorporating not only the express provisions, but also matters of equity, usage and the nature of the obligation.

> So in contract of sale, although the clause that the seller shall be bound to warrant and defend the purchaser from evictions, is not expressed, it will be understood.[42]

Valcke has argued that the different French and English approaches to contractual interpretation are reflective of the different subjective and objective approaches to contract law, and reveal fundamental differences in 'thought structures'.[43] She thus argues that:

> French legal actors tend to conceptualize the normative dimension as both dominant and clearly delineable from the factual dimension ('fact/NORM'), whereas English legal actors tend to conceptualize the normative dimension as ancillary to, and subsumed within, the factual dimension ('FACT(norm)').[44]

Lord Hoffmann drew upon Valcke's analysis in the *Persimmon Homes* case in order to emphasise how these deep-seated differences entailed that caution should be exercised in transposing comparative law solutions in this area:

> French law regards the intentions of the parties as a pure question of subjective fact, their *volonté psychologique*, uninfluenced by any rules of law. It follows that any evidence of what they said or did, whether to each other or to third parties, may be relevant to establishing what their intentions actually were. There is in French law a sharp distinction between the ascertainment of their intentions and the application of legal rules which may, in the interests of fairness to other parties or otherwise, limit the extent to which those intentions are given effect. English law, on the other hand, mixes up the ascertainment of intention with the rules of law by depersonalising the contracting parties and asking, not what their intentions actually were, but what a reasonable outside observer would have taken them to be. One cannot in my opinion simply transpose rules based on one philosophy of contractual interpretation to another, or assume that the practical effect of admitting such evidence under the English system of civil procedure will be the same as that under a Continental system.[45]

In Jersey, the English case law has been influential in shaping the approach of the Jersey courts. The adoption of the English law technique might, however, be questioned: how valid is the common law objective approach, given that, as we have seen, the Jersey courts have firmly nailed their colours to the subjective mast?[46] As a consequence, one wonders whether it fits well with the 'thought structures' of Jersey law. This issue is played out more directly in the sphere of implied terms.

[42] Pothier, *Traité Des Obligations*, part 1, ch 1, para 95. This is the translation provided by the Royal Court in *Grove v Baker* 2005 JLR 348, 355.

[43] For an evaluation of the 'thought structures' approach, see S McEvoy, 'Descriptive and Purposive Categories of Comparative law' in P-G Monateri, *Methods of Comparative Law* (Cheltenham, Edward Edgar, 2012) 144.

[44] C Valcke, 'On Comparing French and English Contract Law: Insights from Social Contract Theory' (2009) IV *Journal of Comparative Law* 69.

[45] *Chartbrook Ltd v Persimmon Homes Ltd* [2009] UKHL 38, [39].

[46] See, however, the recent decision of the Jersey Court of Appeal in *Home Farm Developments Ltd v Le Sueur* [2015] JCA 242, which has generated some uncertainty on this issue. See further Chapter 3 above at pp 45–46.

## B. General Principles Regarding Implied Terms

The approach to implied terms in different legal systems is also very diverse. Indeed, in French law, the distinction between express and implied contractual terms is rarely made. In English law, on the other hand, the notion of implied terms has generated voluminous cases and commentary. As is well known, terms may be implied into contracts in a variety of ways. Implied terms can arise by operation of law, whereby 'the law (sometimes by statute, sometimes through the common law) effectively imposes certain terms into certain classes of relationship'.[47] Implied terms can also arise by virtue of the operation of custom or trade usage.[48] Terms implied in fact have generated more debate. The classic rules concerning the implication of terms into a contract can be found in a classic series of cases,[49] the rules of which have been revisited in more recent times. Restrictions on space prevent an in-depth analysis of this area within this context. However, a word will be said on the topic of when courts will *imply terms in fact* into contracts.

In implying terms in fact into contracts, much reliance has been placed on Lord Simon's summary of the exercise facing the courts found in the Privy Council case of *BP Refinery (Westernport) Pty Ltd v President, Councillors and Ratepayers of the Shire of Hastings*.[50] Lord Simon held that for a term to be so implied:

> (1) it must be reasonable and equitable; (2) it must be necessary to give business efficacy to the contract, so that no term will be implied if the contract is effective without it; (3) it must be so obvious that 'it goes without saying'; (4) it must be capable of clear expression; (5) it must not contradict any express term of the contract.

A minor storm has been generated in this area by Lord Hoffmann's judgment in the Privy Council in *Attorney-General for Belize v Belize Telecom Ltd*,[51] in which he criticised the 'officious bystander' and 'business efficacy' tests, and instead provided a simplified restatement, consonant with that in interpreting an express term, whereby a contract should be construed by its reasonable addressee with knowledge of the background to the contract:

> [I]n every case in which it is said that some provision ought to be implied in an instrument, the question for the court is whether such a provision would spell out in express words what the instrument, read against the relevant background, would reasonably be understood to mean.[52]

[47] *Marks and Spencer plc v BNP Paribas Securities Services Trust Company (Jersey) Limited* [2015] UKSC 72, [15] (per Lord Neuberger).

[48] See generally Andrews (n 20) paras 13.17–13.19.

[49] *Shirlaw v Southern Foundries Limited* [1939] 2 KB 206; *Lister v Romford Ice & Cold Storage Co Ltd* [1957] AC 555; *Liverpool City Council v Irwin* [1977] AC 239.

[50] *BP Refinery (Westernport) Pty Ltd v President, Councillors and Ratepayers of the Shire of Hastings* (1977) 52 ALJR 20, 26.

[51] *Attorney-General for Belize v Belize Telecom Ltd* [2009] UKPC 10.

[52] Ibid, [21.]

Some commentators were strongly supportive of this approach,[53] others have instead opined that the judgment was to 'be treated with caution'.[54] What might have seemed like a departure from the *BP Refinery* test[55] has, however, been placed in context more recently in the Supreme Court decision of *Marks and Spencer plc v BNP Paribas Securities Services Trust Company (Jersey) Limited*,[56] in which their Lordships negated any (perceived or real) change in the law associated with *Belize Telecom*. Reaffirming the traditional approach, Lord Neuberger affirmed that *Belize Telecom* did not result in a 'dilution of the requirements which have to be satisfied before a term will be implied'.[57] Lord Carnwath opined that: '[T]he judgment [in *Belize Telecom*] is not to be read as involving any relaxation of the traditional, highly restrictive approach to implication of terms.'[58] As to Lord Hoffmann's suggested approach, Lord Neuberger said that the *Belize Telecom* formulation was 'quite acceptable' provided the reasonable reader 'would consider the term to be so obvious as to go without saying or to be necessary for business efficacy'.[59] This sounds very much like a retrenchment to the traditional approach.

Much of these developments have yet to reach the Channel Islands' shores. In Jersey, the basic rule concerning implied terms may be found in two Jersey cases, *Sibley v Berry*[60] and the more recent *Grove v Baker*.[61] In these cases, the judiciary staunchly relied upon the classic English cases.

In *Sibley v Berry*,[62] the Court of Appeal considered an appeal by the widow of a man who had lent money to the respondent free of interest in order to enable her to buy a house. There had been no written contract. The evidence was, however, that it was an indefinite loan which was repayable upon the sale by the respondent of the house which she had purchased. The principal question for the court was whether a term could be implied into the contract requiring the respondent to sell the house or, alternatively, stipulating that the loan was repayable on reasonable notice.

[53] D McLauchlan, 'Construction and Implication: In Defence of Belize Telecom' [2015] *LMCLQ* 203. For a response, see JW Carter and W Courtney, 'Belize Telecom: A Reply to Professor McLauchlan' [2015] *LMCLQ* 245.

[54] Andrews (n 20) para 13.16. See also P. Davies, 'Recent Developments in the Law of Implied Terms' [2010] *LMCLQ* 140 as well as discussion in the Singapore Court of Appeal in *Foo Jong Peng v Phua Kiah Mai* [2012] 4 SLR 1267, [29]–[35.]

[55] Which Lord Hoffmann considered as 'best regarded, not as series of independent tests which must each be surmounted, but rather as a collection of different ways in which judges have tried to express the central idea that the proposed implied term must spell out what the contract actually means, or in which they have explained why they did not think that it did so' [27].

[56] *Marks and Spencer plc v BNP Paribas Securities Services Trust Company (Jersey) Limited* [2015] UKSC 72.

[57] Ibid, [24.]

[58] Ibid, [66.]

[59] Ibid, [23.]

[60] Unreported, 7 July 1987.

[61] *Grove v Baker* 2005 JLR 348

[62] Unreported, 7 July 1987.

The Court of Appeal examined the principles applied by the English courts, as laid down by the House of Lords in *Liverpool City Council v Irwin*,[63] and identified the following three situations in which terms may be implied:[64] established usage; necessity; and according to the intention of parties. The Court held that it was impossible to imply a term stipulating that the loan was repayable on reasonable notice. A court may not imply a term contradictory to the express terms of an agreement, and a term to repay on reasonable notice was in contradiction with the express term agreed between the parties that the loan was to be repayable on the sale of the property. As for the argument that there should be a term implied whereby the respondent would be required to sell the house on reasonable notice, the Court did not consider that this term could be implied based on any of the grounds laid down in *Liverpool City Council v Irwin*. On the contrary, the loan in question was expressed by the parties to be an indefinite loan 'without any strings at all'. The Court thus held that:

> [O]nce the true nature of the original transaction is grasped, it appears to me that the absence of any such right does not make the transaction futile or inefficacious or absurd, but is perfectly consistent with the nature which the parties apparently intended it to have.[65]

The leading case on this issue is now *Grove v Baker*.[66] This case involved a loan agreement which made provision for interest to be paid on the loan but which did not provide for the repayment of the capital amount. The plaintiff lender argued, inter alia, that there was an implied term that the loan was repayable on demand. The Court applied the decision in *Sibley v Berry*, and again relied upon *Liverpool CC v Irwin*.[67] The Court held that the contract in this case was a commercial one between business partners and that, in the absence of an express provision, it was implied that the capital was repayable on formal demand by the lender.[68] More recent cases have accepted that *Grove v Baker* remains the leading case in Jersey on implied terms.[69]

These cases illustrate that the Jersey courts seem wedded to the traditional English law approach. And yet how consistent is that with the underpinning precepts of Jersey law? We have already questioned above whether the general approach to contractual interpretation should really be premised upon a purely

63 *Liverpool City Council v Irwin* [1977] AC 239

64 The English case also referred to the implication of 'reasonable terms', but in more cautious terms, and this has not been taken up in the Jersey law: see eg *Jersey Civil Service Assn v Establishment Cttee* (unreported, 19 October 1994).

65 Unreported, 7 July 1987, 10.

66 *Grove v Baker* 2005 JLR 348.

67 *Liverpool CC v Irwin* [1977] AC 239

68 *Grove v Baker* 2005 JLR 348, 358.

69 In *EVIC v Greater Europe Deep Value Fund II Limited* [2012] JRC 146, the Royal Court noted that 'the parties agreed that the leading authority in Jersey is *Grove-v-Baker* 2005 JLR 348', and then went on to cite the two situations in which a term can be implied into a contract as set out above at [44]–[45].

objective approach *à la common law*.[70] Similar considerations would apply to the position of implied terms. In a legal system which has asserted that a subjective approach should be taken to contract law,[71] it would seem important to prioritise the parties' subjective views rather than the external, abstract objective approach (albeit imbued with the knowledge of the background to the contract).[72] There have indeed been traces of such an approach in the Jersey cases. In the case of *Cunningham v Sinel*,[73] an issue arose as to whether a supplier of legal services must act with reasonable care and skill. It was held that:

> [I]n the absence of express terms to that effect [that supplier of legal services will act with reasonable care and skill], the Court may be satisfied that the will or *volonté* of the parties to make the contract at all was such that such a term should be implied.[74]

It will thus be apparent from this statement that the actual will of the parties is central to the implication of the relevant term—thereby reflecting the subjective philosophy that we have traced above.

## C. Application in Practice

A number of examples may be given of the concrete application of these principles. In building contracts, the Royal Court held in *Osmand v Wood and Estate of Verner*[75] that, under terms implied into construction contracts by customary law, a contractor is obliged to undertake the building work in good time, to do it well and to take all reasonable care in the use of materials. However, in *Donnelly v Randalls Vautier Ltd*,[76] concerning a fixed-price contract to build pétanque pitches, the Court declined to imply a term based on trade usage that the defendant would pay for extra work caused by unforeseen circumstances.

It has also been held in the sphere of the provision of services that a term will be implied that the service provider acts with reasonable care and skill. This is the case in respect of the provision of legal services,[77] and in the banking sphere it was

[70] Recognising, though, the debate as to how objective the English contract law standard really is: see generally Valcke (n 44).

[71] In the case of *O'Brien v Marett*, the Court of Appeal held that 'the Jersey law of contract determines consent by use of the subjective theory of contract'. *O'Brien v Marett* [2008] JCA 178, [55]. See, however, the recent Court of Appeal decision in *Home Farm Developments Ltd v Le Sueur* [2015] JCA 242 in which, contrary to the previous case law (analysed in Chapter 3 above, at 31–32) it was stated in a postscript that 'there are potentially powerful arguments against the adoption of a subjective test. We cannot express a concluded view as to which arguments ought to prevail, but we do express the view that the arguments have yet to be deployed, and as a result the point has not yet been definitively resolved' ([59]).

[72] As Andrews points out, the English courts when finding terms implied in fact, are not applying *stricto sensu* a test of reasonableness but rather one of necessity: Andrews (n 20) para 13.12.

[73] *Cunningham v Sinel* [2011] JRC 015.

[74] Ibid, [18]

[75] *Osmand v Wood and Estate of Verner* 1991 JLR N6c.

[76] *Donnelly v Randalls Vautier Ltd* 1991 JLR 49

[77] *Cunningham v Sinel* [2011] JRC 015.

held in the case of *Izodia Plc v Royal Bank of Scotland Intl Ltd*[78] that there was an implied term in the contract between a bank and its customer that the bank will observe reasonable skill and care in executing the customer's orders.[79]

It is also important to note that under the Supply of Goods and Services (Jersey) Law 2009, a number of terms are implied into contracts for the sale of goods and services by operation of that legislation.[80] Under the customary law, the latent defect warranty was implied by operation of law, which is an interesting comparative law study in itself, and which we will turn to now.

## IV. Warranties: The Case of *Vices Cachés*

The latent defect warranty, or *vice caches*, is a fascinating comparative law case study.[81] Deriving from the Roman law remedy of *actio redhibitoria*,[82] it was transposed through the work of Pothier and Domat into modern French law first through codification, followed by a radical expansion of the doctrine through a striking example of judicial law-making.[83] Within Jersey, it represents another prime example of the courts resorting to civil law concepts to underpin core areas of contract law. We will thus examine how, relying heavily on the writings of Pothier and Domat, as well as local commentators such as Poingdestre, the Jersey courts developed the customary law of *vices cachés*. In formulating the law in this sphere, the Jersey courts have thus explicitly drawn upon modern French law. Indeed, reference is also sometimes made by the courts to Pothier's terminology of '*vices rédhibitoires*'.[84]

### A. *Vices Cachés*—General Principles and Comparative law dimension

The doctrine of *vices cachés* is a well-known feature of law of obligation in civil law jurisdictions.[85] In essence, it entails that, on the sale of property or goods, there is an implied warranty that there are no hidden defects in the item sold.[86] If a defect

[78] *Izodia Plc v Royal Bank of Scotland Intl Ltd* 2006 JLR 346.

[79] Ibid, 397.

[80] Warranty as to title (Art 21 of Supply of Goods and Services (Jersey) Law 2009); Warranty as to description (Art 22); Warranty about sale by sample (Art 25); Warranty as to quality or fitness (Art 23).

[81] See generally J Bell, *French Legal Cultures* (London, Butterworths, 2001) 79–88.

[82] Zimmermann (n 15) 317.

[83] It is thus an interesting counter-example to the traditional French perception of the judge as Montesquieu's *bouche de la loi*. See generally Bell (n 81) 79–88.

[84] See eg *Kwanza Hotel Limited v Sogeo Company Limited* (1983) JJ 105, 115–17.

[85] See generally Bell (n 81) 79–88.

[86] For the complicated relationship between liability for latent defects and for 'defects of conformity', see S Whittaker, *Liability for Products* (Oxford, OUP, 2005) 71–72.

is so present, then liability will attach to the vendor, unless the defect could have been discovered on examination by a reasonably prudent purchaser.

Deriving from Roman law, as we have seen, the doctrine of *vices caches* is the oldest and one of most important bases for liability in respect of failures in quality of property sold.[87] In French law, liability for defective goods is governed by several provisions set out in the Code civil, and referred to as 'latent defect warranty' ('garantie contre les vices cachés').[88] With respect to latent defects, Article 1641 of the Code civil provides that the seller guarantees goods sold against hidden defects rendering the goods improper for the use for which they are intended.[89] Four conditions must be met for the warranty to apply:[90] (1) the product is defective; (2) the defect was hidden; (3) the defect was present prior to the transfer of property in the goods; (4) the defect is material enough to render the product unfit for use or to materially reduce its value.[91]

Developing these basic provisions, the scope of the doctrine has been expanded due to a series of factors. In principle, whilst contractual liability evidently requires the existence of a sales contract between the defendant and claimant, the 'latent defect warranty' has been extended by the French courts to all buyers and sub-buyers in the distribution chain and to other persons to whom property is transferred. A consumer can thus sue the manufacturer directly for latent defects in products sold to him by a retailer by means of an *action directe*.[92]

In French law, a variety of remedies are available for the breach of this warranty, including recovery of the purchase price (and return of the property), reduction of the price and a damages claim.[93] In order for damages to be awarded, the Code civil lays down the condition that the seller knew of the defect at the time of sale.[94] However, the French courts have softened the burden of having to prove knowledge by applying an evidential presumption that professional sellers should, due to their special professional expertise, be aware of, at the time of sale, latent defects in the products they sell.[95] As Taylor has explained, this has subsequently been transformed into a substantive rule: professional sellers are strictly liable to

[87] Ibid, 69 et seq.

[88] See Arts 1625, 1641–1648 Code civil.

[89] 'The seller is held to warrant against latent defects in the thing sold which make it improper for the use for which it is intended or which so impair such use that the buyer would not have acquired it, or would only have paid a lower price, if he had known of them.'

[90] See Arts 1641–48 Code civil.

[91] For more detailed appraisal of these pre-conditions, see Whittaker (n 86) 73–79.

[92] Cass com, 24 nov 1987, *Bull civ* IV, no 250. See generally M Fabre-Magnan, *Droit des Obligations: Contrat et Engagement Unilatéral* (3rd edn, Paris, PUF, 2012) 547–53.

[93] This has been supplemented by provisions providing for a guarantee of conformity: see Arts L.211-1 et seq, Code de la consommation.

[94] Art 1645 Code civil: 'Where the seller knew of the defects of the thing, he is liable, in addition to restitution of the price which he received from him, for all damages towards the buyer.'

[95] Cass civ 1ère, 24 nov 1954 JCP 955.II.8565. See generally on this topic, P Le Tourneau, *Droit de la Responsabilité et des contrats* (9th edn, Paris, Dalloz, 2014/15) paras 6069–132.

the buyer for damage caused by hidden defects in the goods.[96] The broad notion of 'professional seller' ensures that this rule extends to both manufacturers of a product but also professional resellers (eg a distributor or retailer).

## B. Jersey: The Older Authorities

Unsurprisingly, given its Roman law roots, we find references to civil law sources in many of the relevant Jersey commentaries on *vices cachés*. Poingdestre is recorded as writing:

> Tout home qui a vendu, baillé, assigné, cedé, eschangé, engagé, hypothequé, ou allotty en partage & division de chose comune; est tenu a garantir la chose vendue, baillée, assignée, cedée, eschangée, engagée, hypothequée ou allottie pour ledit Partage ou division; non seullement quant à la proprieté & possession, mais aussy quant aux charges, empeschements & servitudes qui la diminuent de valleur, & la rendent moins estimable.[97]

The Jersey courts have also accorded importance to civil law writers such as Domat on 'de la redhibition, & diminution du prix' in his book *Loix Civiles*.[98] Pothier's work has been particularly influential. Pothier examines this doctrine in particular in *Traité du Contrat de Vente:*

> Le vendeur, par la nature du contrat de vente, est tenu de garantir l'acheteur, que la chose vendue est exempte de certains vices qui sont de nature à rendre ou presque inutile ou même quelquefois nuisible, l'usage pour lequel cette chose est dans le commerce.
>
> …
>
> Ces vices que le vendeur est tenu de garantir se nomment rédhibitoires, parce que l'action qui naît de cette garantie est une action rédhibitoire, c'est-à-dire une action pour laquelle l'acheteur conclut contre le vendeur à ce qu'il soit tenu de reprendre la chose vendue, et de lui rendre le prix.[99]

[96] S Taylor, 'The Harmonisation of European Product Liability Rules: French and English Law' (1999) 48 *ICLQ* 419, 425.

[97] In *Lois et Coûtumes*, 102 (referred to in *Kwanza Hotel Limited v Sogeo Company Limited* (1983) JJ 105, 113–14). Translation: 'Any man who has sold, leased, assigned, transferred, exchanged, engaged, placed as security, mortgaged, or allotted in division a common thing must guarantee that which is sold, leased, assigned, transferred, exchanged, engaged, placed as security, mortgaged or allotted for the said division; not only in respect of the ownership and possession, but also in respect of any legal charge, defect and servitudes which decrease its value and make it less valuable.'

[98] See vol 1, book 1, title II, *Du Contrat du Vente*, s XI, para 11 at 49, cited in *Kwanza Hotel*, ibid.

[99] Para 203: 'Due to the nature of a sales contract, the vendor must guarantee to the buyer that the thing sold is free of any defect likely to render it either useless or harmful in respect of the use for which the item was sold. … The defects that the vendor must guarantee are called *rédhibitoires* because the action arising from this warranty is a *rédhibitoire* action, that is to say an action whereby the buyer claims that the vendor should take the item sold back and reimburse him'

Pothier then goes on to describe the relevant elements of an action for breach of this guarantee by a purchaser:

> Pour qu'un vice de la chose vendue donne lieu à la garantie, il faut le concours de quatre choses: 1° que le vice soit du nombre de ceux qui, selon l'usage des lieux, passent pour rédhibitoires; 2° qu'il n'ait pas été connu à l'acheteur; 3° qu'il n'ait pas été excepté de l'obligation de garantie par une clause particulière du contrat; 4° qu'il existe au temps du contrat.[100]

In Jersey, the customary law of *vices cachés* has now been supplemented by statutory protection for consumers deriving from the Supply of Goods and Services (Jersey) Law 2009. We will first examine the Jersey case law, before looking at the effect of the new statutory provisions.

## C. The Jersey Law Approach to *Vices Cachés*

The doctrine of *vices cachés* was initially invoked in two Jersey cases, *Scarfe v Walton*[101] and *Wood v Wholesale Electrics (Jersey) Limited*.[102] The leading case now is *Kwanza Hotel Limited v Sogeo Company Limited*,[103] which we have already examined above.[104] This concerned a dispute over the sale of a guest house. The house had a chalet attached to it which was described in the advertising materials as the owner's accommodation, whereas, in reality, there was no permission for the chalet to be used in such a way. After having referred to the various commentaries and the modern French law, the Court of Appeal summarised the principles of Jersey law on *vices cachés* as follows:

> The doctrine applies not only to physical faults, but also to legal limitations of the enjoyment by the purchaser of the thing sold. This was clearly the view of Poingdestre. A fault is not 'hidden' if the purchaser could have discovered it either by examining the thing sold himself or (as Pothier expressly said) by getting it examined by somebody better qualified. The critical question is whether the fault would have been revealed by an examination, more than superficial but less than minute, such as a reasonably careful purchaser could have made either himself or through someone appointed for the purpose. This does not mean an examination involving taking the thing sold to pieces or, on the sale of a building, such steps as taking up floors or removing wall coverings.[105]

[100] Para 205: 'For a defect in the item sold to be covered by the warranty, four conditions must be met: 1) that the defect must be considered *rédhibitoire* in accordance with local customs 2) the defect is not known to the buyer 3) the defect is not excluded from the warranty under a specific clause of the contract 4) the defect exists at the time of the contract.'

[101] *Scarfe v Walton* (1964) JJ 387.

[102] *Wood v Wholesale Electrics (Jersey) Limited* (1967) JJ 415.

[103] *Kwanza Hotel Limited v Sogeo Company Limited* (1983) JJ 105.

[104] See p 107 above.

[105] *Kwanza Hotel Limited v Sogeo Company Limited* (1983) JJ 105, 119.

In the instant case, the court held that there was no *vice caché* in the property sold. The description of the chalet as 'owner's accommodation' was merely descriptive. Even if it had not been, a duty of investigation exists and therefore a defect which is discoverable could not constitute a *vice caché.*[106]

Another decision illustrates the need for the defect to be hidden at the time of sale. In *Dempster v City Garage Ltd*,[107] a car was discovered after purchase to have substantial corrosion to its chassis. The Royal Court held that the corrosion would have been revealed by an examination prior to the sale. Consequently, the fault was not a *vice caché* and there could be no *résolution* of the contract. However, this decision seems to lay down a rather exacting standard of examination of the relevant goods. Indeed, on the Court's view, the duty of examination would seem to extend to the removal of the underseal of the car so as to reveal the corrosion!

In summary, the successful application of the doctrine would seem to presuppose[108] that: there was a defect[109] in the property sold; the defect existed at the time of the contract; the purchaser did not know of the defect; the warranty against hidden defects has not otherwise been negated by the parties, eg by agreement (eg the *tout tel* clause in property contracts);[110] and the purchaser could not reasonably be expected to have discovered the defect—thus, unlike in respect of the doctrine of misrepresentation, the purchaser is under a duty of verification, to exercise the degree of care reasonably expected of a prudent purchaser ('more than superficial but less than minute').[111] The customary law doctrine of *vices cachés* would now seem to have been displaced by the statutory provisions.

## D. Warranties under the Statutory Regime[112]

A variety of warranties are now set out in the Supply of Goods and Services (Jersey) Law 2009. This legislation applies to all 'onerous'[113] contracts for the

[106] Ibid: 'As the learned Bailiff observed, whether statutory consents for the existing use of property have been issued 'is a matter of record which can easily be verified.'

[107] *Dempster v City Garage Ltd*, 24 March 1992, unreported.

[108] Note also the doctrine of *réception* in Jersey, a corollary to the concept of *vices cachés*, according to which in case work undertaken by a contracting party is evidently defective (as opposed to hidden or *caché*), then the unilateral act by the other contracting party by which he or she approves works undertaken by a contractor prevents the contracting party from later claiming a breach of contract and seeking a remedy. See eg *Warner v Hendrick* 1985–86 JLR 366.

[109] Including 'legal limitations' as well as physical faults: see *Kwanza Hotel Limited v Sogeo Company Limited* (1983) JJ 105.

[110] Ibid.

[111] Ibid.

[112] See generally T Hanson and C Marr, 'An Introduction to the Supply of Goods and Services (Jersey) Law 2009' (2009) 13 *Jersey and Guernsey Law Review* 347.

[113] Defined in the law as a 'contrat à titre onéreux' (Art 1). This would seem to be an insufficient definition of this complex concept. See discussion of lucrative and onerous transactions, albeit in the very different context of an *action paulienne* (avoiding the defrauding of creditors), in Chapter 5 above, at p 80.

sale of goods entered into on, or after, 1 September 2009. The legislation imposes various warranties on the seller of goods, including: warranty as to title;[114] warranty as to description;[115] warranty about sale by sample;[116] and warranty as to quality or fitness.[117] In terms of latent defects, it is the latter warranty that is of interest, and we will thus examine this further here. A distinction is made between sales of goods in the course of business and private sales.[118]

## E. Sales of Goods in the Course of a Business

It is provided in the legislation that where a seller supplies goods under a contract of sale *in the course of a business*, there is an implied term to the effect that 'the seller warrants that the goods supplied under the contract are of satisfactory quality'.[119] According to the 2009 Law, goods are of 'satisfactory quality'[120] 'if they meet the standard that a reasonable person would regard as satisfactory, taking account of any description of the goods, the price for them (if relevant) and all other relevant circumstances'.[121] In the event that the purchaser is a consumer, then such circumstances may include public statements (including labelling or adverts) as to the specific characteristics of the goods.[122]

Unlike under customary law, there is therefore no longer a requirement for the purchaser to examine the goods purchased, though it is specifically provided that *if* the purchaser nonetheless chooses to examine the goods, the warranty will not cover those defects that *that* examination ought to have revealed[123] (thereby discouraging inspection). The legislation also addresses the position where the buyer uses the good for a particular purpose. It is provided that, subject to certain specified exceptions, where a seller sells in the course of business and the buyer makes it known expressly or by implication the particular purpose for which the goods are being bought, the seller warrants that the goods are reasonably fit for

[114] Inter alia that the seller has a right to sell the goods and that those goods are free of charges. See further Art 21.

[115] Inter alia that the goods will correspond with the description. See further Art 22.

[116] Inter alia that the bulk of the good will correspond with the sample in quality. See further Art 25.

[117] The legislation lays down as the basic principle in Art 23(1) that there 'is no warranty about the quality or fitness for any particular purpose of the goods supplied under a contract of sale of goods'. However, various important exceptions are made to this basic rule, thereby providing for important warranties as to quality and fitness.

[118] Finally, the legislation provides for various warranties in respect of the supply of services, including warranty about care and skill (Art 28); warranty about time for performance (Art 29).

[119] Art 23(3).

[120] 'Quality' is defined in Art 4.

[121] See Art 20(1).

[122] See Art 20(2) and (3).

[123] Art 23(4)(b). Note that under Art 63, the buyer has a right to examine goods. Under Art 64, a buyer will be considered to have accepted goods if, inter alia, he has had 'a reasonable opportunity of examining them'.

that particular purpose, whether or not that is a purpose for which such goods are commonly supplied.[124]

## F. Private Sales

The Jersey provisions extend the benefit of the legislation to sales by those who are *not* selling in the course of business.[125] The private seller will be liable under the conditions already enunciated as regards business sales, but only to the extent that the seller was *aware* of the relevant defects.[126]

## G. Conclusion

It will be apparent from the foregoing that there is clearly some degree of overlap in the protection afforded by the statutory warranty of satisfactory quality and the customary law warranty against latent defects (*vices cachés*). Continuity with the previous regime is not that surprising given that, in this sphere, Pothier's own influence on the UK Sale of Goods Act is well known. Zimmerman thus notes that 'Sir Mackenzie Chalmers, the "father" of the Sale of Goods Act, had a very high regard for Pothier's *Traité du contrat de vente*'.[127] Indeed, Chalmers wrote in the introduction to his treatise that:

> I have made frequent reference to Pothier's Traité du contrat de vente. Although published more than a century ago—for Pothier died in 1772—it is still probably the best reasoned treatise on the law of sale that has seen the light of day.[128]

Despite this continuity, differences in the regimes do exist, and this begs the question as to the remaining relevance of the customary law regime. There may perhaps be an argument that the warranty against latent defects could be subsumed within the broader concept of an implied term of satisfactory quality. Indeed, this seems to have been the intention of the statutory drafters as well. The 2009 Law explicitly states that the basic principle according to which there is no warranty about the quality or fitness of any good supplied 'shall have effect … (a) despite any rule of customary law'.[129] This would seem therefore to exclude the operation of *vice cachés*. From one perspective, this is an understandable approach to take: the policy of clarification underpinning the law would be difficult to achieve if the different common law rules applied in parallel.

[124] Art 23(5).

[125] Under Jersey customary law, the guarantee that goods are free of *vices cachés* arises whether or not a seller is acting in the course of business or in a private capacity.

[126] See Art 24(1).

[127] See Zimmerman (n 15) 336.

[128] MD Chalmers, Introduction to the First Edition, in *Chalmers' Sale of Goods Act 1893* (11th edn, London, Butterworths, 1931) vii, x.

[129] Art 23 (2)(a).

On the other hand, a later provision of the 2009 Law does foresee that the rules of customary law may continue to apply. It is thus laid down in Article 95(2) that: 'The rules of customary law, except in so far as they are inconsistent with this Law, continue to apply to contracts of sale of goods, contracts for the supply of services and hire-purchase agreements.' Are the customary law rules on *vices cachés* 'inconsistent' with the new legislation? There would certainly be advantages, in certain circumstances, in relying upon the customary law position. For the statutory warranty to apply in case of private sales, it must be shown that the seller was *aware* of the relevant defects, whereas under the common law rule, knowledge of the seller is not a requirement. Moreover, we have seen that—under modern French law at least—concerning the contract between the defendant and claimant, the warranty can be extended to all buyers and sub-buyers in the distribution chain,[130] by means of an *action directe*.

## V. Exceptions to *la Convention Fait la Loi des Parties*: Intervening to Modify Contractual Terms

In this section, we will examine the exceptional circumstances in which the Jersey courts will defeat the principle of *la convention fait la loi des parties*, and intervene to modify or invalidate contractual clauses. Of relevance here is the case of penalty clauses and exemption clauses, which we will examine in turn.

### A. Exemption Clauses

In previous sections, we have already referred to the primacy of the doctrine of freedom of contract as articulated in the Jersey case law by means of the principle of *la convention fait la loi des parties*. However, the courts may interfere with contractual agreements in exceptional circumstances and this appears to be the case where contractual terms are contrary to public policy.[131]

One further example of judicial intervention is the case of exemption clauses. From a customary law perspective, the Jersey courts have accepted to strike down exemption clauses in certain scenarios. Exemption clauses were initially held to be inapplicable in case of attempted exclusion of liability for fundamental breaches.[132] Subsequently, the Jersey courts have instead proceeded on the basis of the construction of the parties' intentions,[133] holding that 'the law is certainly

[130] At p 130 above.

[131] *Basden Hotels Ltd v Dormy Hotels Ltd* (1968) JJ 911.

[132] *United Dominions Corp Ltd v Pinglaux* (1969) JJ 1123.

[133] *Lydan Developments Ltd v Medans* 1992 JLR 135.

at the very least that the applicability of an exemption clause is a question of construction, depending on the intention of the parties'.[134] In a case anticipating the shift in Jersey to a subjective approach,[135] the Royal Court applied the parties' intentions approach, in respect of a lease of a pick-up truck, to render inapplicable a clause purporting to exclude liability as to the condition, fitness for purpose or reliability of the vehicle (which turned out to be dangerously unfit to be on the highway).[136]

The recent statutory intervention has also had an impact on this area, and under the combined effect of both the Supply of Goods and Services Law 2009, as well as the more recent Supply of Goods and Services (Jersey) Regulations 2010, there is a statutory prohibition on the unilateral exclusion of certain implied warranties by businesses when they are dealing with consumers.[137] In business-to-business contracts, the Regulations provide that exclusion clauses must be fair and reasonable.[138]

## B. The Position of Penalty Clauses

The topic of contractual penalties has been the subject of comparative law analysis,[139] and has also been the subject of a number of interesting cases in Jersey. The starting point for analysis is the discussion on this topic found in the writings of Pothier, as this was both influential on the subsequent rules in the French Code civil and has also become the centrepiece of the Jersey courts' analysis in this sphere.

Pothier defines an *obligation pénale* as 'celle qui naît de la clause d'une convention par laquelle une personne pour assurer l'exécution d'un premier engagement, s'engage, par forme de peine, à quelque chose en cas d'inexécution de cet engagement'.[140] Pothier goes on—characteristically—to provide colourful examples of the operation of an *obligation pénale*,[141] and then sets out a series of principles applying to this rule. Over and above principles such as the accessory nature of the *obligation pénale*,[142] Pothier provides for the ability of the judge to

[134] Ibid, 141.

[135] See discussion in Chapter 3 above, at pp 44–46.

[136] *Lydan Developments Ltd v Medans* 1992 JLR 135.

[137] Regulation 4 applies to consumer contracts.

[138] Regulation 5.

[139] See eg see Beale et al (n 14) 1051 et seq.

[140] Pothier, *Traité des Obligations*, part II, ch V, para 337: '[T]hat which arises from the clause of a contract according to which, in order to assure the performance of an obligation, a person agrees as a penalty, to undertake something in case of inexecution of that obligation.'

[141] Involving the loan of a horse, subject to payment of a penalty clause in case of injury to the horse: ibid.

[142] So that the annulment of the primary contractual obligation ipso facto results in the annulment of the *obligation pénale*.

modify the amount of the penalty to be paid,[143] given that its 'nature is to substitute the award of damages'.[144]

Under English law, contracting parties may also make provision for the consequences of a breach of contract by including a clause which quantifies or liquidates the sum payable. Whilst the courts will traditionally enforce a liquidated damages clause which represents a genuine pre-estimate of the loss caused to one party on breach, they will not order payment of a sum which, although agreed, is disproportionate to the injury suffered, and is thus a penalty clause.[145] This rule, stemming from Lord Dunedin's famous speech in *Dunlop Pneumatic Tyre Co Ltd*, has been described as achieving 'the status of a quasi-statutory code in the subsequent case-law'.[146] It has, however, been criticised in the recent case of *Cavendish Square Holding BV v Talal El Makdessi*,[147] in which Lords Neuberger and Sumption held that: '[T]he law relating to penalties has become the prisoner of artificial categorisation, itself the result of unsatisfactory distinctions: between a penalty and genuine pre-estimate of loss, and between a genuine pre-estimate of loss and a deterrent.'[148] Their Lordships criticised this approach, opining that:

> The real question when a contractual provision is challenged as a penalty is whether it is penal, not whether it is a pre-estimate of loss. These are not natural opposites or mutually exclusive categories. A damages clause may be neither or both. The fact that the clause is not a pre-estimate of loss does not therefore, at any rate without more, mean that it is penal. To describe it as a deterrent … does not add anything.[149]

Their Lordships opined instead that in determining 'whether the clause impugned was "unconscionable" or "extravagant"',[150] the focus should be on 'what was the nature and extent of the innocent party's interest in the performance of the relevant obligation'.[151] Their Lordships thus recognise that a party can, in some circumstances, have a legitimate interest in enforcing performance which goes beyond simply being compensated for losses.

Their Lordships thus held that:

> The true test is whether the impugned provision is a secondary obligation which imposes a detriment on the contract-breaker out of all proportion to any legitimate interest of the innocent party in the enforcement of the primary obligation. The innocent party can have no proper interest in simply punishing the defaulter. His interest is in performance

[143] Pothier, *Traité des Obligations*, part II, ch V, para 345.
[144] Ibid, para 345.
[145] See generally *Dunlop Pneumatic Tyre Co Ltd v New Garage and Motor Co Ltd* [1915] AC 79.
[146] *Cavendish Square Holding BV v Talal El Makdessi* [2015] UKSC 67, [22].
[147] *Cavendish Square Holding BV v Talal El Makdess* [2015] UKSC 67.
[148] Ibid, [31].
[149] Ibid.
[150] Ibid, [22].
[151] Ibid, [23].

> or in some appropriate alternative to performance. In the case of a straightforward damages clause, that interest will rarely extend beyond compensation for the breach, and we therefore expect that Lord Dunedin's four tests would usually be perfectly adequate to determine its validity. But compensation is not necessarily the only legitimate interest that the innocent party may have in the performance of the defaulter's primary obligations.[152]

If a term in a contract is held to be a penalty clause, then it will not be enforced and the innocent party will be confined to damages as per orthodox principles—the courts considering that the promise is sufficiently compensated by being indemnified for his actual loss.[153]

Whereas in English law, a clause which provides for a penalty is invalid, in French law in contrast, the penalty clause can be enforceable but will be subject to reduction by the court. In French law, the notion of a *clause pénale* is covered by Article 1231-5 of the new Code civil which states that when the agreement provides that the party who fails to perform shall pay a certain sum on account of damages, no larger or smaller sum can be awarded to the other party. In this sense, a contractual *clause pénale* may fix both a ceiling and a floor to damages, and may thereby benefit either party. It is consequently much wider than the English notion of a penalty clause.[154] Article 1231-5 of the new Code civil also provides that where a *clause pénale* takes the form of a term imposing the payment of a certain sum of money by way of damages, the judge may 'even of his own initiative' diminish or increase the agreed penalty if it appears 'manifestly excessive or derisory'. Any contractual provision to the contrary is deemed inoperative.

In Jersey, the courts have long accepted to reduce contractual penalties if the amount provided for is excessive.[155] In so doing, the courts have again drawn heavily upon Pothier, and have thus held that a penalty will not be considered to be excessive unless it exceeds the maximum damages which the creditor would have suffered as a result of the breach of the principal obligation.[156] The Jersey courts have contrasted this with the position where the contractual sum in question was designed to represent a genuine pre-estimate of the damage likely to ensue from the breach, in which case the clause would be upheld.[157] This approach was approved by the Royal Court in the case of *Doorstop Ltd v Gillman and Lepervier Holdings Ltd*.[158] In this case, which concerned a commercial loan for the completion of a property development, various aspects of the interest level attached to the loan were considered by the Court to be excessive and

[152] Ibid, [32].

[153] M Furmston, *Cheshire, Fifoot & Furmston's Law of Contract* (16th edn, Oxford, OUP, 2012) 785–86.

[154] See L Miller, 'Penalty Clauses in England and France; A Comparative Study' (2004) 53 *ICLQ* 79.

[155] *Basden Hotels Ltd v Dormy Hotels Ltd* (1968) JJ 911.

[156] *Viscount v Treanor* (1969) JJ 1243, 1245.

[157] *Hyams v Russell* (1971) JJ 1891.

[158] *Doorstop Ltd v Gillman and Lepervier Holdings Ltd* [2012] JRC 199.

thus the level of interest in relation to the loans was capped.[159] This approach has received support in subsequent cases,[160] though it does in practice entail the Jersey courts extending their control of penalty clauses so as to allow them to rewrite the level of contractual interest rates. As has already been noted,[161] this approach does correspond with the broader conception of the judge in Jersey in terms of reappraising contractual bargains. Consistently with the broader approach in the Jersey law of contract, Jersey courts will intervene, in specific circumstances, to remedy the economic imbalance in a contractual bargain. The Jersey judiciary are thus prepared to undertake a more interventionist role than would be readily assumed in a common law context.

[159] The Royal Court held that it would be 'unconscionable to give judgment for interest rates which are not moderate or reasonable': *Doorstop Ltd v Gillman and Lepervier Holdings Ltd* [2012] JRC 199, [40].

[160] See *Hard Rock Limited v HRCKY Ltd* [2013] JRC 244B.

[161] See further discussion in Chapter 2, at pp 31–32.

# 7

# Comparing Remedies

## I. Introduction

The sphere of remedies is a very fertile one from a comparative law perspective.[1] But it is also a complex and challenging one, as the very term 'remedy' has created a degree of debate in many legal systems. The common law is perhaps most naturally at home with the concept of remedies. Indeed, the importance of a remedies-based approach is underlined by the traditional common law adage under which 'where there is a remedy there is a right' (*ubi remedium ibi ius*), entailing as a necessary corollary that *remedies thus precede rights*.[2] As FH Lawson observed in respect of the common law: 'The rights that are recognised by law have crystallised round the remedies.'[3] A number of factors explain this approach within common law systems, but historical factors are of crucial importance, and in particular the procedural constraints born of the fact that remedies were provided for wrongs via an intricate set of forms of action.[4] As Sir Nicholas Browne-Wilkinson VC held in *Spain v Christie, Manson & Woods Ltd*:

> In the pragmatic way in which English law has developed, a man's legal rights are in fact those which are protected by a cause of action. It is not in accordance, as I understand it, with the principles of English law to analyse rights as being something separate from the remedy given to the individual.[5]

Whilst the notion of 'remedy' has thus been commonly referred to in common law discourse, it has—somewhat paradoxically—rarely been subject to rigorous analysis by the English common lawyers who make use of it.[6] Peter Birks famously

[1] See generally G Treitel, *Remedies for Breach of Contract: A Comparative Account* (Oxford, OUP, 1988); N Cohen and E McKendrick (eds) *Comparative Remedies for Breach of Contract* (Oxford, Hart Publishing, 2005); S Rowan, *Remedies for Breach of Contract* (Oxford, OUP, 2012).

[2] D Friedmann, 'Rights and Remedies' in Cohen and McKendrick (n 1) 4.

[3] See FH Lawson, *Remedies of English Law* (2nd edn, London, Butterworths, 1980) 2. Note, though, Lord Nicholls's point that a remedy may arise in the common law 'where identification of the underlying "right" may be elusive' (*Mercedes Benz AG v Leiduck* [1996] 1 AC 284, 310).

[4] See Lawson, ibid, 2.

[5] *Spain v Christie, Manson & Woods Ltd* [1986] 1 WLR 1120, 1129.

[6] See comments of A Burrows, *Remedies for Torts and Breach of Contract* (3rd edn, Oxford, OUP, 2009) 1; id, *English Private Law* (3rd edn, Oxford, OUP, 2013) 1253. See also the view of a civil lawyer on this lack of rigour: Y-M Laithier, 'Comparative Reflections on the French Law of Remedies for Breach of Contract' in Cohen and McKendrick (n 1) 106.

identified at least five different meanings of the term, and was very sceptical of the value of the notion as a legal term.[7] In contrast, an important strand of literature has developed on the other side of the Atlantic in respect of the law of remedies. Authoritative tomes in the United States have thus analysed remedial provision as a 'transsubstantive' topic,[8] drawing out the principles of remedies applied across different substantive areas of the law. Organised by means of types of remedies (namely injunctions, declaratory judgments, compensatory damages, punitive damages, et al), the underlying theme is to 'see remedies not as a list of responses to specific harms, but as a set of principles exemplified in particular cases and extending beyond them'.[9]

Civil systems have not traditionally adhered to this remedy-centric approach. Indeed, from a perspective of terminology, the notion of 'remedy' is complicated to render into French.[10] The French word, *remèdes*, tends to be used as a synonym of *recours*, ie a recourse—the action available to a plaintiff. As Bell has noted:

> French law identifies rights and then tries to work out appropriate protection … the Code civil sets out the entitlements of an individual and the procedures by which they are enforced are in a totally distinct code, the Nouveau Code de procédure civile.[11]

The differences, however, go beyond mere terminology, and extend also to *mentalités* or mindsets,[12] as is shown in the work of Samuel, who has argued that French jurists start their legal reasoning with the conception of a right and then proceed to finding a way to protect and enforce it, whereas in the common law, remedies 'not only give expression to existing "rights" but on occasions play a creative role in helping to establish new "rights"'.[13] From that perspective, the civil law and common law systems thus seem to encapsulate antithetical approaches: remedies versus rights-based approach.

The remedy-based model in the common law has had a number of consequences. From a more general perspective, the concentration on remedies may have played a role in impeding the systematisation of the law, as a focus is placed upon relief provided by the courts, rather than an attempt—illustrated by the opposing rights-based model which is characteristic of the civilian model—whereby a comprehensive definition of legal rights and duties is the starting approach to understanding the empire of the law.[14]

The highly systematised civil law model, based upon an overarching, general theory of civil law can thus be contrasted with English law, where '[r]ights

[7] P Birks, 'Rights, Wrongs and Remedies' (2000) 20 *OJLS* 1.

[8] D Schoenbrod, A Macbeth, D Levine, and D Jung, *Remedies: Public and Private* (3rd edn, London, Thomson, 2002) 3

[9] Ibid, 4.

[10] On this point, see André Tunc's preface to *Code de Commerce Uniforme des Etats-Unis* (Paris, A Collin, 1971) 17.

[11] J Bell, *French Legal Cultures* (London, Butterworths, 2001) ix.

[12] See generally Chapter 2, at pp 25–32 below.

[13] G Samuel, *Law of Obligations* (Cheltenham, Edward Edgar, 2010) 58.

[14] Friedmann (n 2) 8.

emerge only after the individual decisions granting particular remedies have been synthesised into a coherent set of rules'.[15] As Samuel points out, the remedies model tends to generate a form of thinking where the emphasis is on the factual situation, with a tendency towards analogous reasoning: 'The method of reasoning associated with this model is one of analogy: do the facts of a potential litigation match the factual situation envisaged by the cause of action and remedy?'[16] As other commentators have noted:

> At the root of this obsession with concentrating on remedies, we can observe the fact that English judges and some practitioners see their role as dealing with arrangements which have 'gone wrong.' They are therefore concerned to find a remedy which fits the particular circumstances of the case.[17]

Whilst it is true that today's French-trained lawyers do use more frequently the term *remèdes* (the literal translation of remedies), they do so using the word generically so that it encompasses any legal form of redress. It is also quite obvious that the use of the term comes from a greater circulation of ideas, greater exposure to the common law and more frequent use of English, by students and lawyers. But even then, the French word, *remèdes*, tends to be used as a synonym for the word *recours*, as we have seen, whether it is a legal action (domestic courts), arbitration, mediation or settlement, and irrespective of the situation—breach of contract, tort or regulatory redress. Thus, traditionally, French law envisages a legal action (*une action en justice*) that follows a sanction (for breach of contract or a tort action).[18] It will be said that there is a situation that warrants a sanction. And sanctions follow rights!

## II. Remedies and the Law of Obligations: Comparative Perspectives

Cross-channel differences also seem stark in the specific sphere of contract law. The remedy-based model in the common law has also resulted in a number of practical differences. It is thus well known that the availability of specific relief in England is limited, with specific performance in particular being the exception

[15] D Harris and D Tallon, 'Conclusions' in *Contract Law Today: Anglo-French Comparisons* (Oxford, Clarendon Press, 1989) 387.

[16] G Samuel, 'Legal Reasoning and Argumentation' in J Wright, *International Encyclopedia of the Social & Behavioral Sciences* (2nd edn, Oxford, Elsevier, 2015) 776, 782.

[17] See Harris and Tallon (n 15).

[18] Academics have criticised the prevailing view. In the 1990s, Tallon emphasised the consequences of the traditional view, which he saw as leading to a fragmented approach, as well as creating excessive complexities. D Tallon, 'L'inexécution du contrat, pour une autre présentation', RTDciv 1994, 223. More recently, Laithier's doctoral thesis suggested that remedies should measure the effectiveness of a contract, and that the economic efficiency of a remedy should guide the use of each available remedy: Y-M Laithier, *Etude comparative des sanctions de l'inexécution du contrat* (Paris, LGDJ, 2004).

rather than the rule, whereas in France, in contrast, specific remedies are unequivocally the rule.[19] There has, however, been a growing view in commentaries that the differences in practice concerning specific remedies in French and English law were perhaps less significant than was traditionally believed.[20] This tendency was confirmed judicially by Lord Hoffmann in the case of *Co-operative Insurance Society Ltd v Argyll Stores (Holdings) Ltd*:[21]

> Specific performance is traditionally regarded in English law as an exceptional remedy, as opposed to the common law damages to which a successful plaintiff is entitled as of right. … This is the basis of the general principle that specific performance will not be ordered when damages are an adequate remedy. By contrast, in countries with legal systems based on civil law, such as France, Germany and Scotland, the plaintiff is prima facie entitled to specific performance. The cases in which he is confined to a claim for damages are regarded as the exceptions. In practice, however, there is less difference between common law and civilian systems than these general statements might lead one to suppose.[22]

Doubt has been, however, been cast upon the analysis, and Lord Hoffmann himself confirmed that his viewpoint was primarily based upon judicial hunch rather than analysis: 'I have made no investigation of civilian systems, but a priori I would expect that judges take much the same matters into account in deciding whether specific performance would be inappropriate in a particular case.'[23]

Indeed, as Rowan has argued in a detailed and elegant Franco-British comparative study, the commentators have 'misapprehend[ed] the degree and complexity of the differences between specific remedies in England and France which, on close analysis, are both theoretical *and* practical'.[24] Rowan thus argues that the continuing rarity of specific remedies in English law is illustrative of a lesser commitment to the contractual performance, in the sense of 'the value that is ascribed to the contractual obligation'.[25] She thus explains that:

> English law seeks to ensure that the promisee obtains the economic benefit for which he contracted. As long as he receives this advantage, it does not matter whether the defaulting promisor performs or pays damages. This explains why there is no need to keep the parties 'yoked' together following a breach of contract. Upholding the relationship between the parties is less important than the economic outcome of the contract.[26]

In contradistinction, the French law approach is much more orientated towards upholding the performance interest. Seen as deriving from the principle of enforceability enshrined in the seminal Article 1134(1) of the old French

[19] See generally Rowan (n 1).
[20] See eg G Treitel, *Remedies for Breach of Contract: A Comparative Account* (Oxford, OUP, 1989) 41.
[21] *Co-operative Insurance Society Ltd v Argyll Stores (Holdings) Ltd* [1998] AC 1.
[22] Ibid, 11–12.
[23] Ibid, 12.
[24] Rowan (n 1) 20.
[25] Ibid, 52.
[26] Ibid, 52–53.

Code civil[27] (now Article 1193 of the new Code civil), specific performance is the primary remedy for breach of contract: performance is thus 'its fate; it must be accomplished'.[28] Stemming from the consent-based approach to contract, French doctrinal writers show the potency of specific remedies: Laithier argues that:

> [P]erformance of the contract can only mean specific performance. Considered as an ideal remedy, justified by the power of each individual to bind himself voluntarily under the contract, specific performance thus bears no limits. If its scope is still in fact limited in certain instances, the reasons lie in the means available to implement that remedy—that is, the fact that measures of enforcement may only affect the debtor's property and not his person.[29]

Performance-based policy can be seen in a series of additional features of French law. The reluctance to allow self-help in case of breach of contact can also be seen as a manifestation of this approach. The principle of resort to the courts for termination of a contract, as enshrined in Article 1184 of the old Code civil,[30] is an illustration of this. Laithier again explains the *mentalité* underpinning this approach:

> [M]any legal scholars argue that, since specific performance affects the strength of enforceability, the circumstances for terminating contracts must be reduced. Termination must be judicial so that, once bound, the parties may not set themselves free from the obligations that the contract prescribes. Under the cover of neutrality, it is clear that termination is seen as a remedy of last resort.[31]

## III. Mid-Channel Remedies

Where does the mid-Channel jurisdiction of Jersey sit within this spectrum of different approaches to remedies? The answer is not simple: whilst it might be said that the remedial perspective in Jersey sits somewhere between the two different extremes of English and French law, it is perhaps more accurate to say that all depends upon the exact remedy in question. As we shall see, the cherry-picking temptation of this mid-Channel jurisdiction is vividly illustrated in the sphere of remedies.

It should first be noted, however, that the common law attachment to damages over specific remedies has—by a process of osmosis—infused into Jersey law.

[27] This article provides that 'agreements legally formed have the force of law for those who have agreed to them'.

[28] Attributed by Laithier (n 18) 116, to C Demolombe, *Traité des Contrats ou des Obligations Conventionnelles en Général*, vol 24 (2nd edn, Paris, Durand, 1870) no 490, 471.

[29] Laithier (n 6) 109.

[30] 'Rescission must be judicially demanded, and the defendant may be granted additional time to perform according to the circumstances.'

[31] Laithier (n 6) 117.

In statistical terms, the Jersey cases illustrate a preference for pecuniary remedies, and on the basis of the Jersey law reports, actions for specific performance are relatively rare.[32] It would, however, be wrong to see Jersey as replicating the English law of specific performance, as we shall see below. Indeed, the rejection of English notions of equity could potentially have freed the Jersey courts to pursue a more performance-friendly policy, in line with other civil law jurisdictions. As the remedy of *résolution* illustrates, court control of the termination of contracts has not entirely been relinquished, and might again prove a route for encouraging contractual performance.

This hybrid approach to remedies in Jersey has, however, created complications. It has been difficult to justify a consistent approach across the range of different remedies when the sources and the principles underpinning those sources differ so greatly from one remedy to another. In examining the various remedies available in Jersey law, we will first consider the effect on a contract of the finding of a *vice de consentement*, followed then by a separate analysis on remedies for non-performance.[33]

## IV. Consequences of a Contract Vitiated by a *Vice de Consentement*: Null or Void?

We have already seen that when a contract has been vitiated by a *vice de consentement* of *dol*, *erreur* or *violence*, then the Jersey courts have held that the contract will be undermined, and an action may thus be brought before the courts to have it annulled.[34] Difficulties have, however, arisen in Jersey law about the contours and the content of the exact remedy which arises, with variegated references to both the English law concepts of void and voidable contracts as well as the French concepts of *nullité absolue* and *nullité relative.*

### A. Drawing on the English Law Notion of Void/Voidable Contracts

Reliance has been placed in recent Jersey cases on the English law terminology in the area of void/voidable contracts.[35] A short word will thus be said on that theme. English law has adopted the distinction between 'void' and 'voidable' as a means of

[32] See though the cases referred to in the section on specific performance below, at 157–159.

[33] Various statutory remedies are available under the Supply of Goods and Services (Jersey) Law 2009, which will not be examined here. See generally T Hanson and C Marr, 'An Introduction to the Supply of Goods and Services (Jersey) Law 2009' (2009) 13 *Jersey and Guernsey Law Review* 347, 356.

[34] See Chapter 5 above.

[35] *O'Brien v Marett* [2008] JCA 178, [56].

classifying contracts according to their effect on both the parties to the contract, as well as third parties.[36] Strictly speaking, a void contract should produce no effects whatsoever.[37] Neither party should be able to sue the other on the contract. If goods have been delivered, then those goods (or their value) should be recoverable by means of an action in tort because title will not have passed.[38] If money has been paid, it should be recoverable by an action in restitution because the money was not due.[39]

By contrast, a voidable contract is one where one or more of its parties have the power, by election, either to avoid the legal relations created by the contract or to affirm it, thereby extinguishing the power of avoidance.[40] In English law, contracts are voidable for misrepresentation,[41] duress, undue influence,[42] minority,[43] incapacity,[44] drunkenness[45] or on statutory grounds.[46] If the contract has not yet been performed, the party entitled to void the contract[47] can plead its voidability in an action against him. If the contract has been wholly or partly performed, he can claim to have it set aside, and to be restored to his original position. However, until the right of avoidance has been exercised, the contract is valid.

This distinction has effects on the rights of third parties. Since title does not pass under a void contract, an innocent third party cannot acquire rights as against the original owner of the property.[48] By contrast, if a contract for the sale of goods is merely voidable (eg for fraud) but has not been avoided, the fraudulent party acquires good title to the goods which he can transfer to an innocent purchaser for value.[49]

## B. French Law Concepts of Nullity

As we shall see, French law notions of nullity are also relevant within a Jersey context, and therefore a word will be said about this French law remedy. *Nullité*

[36] *Chitty on Contracts*, vol I: *General Principles* (31st edn, London, Sweet & Maxwell, 2012) para 1-108–1-110.

[37] Ibid, para 1-110.

[38] *Shogun Finance Ltd v Hudson* [2004] 1 AC 919.

[39] The general rule that money paid under a void contract can be recovered back is clearly established; but there has been some difference of opinion as to its legal basis: E Peel, *Treitel: The Law of Contract* (13th edn, London, Sweet & Maxwell, 2011) para 22-014.

[40] *Chitty on Contracts* (n 36) paras 1-082, 1-102.

[41] See generally A Burrows (ed), *Principles of the English Law of Obligations* (Oxford, OUP, 2015) paras 1.175–77.

[42] *Allcard v Skinner* (1887) 36 Ch D 145; *Royal Bank of Scotland v Etridge (No 2)* [2001] UKHL 2 AC 773.

[43] See *Proform Sports Management Ltd v Proactive Sports Management Ltd* [2006] EWHC 2903 (Ch); [2007] 1 All ER 542, [34].

[44] *Chitty on Contracts* (n 36) para 8-001.

[45] *Matthews v Baxter* (1872–73) LR 8 Ex 132.

[46] See eg Auctions (Bidding Agreements) Act 1969 s 3(1); Consumer Credit Act 1974, ss 67–73.

[47] ie bring an action for rescission.

[48] See eg *Cundy v Lindsay* (1878) 3 App Cas 459.

[49] *Phillips v Brook Ltd* [1919] 2 KB 243; *Lewis v Averay* [1972] 1 QB 198; Sale of Goods Act, s 23.

is the remedy that may be sought when one of the preconditions of validity of a contract is lacking.[50] Such a remedy is available in case of a *vice de consentement* of *dol*, *erreur* or *violence*, or where a contract lacks a cause or an *objet*. If an agreement is found to be *nul* by a judge, then it is annulled and is in principle without effect ab initio.

Under French law, a distinction is drawn between a *nullité absolue* and *nullité relative*, which derives from the so-called 'modern theory of nullities'.[51] The distinction is based upon the issue of what interest is protected by the law, and whether it is a private or general interest. The former will lead to the application of a *nullité relative* and the latter to the application of a *nullité absolue.* This is to be contrasted with the historical approach to the question. In the nineteenth century, the articulation between *nullité absolue* and *nullité relative* was based upon a graduation of the sanction according to the seriousness of the *vice.*[52] The more important the *vice*, the stronger the sanction would be (ie *nullité absolue*).

According to the modern approach, in the case of a contract vitiated by a *vice de consentement*, namely *erreur*, *violence* or *dol*, the contract is subject to a relative nullity.[53] On the other hand, where a contract lacks either cause or objet, then the sanction has predominantly been that of a *nullité absolue* because, analysed through the traditional approach to nullity, the lack of cause or object was considered very important. However, there is an argument that, according to the modern theory, the necessity for an obligation to have an object or a cause is designed to protect the parties to a contract, not the general interest. Thus, the appropriate sanction should be *nullité relative.* The case law has thus sometimes adopted such an approach.[54]

However, it should be noted that the differences between *nullité absolue* and *nullité relative* relate to the way in which the nullity may be claimed and not to the resulting effects. This is summarised by Whittaker as follows:

> Where a contract lacks either cause or objet, was induced by *dol*, *erreur* or *violence*, possesses an unlawful cause or (exceptionally) gives rise to lesion it may be brought before a court and annulled. The 'relative or absolute' nature of nullity in any of these cases goes principally to the question of who may bring this action and not to the effects of nullity once declared.[55]

Under French law, *a nullité relative* may only be relied on by the victim of the *erreur*, *violence* or *dol.*[56] An absolute nullity may be relied on by anyone provided

[50] M Fabre-Magnan, *Droit des Obligations: Contrat et Engagement Unilatéral* (3rd edn, Paris, PUF, 2012) 462.

[51] See generally *ibid*, 461 et seq.

[52] See eg *ibid*, 466.

[53] Ibid. Under the new Code civil, mistake and violence give rise to a *nullité relative* (see Arts 1132 and 1141, respectively).

[54] Opting for *nullité relative*: Cass civ 3ème, 29 mar 2006, no 05-16032. Opting for *nullité absolue*: Cass com, 23 oct 2007, no 06-13979.

[55] J Bell, S Boyron and S Whittaker, *Principles of French Law* (2nd edn, Oxford, OUP, 2008) 441.

[56] See eg Fabre-Magnan (n 50) 464.

he or she has an interest. Moreover, *a nullité relative* may subsequently be validated by confirmation on the part of the person protected by the nullity, whereas an absolute nullity can never be confirmed.

In terms of the effects of a nullity under French law, with the contract being considered as null, then in principle it is without effect ab initio.[57] Restitution must thus be made by each party, so that the price paid must be returned. A purported transfer of property by virtue of the contract is also in principle without effect. Thus, property transferred under the contract must, if still in the hands of the other party, be returned. The important difference between *nullité relative* in French law and a voidable contract in English law, therefore, is that, once a *nullité relative* has been pronounced, this has a retrospective effect and may in principle affect the rights of third parties who may have acquired rights to the subject-matter of the contract. On the other hand, a third party may acquire rights under a voidable contract prior to its having been avoided.

This rule in France would have had radical effects on third parties, and thus various exceptions have developed to assuage these. Whittaker describes the principle, and its exception in respect of movable goods, as follows:

> As to corporeal movable property, a very considerable restriction on its potential effect is found in the famous rule that 'in the case of movable property, possession is equivalent to title.' This rule means that a person who receives this type of property in good faith from a non-owner will nevertheless acquire title to it, as long as the owner originally allowed it to leave his possession voluntarily; it therefore protects many persons who receive property from another who possessed title at the time, but who subsequently lost it as a result of the annulment or résolution of the contract.[58]

## C. The Position in Jersey: Searching for the Right Language and Concepts

The Jersey case law has again navigated between the contrasting civil law and common law approaches in this sphere, without always steering a very straight course. There have thus been conflicting statements on the categorisation of the relevant remedy in the law of Jersey. Traditionally, the courts have seemed to make use of the distinction between void and voidable contracts. However, in some cases, most notably *Selby v Romeril*,[59] a preference has been indicated for the French terminology of nullity.

[57] See eg Cass civ 1ère, 15 mai 2001, no 99-20597.

[58] Bell, Boyron and Whittaker (n 55) 451.

[59] *Selby v Romeril* 1996 JLR 210.

## D. Void and Voidable

In developing the law on nullity, the Jersey courts have placed great reliance upon the writings of the Jersey commentators, most notably Le Geyt in *La Constitution, les Lois, et les Usages de Cette Ile*.[60] In this book, Le Geyt drew a distinction between contracts which were to be declared nul ab initio, where there was a 'manifest' and 'evident' nullity, and those which were merely voidable:

> Les Contrats sont nuls, 1° par l'incapacité des contractans, quand ils sont faits par gens en Curatelle ou en Tutelle, ou par des femmes sans l'autorité de leurs maris. 2° Par la qualité de la matière, comme sont les choses saintes et sacrées, et comme celles qui sont contre les bonnes mœurs; par exemple, les promesses faites pour le service future du malade au médecin, du client à l'Avocat ou Procureur, du disciple au maistre d'école, et du prisonnier à son concierge. 3° Un Contrat peut estre nul aussi par manque de formalitez, comme si dans l'isle, en fait d'héritage, il n'étoit pas de passé devant les Juges, selon la Coûtume.[61]

Le Geyt thus labelled these grounds of nullity, covering lack of capacity et al, as 'evident and perpetual nullities' in respect of which 'there is no need for restitution or express revocation because they come with an inherent defect'.[62] He contrasted them with other less important grounds in respect of which the 'defects are neither manifest nor of such great importance',[63] as follows:

> Il y a des Contrats dont les défauts ne sont pas si manifestes, ni d'une si grande importance. Les causes en sont occultes ou douteuses, il y faut de l'examen et de la preuve; tels sont le dol, la lésion d'outre moitié, la crainte, etc, de tout quoy, pour se faire relever, on a besoin du ministère de la Justice, et l'on ne déclare pas le Contrat nul ab initio, mais on le casse comme fait injustement.[64]

It will thus be clear from this excerpt that in Le Geyt's typology, contracts which are vitiated by a *vice de consentement* would *not* be subject to a remedy which resulted in annulment ab initio. The case law interpretation of this statement has been somewhat equivocal.

[60] P Le Geyt, *La Constitution, les Lois, et les Usages de Cette Ile*, tomes 1–4 (reprinted 1846, St Helier).

[61] Ibid, 119. 'Contracts are null 1° because of the incapacity of the contracting parties whenever they are made by individuals under Curatelle or Tutelle, or by women without their husbands' authority. 2° because of the quality of the matter, such as saintly and sacred things, for example the promises made in respect of the future care of a sick person by the doctor, or a client by an advocate or attorney, disciple by the school teacher and prisoner by his keeper. 3° A contract may be null also for lack of formality, such as on the Island, in matters of héritage, it had not been passed before the Court in accordance with the Custom.'

[62] Ibid.

[63] Ibid.

[64] 'There are contracts where defects are neither manifest nor of such great importance. Their causes are obscure or dubious and need to be examined and proved, for instance dol, lésion d'outre moitié, violence etc, and all require the intervention of the Courts to remove them, and it is not possible to declare the Contract null ab initio but it shall be terminated for having been made unfairly.'

Le Geyt's categorisation featured prominently in the important decision of *Deacon v Bower*.[65] In this case, Deacon made a claim to avoid contracts for the sale of building plots which he had entered into during a procedure known in Jersey as a *remise de biens*, which is part of insolvency procedure.[66] On the issue of the setting aside of a contract as *nul*, the Royal Court held that in order for a contract to be void ab initio, it must have had an *inherent defect* which negatives one or more of the essential conditions required to establish a valid legal relationship. The Court gave as examples 'those [defects] mentioned by Le Geyt either due to the incapacity of the parties or some fundamental mistake'.[67] The Court compared the situation where a transaction only had its validity called into question due to the happening of 'some subsequent event',[68] in which case the transaction would be regarded as voidable rather than void ab initio.

The Royal Court in *Deacon v Bower* thus confirmed the analytical framework of void/voidable (rather than nullity) in this area. It should be noted, however, that in doing so, the Royal Court in *Deacon v Bower* proposed a distinction unique to Jersey law, in that it is not a distinction which is recognised by either French or English law. Indeed, even more surprisingly it would not even seem to be the distinction that Le Geyt was drawing in the excerpt above either! According to the interpretation by the Royal Court in *Deacon v Bower*[69] of the classification laid down by Le Geyt, a contract would seem to be voidable where its validity is questioned by a 'subsequent event'. This is contrasted with the case where there was an *inherent defect* in the contract, in which it is void ab initio. On close examination, the Court does not in fact seem to have followed Le Geyt at all in establishing these criteria. As we have seen above, the approach adopted by Le Geyt is somewhat different.

One example will suffice to illustrate the problem. Le Geyt refers explicitly to the *vice de consentement* of *dol* as giving rise to a voidable contract. On the other hand, on the criteria laid down in *Deacon v Bower*, it is difficult to see how *dol* can be anything other than an inherent defect in the contract, which is therefore void ab initio. Whilst Le Geyt considered that contracts which are vitiated by a *vice de consentement* would *not* be subject to a remedy which resulted in annulment ab initio, the Royal Court's test in *Deacon v Bower* of 'inherent defect' as a litmus test for a contract being void ab initio seems inevitably to encompass contracts which are undermined for a defect of consent/*vice de consentement.*

[65] *Deacon v Bower* (1978) JJ 39.

[66] A *remise de biens* is undertaken under the auspices of the Royal Court, and allows a debtor time to get his affairs in order and effect an orderly sale of property.

[67] *Deacon v Bower* (1978) JJ 39, 51.

[68] Ibid, 52.

[69] Ibid.

## E. Reverting to Nullity?

To further complicate matters, it is to be noted that the decision in *Selby v Romeril*[70] represented a different approach of the Royal Court to this question. Indeed, in this case, the Court proceeded on an implicit assumption that the concepts of *nullité absolue* and *nullité relative* were recognised by Jersey law. The Court noted that 'the absence of an objet and indeed of a cause renders the contract null'.[71] The Court referred to the writings of Professor Barry Nicholas in support of the principle that nullity should result in the parties being restored to their original position.[72]

Clearly, the Court in *Selby* drew upon the distinction of *nullité relative/absolue* in its decision. This reference to modern French law on this point was thus more obviously present than in other previous Jersey cases on nullity. This of course reflects the Court's broader position on sources of Jersey contract law in this decision.[73] However, many questions arise from this approach. How does the distinction of *nullité relative/absolue* coexist with the English law concepts of void/voidable contracts? What would the implications of such a distinction be in remedial terms? What would be the position of third parties?

More recent decisions of the Jersey courts, however, have *not* tended to follow the approach in *Selby* on this issue. The Jersey courts have since adopted the void/voidable distinction in a number of subsequent cases.[74] Following the approach in *Deacon v Bower*, it has also been indicated that where a contract is vitiated by a *vice de consentement*, then it should be found to be void ab initio.[75] In the case of *Steelux Holdings Ltd v Edmonstone*,[76] the Royal Court indicated that *dol* or misrepresentation would result in a contract being found void ab initio. The Court of Appeal in *O'Brien v Marett* summarised the impact of this case in even broader terms:

> Steelux v Edmonstone [2005] JLR 152 is recent Jersey authority for the proposition that a vice du consentement (and, á fortiori, erreur obstacle) will render a contract void ab initio, that is to say, it never existed.[77]

On the strength of the recent case law, the void/voidable distinction would seem now to be entrenched as the correct remedial dichotomy in the law of Jersey, over

[70] *Selby v Romeril* 1996 JLR 210.

[71] Ibid, 219.

[72] Which in this case was payment by the defendant to the plaintiffs of compensation in respect of the benefit which the defendant received by way of improvement to the property in question.

[73] See Chapter 2, at p 17 above.

[74] See eg *Bisson v Bisson* (1981) JJ 103; *Steelux Holdings Ltd v Edmonstone* 2005 JLR 152.

[75] See eg *Bisson v Bisson* (1981) JJ 103 (a case of a contract formed under duress—found to be void ab initio).

[76] *Steelux Holdings Ltd v Edmonstone* 2005 JLR 152.

[77] *O'Brien v Marett* [2008] JCA 178 at [56].

and above the notion of nullity. Contracts will be found void ab initio as a matter of Jersey law when: one of the parties lacks capacity (eg a minor); a contract is contrary to public policy as *contre la loi* or *contre bonnes mœurs*;[78] a contract lacks one of the necessary formalities;[79] in a contract for the sale of goods, where the goods have, without the knowledge of the seller, perished at the time when the contract is made.[80] As we have already seen above, recent cases have also confirmed that in case of a contract vitiated by a *vice de consentement*, then it is thus void ab initio. By parity of reasoning, this would also be applicable to a contract which has a valid cause or *objet*, or where there is an unlawful cause.

On the other hand, a contract will merely be voidable where it is entered into by an unsuccessful *remise de biens* (part of the Jersey insolvency procedure)[81] followed by a *dégrèvement*: indeed those were the facts of *Deacon v Bower* itself.[82]

The position in case of *lésion* or *déception d'outre moitié de juste prix* is a more complex one. As we have already seen,[83] two distinct remedial possibilities arise in respect of *lésion*. In the case of a transaction undermined by a *dol réel* (namely where there was solely an undervalue in the sale price, and nothing more), then the primary remedy is for the purchaser to make good the shortfall in the price, so that the undervalue is corrected, and the transaction is thus maintained.[84] In such a case, and as long as the purchaser makes the necessary payment, then the contract remains valid. However, if the purchaser fails to make good the shortfall, then the seller is thus entitled to challenge the transaction, and in such a case the transaction is likely to be viewed as voidable. If, on the other hand, *dol personnel* is made out, and fraud or deception is thus proven, then the Privy Council held that the seller may have the contract rescinded, and the purchaser cannot maintain the contract by virtue of paying the shortfall.[85] This scenario is thus equivalent to that of a *vice de consentement* of *dol*, so that the remedy of void ab initio is consistent with the aforementioned position in respect of *vice de consentement*.

## F. Conclusion

We have noted the conflicting case law on the notion of nullity as to whether void and voidable applies or rather the French distinction between *nullité absolue* and

[78] *Jameson Ltd v Cuming-Butler* (1981) JJ 17.

[79] eg where a contract relating to immovables has not been passed before the Royal Court and registered in the Public Registry.

[80] Art 15, Supply of Goods and Services (Jersey) Law 2009.

[81] A *remise de biens* is undertaken under the auspices of the Royal Court, and allows a debtor time to get his affairs in order and effect an orderly sale of property.

[82] *Deacon v Bower* (1978) JJ 39.

[83] See Chapter 5, at pp 113–118 above.

[84] *Snell v Beadle* [2001] UKPC 5, [40].

[85] Ibid, [40].

*nullité relative.* As we have seen, the degree of confusion over the concepts leads not just to linguistic confusion, but can extend to the extent and scope of the remedy as well.

Even though the Jersey courts in more recent cases seem to have adopted the terminology of English law, by means of the void/voidable distinction, there is a clear divergence between Jersey law and English law as to what will render a contract void ab initio as distinct from merely voidable.

## V. Remedies for Non-Performance

Whilst the sources of Jersey law have generated some confusion as to the remedial consequence of *vice de consentement*, it is within the sphere of remedies for non-performance that Jersey-style cherry-picking is most vividly illustrated. The remedy of specific performance in Jersey is said, somewhat colourfully, to be influenced primarily by French concepts of *équité*, the remedy of damages is governed primarily by English law, whereas *résolution*/termination seems to be somewhere between the two.

### A. Specific Performance

The remedy of specific performance is available in Jersey in appropriate cases and at the discretion of the courts. It is as such specifically provided for in recent legislation.[86] Whilst the remedy is an equitable one in English law, the Jersey courts have not been prepared to equate the Jersey remedy of specific performance wholly with English law principles. Indeed, differences have been underlined by the judiciary,[87] and in the case of *Trollope v Jackson*, the Royal Court went further in underlining the specificity of the remedy of specific performance from a customary law perspective, and held that: 'In our view, the word "equity" in Jersey corresponds mainly to the French *équité*.'[88] This is an unusual solution to have adopted in that it combines a quintessentially equitable remedy under English law,

[86] For a statutory recognition of specific performance within the context of a contract for sales of goods, see Art 87(1), Supply of Goods and Services (Jersey) Law 2009, which provides that: 'In any action for breach of contract to deliver specific or ascertained goods a court may, if it thinks fit, on the plaintiff's application, order that the contract shall be performed specifically, without giving the defendant the option of retaining the goods on payment of damages.'

[87] See more generally on distinctiveness of Jersey law vis-à-vis English equitable principles: *Wimborne (Viscount), Ex p*, (1983) JJ 17, where it was held that 'although as I have said, the Royal Court has declared itself a Court of Equity, that does not mean to say that all the principles developed in the English Court of Chancery must necessarily apply' (22).

[88] *Trollope v Jackson* 1990 JLR 192, 198. See also *Ex parte Viscount Wimborne* (1983) JJ 17, 19–22.

with principles of a civil law nature. That unusual hybrid does serve to underline the Jersey judiciary's attachment to civil law origins, and its distinctiveness from the position of English law.

The hybrid nature of the remedy may, however, generate difficulties. First and foremost, a major challenge in adopting French *équité* as a reference point is that the notion of *équité* is by no means a clear and precise one itself in France![89] Indeed, it is the imprecision of the concept of *équité*, mixed with the traditional distrust of judicial powers in France, which has in fact engendered a certain suspicion of the concept by French jurists.[90] The notion of *équité* has nonetheless featured in the French law of contract, where it has been closely associated with the ubiquitous requirement of good faith.[91] Commentators have suggested that it reflects broader considerations than good faith, such as principles of 'justice'.[92] Returning to the Jersey context, it is then perhaps not quite so surprising that, in respect of such a typically English equitable remedy, references are made to *équité* as encapsulating open-textured notions of justice. Indeed, in the aforementioned case of *Trollope v Jackson*, the Royal Court ultimately elided the concept *équité* with that of 'fairness'.[93]

There have been few cases in Jersey on specific performance and thus the relevant law is not detailed. However, it is recognised that the award of the equitable remedy of specific performance is, as in English law, subject to the discretion of the court.[94] In exercising the equitable remedy under customary law, the Jersey courts will only award a remedy of specific performance where it is shown that damages would be an inadequate compensation.[95] In Jersey, the discretionary exercise of the remedy of specific performance depends partly upon the assets concerned in the contract. In the case of *Gallichan v Gallichan*, it was decided that the Jersey courts would not grant specific performance in respect of a sale of land,[96] or more broadly any 'agreement to create or extinguish an interest in land'.[97] The reason for this stems principally from the fact that a contract for land must be passed by the Royal Court in Jersey.[98]

[89] See generally C Albiges, *De l'Equité en droit privé* (Paris, LGDJ, 2000).

[90] Ibid.

[91] See eg the discussion in F Terré, P Simler, and Y Lequette, *Droit civil: Les Obligations* (8th edn, Paris, Dalloz, 2002) para 442.

[92] Ibid.

[93] *Trollope v Jackson* 1990 JLR 192, 198. See also the eliding of the concept with broader natural justice considerations in *Ex parte Viscount Wimborne* (1983) JJ 17, 19–22.

[94] *Co-operative Insurance Society Ltd v Argyll Stores (Holdings) Ltd* [1998] AC 1, 11.

[95] *Trollope v Jackson* 1990 JLR 192, 198.

[96] Ibid, 62: 'A and B enter into a contract for the sale of land. … The law of Jersey will not compel either A or B to fufil the contract by passing a 'contract' before the court.'

[97] 'What, however, is clear from the authorities is that, although the Royal Court is a court of equity, it cannot order the creation or extinguishment of an interest in land arising out of an agreement; in other words, an agreement to create or extinguish an interest in land is not specifically enforceable' (*Felard Investments Ltd v Church of Our Lady* (1979) JJ 19, 24).

[98] As explained in the case of *Taylor v Fitzpatrick* (1979) JJ 1, 15.

It is clear therefore that the availability of specific performance is limited. The immediate constraint on the scope of specific performance is the subsidiary nature of the remedy in that it may only be awarded where damages are inadequate. As in English law, this considerably narrows the scope of specific performance, as does the exclusion of transactions relating to real estate. Unsurprisingly, therefore, there are few cases on specific performance in the Jersey law reports. In remedial terms, more cases are found on the remedy of damages.

## B. Damages

Whilst a separate book could be written on the comparative law of damages,[99] that exercise is rendered unnecessary in Jersey law by the fact that the Jersey courts have made it clear that the rules on damages under Jersey law follow closely the relevant English case law. A recent example of this approach may be found in the case of *Café de Lecq Ltd v Rossborough Ltd*,[100] which concerned the breach of an agency contract between an insurance broker and its client, in which extensive reference was made by the Royal Court to English cases on issues of quantum.[101]

The basic principles of damages in Jersey contract law have been drawn directly from English case law. The Jersey courts have thus applied the principle of *restitutio in integrum*, thereby recognising that the appropriate measure of damages is the sum required to restore the victim to the financial position in which he would have been had the contract been performed.[102] The Jersey courts have adopted the English law rules on remoteness, so that recovery can be made for loss arising from breach, or such as may reasonably be supposed to have been in the contemplation of both parties at the time of contract as the probable result of a breach.[103] Even English law rules are not always of the purest pedigree, however: it is well known that the court in *Hadley v Baxendale*[104] drew upon the French law rule laid down in Articles 1149–50 of the original Civil Code.

Damages may be awarded, as they are in English and French law, for the lost chance of a gain occasioned by the breach of contract,[105] where the chance in

[99] See eg M Fontaine and G Viney (eds), *Les Sanctions de l'inexécution des obligations contractuelles* (Brussels, Bruylant, 2001); L Reiss, *Le juge et le préjudice, Etude comparée des droits français et anglais*, (Thesis, Université Paris 1, 2002); Rowan (n 1) ch 3.

[100] *Café de Lecq Ltd v Rossborough Ltd* [2012] JRC 053.

[101] Such as the English case of *Allied Maples Group-Simmons & Simmons* [1995] 1WLR 1602 on loss of a chance ([54]).

[102] *Snell v Thacker* [2006] JCA 164 (Court of Appeal). A similar rule is applicable in French law under the *principe de réparation intégrale du prejudice*.

[103] See *Denney v Hodge* (1971) JJ 1915.

[104] *Hadley v Baxendale* (1854) 9 Exch 341.

[105] *Grunhalle Lager Intl Ltd v Tascan Trading Ltd* (1981) JJ 1; *Snell v Thacker* [2006] JCA 164 (Court of Appeal).

question is 'a real or substantial chance, as opposed to a fanciful or speculative one'.[106] This causal link will fail if the loss instead resulted from the plaintiff's own shortcomings.[107] There is also a duty to mitigate loss under Jersey law.[108] In that sense, in order to understand the more detailed rules on quantum, it suffices to look to *Chitty*! However, the direct drawing upon English law in this way does raise awkward questions as to the integrity of the sources of law. We have already noted in an earlier chapter[109] that the status of English law as an authority in Jersey is, in strict terms, questionable.[110] Over and above that position, reliance on English law exclusively in terms of damages is particularly problematic given the explicit resort to civil law concepts in other remedial provisions such as specific remedies, as seen above. That is likely to give rise to charges of cherry-picking over consistency.

Set against that position, however, are other explanations which might be given for resort to the English rules. It might thus be argued that the reliance on English law is understandable given the difficulty of ascertaining rules of quantum in French law, due partly to the pithy style of judgments,[111] but mostly due to the fact that in French civil procedure, the lower French courts exercise a *sovereign power of assessment* as to the quantum of damages.[112]

## C. Résolution/Termination for Breach of Contract

### (i) Comparative Introduction

The starkest example of the impact of competing sources in the sphere of remedies in Jersey is that of termination for breach of contract. This is perhaps unsurprising given that English and French law differ so greatly on the issue of the remedies for termination of a contract. As is well known, English law allows a broad right to terminate in respect of failure to perform, whereas in France there is a certain reluctance to allow termination, as well as a significant role attributed to the courts in determining the fate of contracts which have been breached. This in turn

[106] *Café de Lecq Ltd v Rossborough Ltd* [2012] JRC 053 ([54]), citing the English case of *Allied Maples Group v Simmons & Simmons* [1995] 1 WLR 1602.

[107] Ibid.

[108] In application of this principle, the party anticipating or suffering loss from breach has a duty to take reasonable steps to mitigate. *Bisson v Gibbins* (1963) JJ 329.

[109] See Chapter 2, at 20–23 above.

[110] See recent judicial statements uttering this: *Incat Equatorial Guinee Ltd v Luba Freeport Ltd* [2010] JRC 0834, para 24.

[111] Though there have been some recent changes in France, particularly before the administrative courts, prompted by the report of the Conseil d'Etat: *Groupe de Travail sur la Rédaction des Décisions de la Jurisdiction Administrative* (Paris, Conseil d'Etat, April 2012).

[112] P Le Tourneau, *Droit de la Responsabilité et des Contrats* (Paris, Dalloz, 2012) para 2507. And as such is a matter of fact which is unchallengeable before the appeal courts.

reflects the respective differences of the two systems in terms of commitment to the protection of contractual performance.[113]

We will focus here on the French approach. A number of traditional remedies could be sought in French law so as to unravel parties' contractual relations, including, as we have already seen, *nullité*, and also *rescission*,[114] *rédhibition*[115] and *résolution*.

The approach has been clarified and streamlined in the new French Civil Code. Article 1217 of the new Civil Code thus provides a list of remedies in case of non-performance of contractual obligations, whereby a party towards whom an undertaking has not been performed or has been performed imperfectly may:

— suspend performance of his own obligations;
— seek specific performance in kind of the undertaking;
— request a reduction in price;
— initiate the termination of the contract;
— claim compensation for the consequences of non-performance.

*Résolution* has the greatest relevance in the current context, and refers to the retroactive termination of a contract for imputable non-performance. Termination has traditionally been of a judicial nature in French law. Article 1184 of the old Civil Code thus laid down that the remedy of *résolution* was available where, in a bilateral contract, one party has failed to perform his contractual obligations.[116] From Article 1184, and the relevant case law, *résolution* necessitates a decision of the court which will determine, within the judge's sole and sovereign discretion, whether the debtor's non-performance is sufficiently serious[117] to justify termination. Resort to the court is thus in principle required, and this is closely linked to the fact that the essence of a contract is seen as performance, its binding nature is the 'law of the parties'[118] and thus an order of the court is required to free contracting parties therefrom.[119] As is provided in Article 1193 of the new Civil Code, what has been created by the parties can only be undone by the parties' mutual consent, unless otherwise provided for in legislation.[120] Unlike the remedy of *nullité*, where, as we have seen, the court has no discretion in terms of the remedy awarded, in the case of *résolution* there are a number of intermediate

[113] See generally Rowan (n 1).

[114] Now primarily used in the context of *lesion*, as referred to by Art 1674 Code civil.

[115] An action used in the context of *vices caches*–see eg Art 1648 Code civil.

[116] The innocent party has a choice between claiming enforcement of the contract and instead opting for a *résolution*, whereby the contract may be terminated and damages claimed.

[117] Cass civ, 15 juil 1999, Bull civ I no 245.

[118] Previously Art 1134 of the Code civil. The wording of the Art 1193 of the new Code civil is as follows: 'Les contrats ne peuvent être modifiés ou révoqués que du consentement mutuel des parties, ou pour les causes que la loi autorise.'

[119] See generally Rowan (n 1) 82.

[120] Contracts 'can be modified or revoked only by the parties' mutual consent or on grounds which legislation authorises'.

solutions, short of full termination, such as prospective termination, known as *résiliation*.[121]

There are, however, a number of exceptions to the judicial nature of termination.[122] First, and foremost, French contracts commonly now contain *clauses résolutoires*, whereby the parties provide in the contract for the circumstances under which termination may occur and, crucially without need to resort to the courts.[123] It should be noted that, departing as they do from classic principles, the courts have acted cautiously in this respect, with a result that they have thus interpreted such clauses narrowly (thereby requiring clear and unequivocal language), underlining that—like all contracts—they should be exercised in good faith[124] and notably that a formal notification letter is issued before a party relies on the clause.[125]

Second, there has been a developing case law whereby creditors have been authorised unilaterally to bring to an end a contract in case of serious non-performance. This self-help remedy (known as *résolution unilatérale or extrajudiciaire*) avoids the need to resort to the courts, though the action is at the party's own risk and the other side may themselves bring proceedings to contest the rupture. In respect of this case law, which commenced in 1998,[126] the court requires proof of *gravité du comportement* (serious misbehaviour).[127] Commentators have argued that the notion of *gravité du comportement* is to be distinguished from a mere breach of contract, though matters are not entirely clear.[128] Recent case law has provided some illustrations of sufficiently serious misbehaviour,[129] though there is still some debate in the commentaries about the exact contours of the notion,[130] and the case law is still relatively thin. The other party may always challenge the unilateral *resolution*, and the court will then determine whether termination was justified or not (and in the latter case grant a remedy of damages).

The new Civil Code draws together these developments by providing that the termination of a contract may result from a termination clause, by a notice given to the debtor by the creditor or by an action brought before the courts.[131]

[121] See in detail, Bell, Boyron and Whittaker (n 55) 357–59

[122] Ibid.

[123] As is explicitly recognised in Art 1224 of the new Civil Code.

[124] Cass civ 1ère, 31 jan 1995, no 92-20654.

[125] Fabre-Magnan (n 50) 656–57.

[126] Cass civ 1ère, 13 oct 1998, *Bull civ* I, no 300, Dalloz, 1999.198.

[127] The Court stated that 'the serious nature of the conduct of one party to a contract may justify the other party in putting to an end that contract unilaterally at his own risk' (ibid).

[128] Rowan (n 1) 86.

[129] *Résolution* without intervention of the court was justified when 'the apparent defaults of packaging for a perfume commercialized at a high price implied a flawless product' (Cass com, 30 juin 2009, no 08-14944); a similar result was found where a food manufacturer supplied on many occasions food which was not fit for consumption (Cass civ, 24 sep 2009, no 08-14524).

[130] B Fages, *Droit des Obligations* (4th edn, Paris, LGDJ, 2013) 237–38.

[131] See Art 1224. The latter two causes of termination, namely notice and judicial intervention, require 'non-performance [which] is sufficiently serious'.

In a later section, self-help is explicitly provided for, as it is stated that when the breach occurred, a creditor may give notice to the debtor that if the breach is not remedied within a reasonable period, the contract will be terminated (without requiring resort to the courts).[132]

The common law allows, as is well known, for a contracting party to terminate a contract where there is failure of performance, renunciation or impossibility. The rules for termination for failure to perform are complex, but in essence allow for contracts to be brought to an end where a contract term is of essential importance (a contract term known as a 'condition'). These are contrasted with 'warranties', which are of lesser importance. The process of categorisation of the term as a condition can occur by statute,[133] by the courts or more commonly by the parties themselves, in the latter scenario by expressly labelling a term as a condition. There has subsequently emerged an additional series of terms, known as 'intermediate' terms,[134] in respect of which the breach must be shown as going 'to the root of the contract' so as to justify termination.

Moreover, it is also clear that contracting parties are afforded a great degree of freedom in determining contractually how and when the right to termination should arise. In many circumstances, this will occur by means of the inclusion of an express termination clause in the agreement. This is standard practice in commercial contracts, which will commonly provide details as to the circumstances and consequences of such a termination.[135] There are very few constraints on the use of termination clauses, and they are usually considered to supplement rather than oust the common law regime.[136] As Rowan has pointed out, this liberal approach concerning termination clauses contrasts somewhat with the courts' degree of scrutiny in respect of other express terms concerning remedies, such as penalty clauses and specific performance clauses, and she thus draws the conclusion that this 'seems to give the parties freedom to end their contract but not to keep it alive'.[137]

### *(ii) The Jersey Law on* Résolution

Jersey law has been caught between these competing approaches to termination in the different systems. To understand the dilemma, it will be necessary to examine the Jersey case law in some detail.

[132] See Art 1226.

[133] See eg Sale of Goods Act 1979 which designates the implied terms of satisfactory quality and fitness for purpose as conditions.

[134] *Hong Kong Fir Shipping Ltd v Kawasaki Kisen Kaisha Ltd* [1962] 2 QB 26; *Bremer Handelsgesellschaft mbh v Vanden Avenne-Izegem PVBA* [1978] 2 Lloyd's Rep 109

[135] See eg M Anderson and V Warner, *Drafting and Negotiating Commercial Contracts* (London, Bloomsbury Professional, 2011).

[136] Rowan (n 1) 76.

[137] Ibid.

Initial case law in Jersey seemed to indicate a preference for the common law. The Royal Court in *Hamon v Webster*[138] thus held that, except in relation to leases where special rules apply, the Jersey courts prefer the English law approach.[139] The judge referred to older cases in this respect,[140] and also cited the critique of French law in *Rossborough (Insurance Brokers) Limited v Boon*,[141] in the following terms:

> To insist that, however serious the breach by the other party, a party to a contract cannot treat the contract as being at an end so that he is relieved of his obligation to continue to perform his side of the bargain, but has to go to court to seek a discretionary decision as to whether the contract should in fact be ended, would seem to be very undesirable. It would mean that the innocent party would not know where he stood until a decision by the court some months or even years later. We must emphasize that we have not heard any argument on this matter but our initial reaction is that we would be reluctant to find that the law of Jersey was to such effect unless there were binding precedent to say so. The court should develop the law of contract in accordance with the requirements of a modern society in so far as it is open for it to do so. The French approach would appear to leave all the parties in a state of complete uncertainty.[142]

The Court in *Hamon v Webster*[143] went on to note that the parties under French law were free to derogate by contractual clause from the standard approach, but added its own critique to the French courts' restrictive interpretation of such clauses:

> It is true that the parties appear to be free under French law to agree that a lesser breach will give rise to a right of termination, but it is clear that the French courts will interpret such a provision very restrictively. We see no advantage in this. On the contrary, it would appear to be contrary to the maxim '*la convention fait la loi des parties.*' We see no reason why the Court should seek to fetter the freedom of the parties to agree what they wish in this respect.[144]

After a review of the relevant case law, the Royal Court held that Jersey law was the same as English law in this area. Save in respect of leases (where an application to the court was necessary),[145] the Court held that an innocent party may terminate a contract where the breach is one which *goes to the root of the contract* or where the contract itself specifically provides that he will have a right to terminate the contract in respect of the breach in question.

While this entails that the innocent party need not have recourse to the courts, it does not mean that the innocent party is completely free of judicial control.

[138] *Hamon v Webster*, unreported, 19 July 2002.

[139] Ibid, para 67.

[140] In particular *New Guarantee Trust Finance Limited v Birbeck* (1977) JJ 71, and *Hanby v Moss* (1966) JJ 625.

[141] *Rossborough (Insurance Brokers) Limited v Boon* 2001 JLR 416.

[142] Ibid, 430.

[143] *Hamon v Webster*, unreported, 19 July 2002.

[144] Ibid, para 69.

[145] See *Beghins Shoes v Avancement Ltd* 1994 JLR 15, para 19.

The party in breach may always challenge the termination of the contract on the grounds that the breach was not sufficiently serious or did not fall within the category specified in the contract. However, it was noted that it would be exceptional for the courts to intervene in such a way: in most cases the position would be clear.[146]

In the case of *Grove v Baker*,[147] the plaintiffs brought an action against the defendant seeking repayment of a loan and the accumulated interest. The loan agreement had provided for payment of the interest but made no provision for the repayment of capital. The plaintiff alleged that the defendant's failure to make timely interest payments on three separate occasions constituted a fundamental breach of the contract, which entitled them to treat it as terminated (or *résolu*) and to demand repayment of the capital.

The Royal Court accepted the rule as expounded in *Hamon v Webster*[148] that termination is permitted without going to court where the breach is sufficiently serious or the contract gives a specific termination right covering the breach in question. The Royal Court did not agree, however, with the proposition that the law of termination of contract followed *exactly* the English model. The Court held that whilst the law relating to *résolution* is not dissimilar to the English remedy of termination for breach, it is different in that the remedy of *résolution* in Jersey law is available at the discretion of the court whenever the failure to comply with an obligation can be said to be sufficiently serious to justify a cancellation of the contract.

The Court then described the relevant test as follows:

> A trivial or insignificant failure to comply with an obligation would not be sufficient. The failure must go 'to the root of the contract' (*Hamon v Webster* and *New Guar Trust Fin Ltd v Birbeck (5)* (1977 JJ at 83)), or involve 'a breach of a fundamental condition' (*Hanby v Moss (2)*) or be 'sufficiently serious to justify the termination of a contract' (*Hotel de France (Jersey) Ltd v Chartered Institute of Bankers (3)*).[149]

In that case, the Court did not consider that the failures to pay interest on the due dates were cumulatively sufficiently serious to justify the contract of loan as having been terminated.[150] Timely payment of interest was not stipulated as being of the essence of the contract. Whilst the plaintiffs could sue for the overdue interest, they were not entitled to reclaim the capital by treating the contract as terminated.

146 Ibid, *Hamon v Webster*, unreported, 19 July 2002, para 71.
147 *Grove v Baker* 2005 JLR 348.
148 *Hamon v Webster*, unreported, 19 July 2002.
149 *Grove v Baker* 2005 JLR 348, 355.
150 Ibid, para 18.

### (iii) Reconciling the Position

These two approaches to the issue of *résolution* in *Hamon v Webster* and in *Grove v Baker* leave many issues unclear. This is particularly so as far as the role of the Royal Court is concerned. In *Hamon v Webster*, it was clearly contemplated that the judicial role would be reduced. It would be exceptional for the courts to be involved in termination and if such were the case, it would intervene ex post facto so as to determine whether the party who terminated the contract was right to do so. The approach of the Royal Court in *Grove v Baker* is somewhat different. As we have seen above, the Royal Court seemed to suggest that the remedy of *résolution* would only be awarded *at the discretion of the Court*. This would suggest that an intervention of the Court was required, so that the discretion in question was actually exercised. It is difficult to see how these different approaches are to be reconciled. This is again an example of where Jersey finds itself torn between two radically different approaches in civil and common law, and the result is that neither one nor the other has been adopted.

There has been commentary on the issue of whether to follow the French or English position. Some commentators in Jersey believe that the French approach may lead to expense, delay, inconvenience and uncertainty.[151] However, others have pointed out that in practice the French approach works perfectly well in France and that it would be odd if contracts were formed under French legal principles but terminated under English legal principles.[152] It should also be pointed out here that the principle under French law of judicial termination has been chipped away—both where a contractual clause provides otherwise but crucially, as we have seen above, in respect of the exception allowing for unilateral *résolution* in case of sufficiently serious misbehaviour.

## VI. General Conclusion on Remedies

The difficulties arising from the conflicting case law on nullity have already been noted above, and we will not dwell upon those issues again here. In terms of remedies for non-performance, the approach is also by no means crystal clear. The Jersey Royal Court has adopted a casuistic approach to sources and rules in this area of the law. In that sense, the Jersey courts seem to have replicated the common law focus upon the relief provided by the courts, rather than the more systematised civil model. Indeed, the structure and scope of the analysis above in respect of non-performance is indeed structured around the remedies to be obtained by

[151] See T Le Cocq, 'Resolving Contracts: The *Hotel De France* Case' (2000) 4 *Jersey Law Review* 151
[152] J Kelleher '*Résolution* and the Jersey Law of Contract' (2000) 4 *Jersey Law Review* 266.

the innocent party. There is very little evidence within the case law of an attempt to weave together the various remedies within a holistic account of remedies. Indeed, the only really broad underpinning discussion concerns the ubiquitous tectonic clashes of common law and civil law influences.

The question of sources has not been resolved entirely, and this has inevitably generated a certain inconsistency in treatment. Interrelated remedies such as damages and specific performance are said to be governed by English law principles on the one hand, and French law influences, on the other. In shaping the remedy of resolution, the courts seem to have adopted a fusion of the twin influences, albeit in different, successive cases!

In terms of content of the remedial provisions, clarity is by no means served. As we have already seen, in respect of the Jersey remedy of specific performance, French law principles of *équité* are said to underpin the law of Jersey. Not only does that combine a quintessentially equitable remedy under English law with principles of a civil law nature, but the exact content of *équité* under French law is by no means crystal clear. Similarly, in the sphere of *résolution*/termination, there is still continuing uncertainty as to the precise role of the courts in the overall process.

The continuing uncertainty is a product of several factors. First, and foremost, the primary culprit must be found in the lack of clarity as to the sources of the Jersey law of contract which, as we have seen in other areas, has also had a collateral effect on the substantive law.

Second, however, it is also relevant to point to a lack of certainty as to the fundamental underlying principles of Jersey law, in particular the weight attached to the performance interest in contractual matters. We have seen that in statistical and substantive law terms, the Jersey cases illustrate a preference for pecuniary remedies, and on the basis of the Jersey law reports, actions for specific performance are relatively rare.[153] That limited resort to the specific relief in Jersey can be contrasted with French law where specific remedies are unequivocally the rule.[154] In that sense, it might be concluded that in Jersey law, as in English law, the commitment of the courts to the performance interest is somewhat weak. Whilst the rejection of English notions of equity could potentially have freed the Jersey courts to pursue a more performance-friendly policy, in line with other civil law jurisdictions, it would seem clear that specific performance is still viewed as a subsidiary remedy, awarded only where damages are inadequate and in respect of which transactions relating to real estate have been excluded. However, the position is not entirely unequivocal. As the remedy of *résolution* illustrates, the control exercised by the courts over the termination of contracts has not entirely been relinquished, and might again prove a route for encouraging contractual

[153] See, though, the cases referred to in the section on specific performance below, at 157–159.
[154] See generally Rowan (n 1).

performance. If, as has been suggested in the case of *Grove v Baker*, the remedy of *résolution* can only be awarded at the discretion of the courts, then that would leave room for the courts to suggest intermediate solutions, such as giving the debtor more time to perform his obligations.[155] The Jersey courts could thereby illustrate their commitment to the performance interest in such a scenario. It remains to be seen how the doctrine of remedies evolves in the next few years in Jersey. Whilst many uncertainties remain, one thing that is certain is that this area is ripe for reform. It is this issue to which we now turn, from a more general perspective.

[155] Art 1228 of the new Code civil.

# 8

# Comparative Law Lessons and Reform Issues

## I. Comparative Law Themes

### A. Comparative Law in Action

For a comparatist, the Jersey law of contract is a fascinating example of comparative law in action. The customary law of Jersey, with its origins in Normandy but highly influenced by both common law and modern civil law sources, is an absorbing and intriguing example for comparative lawyers. Situated geographically and culturally mid-Channel, between the tectonic plates of civil law and common law, this jurisdiction is illustrative of an open-minded and diverse approach to sources of law. With its hybrid interaction of such different legal systems within a micro-jurisdiction, this jurisdiction is in many ways the Galapagos Islands for comparatists!

The distinctive and hybrid nature of the Jersey legal system is reflected in the various features of the jurisdiction, including the sources of law, patterns of legal reasoning, the impact of doctrinal writers, as well as a somewhat different philosophy as to contract law. As we have seen, the sources of law in Jersey generally, and in respect of Jersey contract law specifically, are multilayered, overlapping and heterogeneous; and this has had a significant impact on the mindset or *mentalité* of Jersey lawyers. Although in recent times most Jersey lawyers are by education and origin common lawyers, this book has argued that, by virtue of their training to become Jersey advocates and through the exercise and practice of Jersey customary law, the outlook of Jersey lawyers is actually very different from that of 'ordinary' common lawyers. This specificity can partly be attributed to substantive law, as is clear from those areas where a distinctive set of civil and customary law-inspired legal rules have developed, such as within the law of property.[1] However, even in those areas of Jersey law where the English common law has increasingly had a predominant influence, such as the sphere of

[1] R MacLeod, *Property Law in Jersey* (Thesis, University of Edinburgh, 2012).

extra-contractual liability, known in Jersey as tort law (and not delict!),[2] the civil law influences are still apparent.[3]

Another key characteristic of Jersey law is the importance of *la doctrine*. Described by one eminent Channel Islands jurist as 'authoritative works explaining or interpreting the law',[4] this aspect of the system again sets it apart from common law jurisdictions. We have already noted the presence and importance of local commentaries, such as the 'distinguished duo of Lieutenant Bailiffs',[5] Le Geyt and Poingdestre, in the late seventeenth and early eighteenth centuries, or more recently Charles Le Gros.[6] Even more striking, however, is the reliance placed upon civil law authorities such as Domat, Terrien or Pothier. References to Domat feature in many contract cases,[7] but it is Pothier, the 'surer'[8] guide to Jersey contract law, whose influence has been particularly significant, with one leading commentator calculating that Pothier has been cited in *half* of the contract law cases before the Jersey Royal Court since 1950.[9] Whilst at first blush it might seem unusual that a treatise from a different era and from a different legal system should be relied upon so heavily, this approach on closer analysis connects the Jersey system further to its civil law roots. Civil law cultures have traditionally been very receptive to *la doctrine*,[10] and we have examined the intellectual and legal foundations

[2] In the case of *Jersey Financial Services Commission v AP Black (Jersey) Ltd* 2002 JLR 294, it was noted that: '[A] *délit* has a different meaning in Jersey. A *délit* is a criminal offence and not a civil wrong' ([26]) (overturned on different grounds in *Jersey Financial Services Commission v AP Black (Jersey) Ltd* 2002 JLR 443).

[3] Indeed in the 1953 case of *Guernsey States Insurance Authority v Ernest Farley and Son Ltd* (1953) JJ 47, the Jersey court was able to say that: 'The word "tort" is used here in the sense in which it is commonly used by English lawyers when they speak of the Law of Torts as opposed to the Law of Contracts. On grounds of convenience this may be permitted, provided that it is done without losing sight of the fact that this is a Jersey court administering Jersey law' ([48]). By the early twenty-first century, the Court of Appeal, however, held that there was a great degree of proximity between the two systems, including the 'the three essentials of duty, breach of duty and damage. Whatever differences there may be between Jersey law and English law as to the range of torts on which reliance may be placed under either legal system, torts under each system involve the existence of those three essentials' (*Jersey Financial Services Commission v AP Black (Jersey) Ltd* 2002 JLR 443, [21]). It is also clear that in respect of 'the tort of negligence, Jersey follows the law of England' (*Arya Holdings Ltd v Minories Finance Ltd* (1997) JLR 176, 181). However, note the cause of action of *voisinage*, whereby a neighbour must not use his property so as to damage neighbouring property: see *Rockhampton Apartment Limited v Gale and Clarke* [2007] JLR 332; *Fogarty v St Martin's Cottage Limited* [2015] JRC 068. *Voisinage* has been characterised as arising from quasi-contract: *Classic Herd Limited v Jersey Milk Marketing Board* 2014 (2) JLR 487, [16].

[4] See Sir P Bailhache, 'Jersey: Avoiding the Fate of the Dodo' in S Farran, E Orucu and S Patrick, *A Study of Mixed Legal Systems: Endangered, Entrenched or Blended* (Farnham, Ashgate Publishing, 2014) 92, fn 17. Sir Philip Bailhache was Bailiff of Jersey from 1995 to 2009, and is now a Senator and Minister for External Relations.

[5] Ibid, 111.

[6] Le Gros, *Traité du Droit Coutumier de L'Ile de Jersey* (1943).

[7] eg *Sutton v Insurance Corporation of the Channel Islands Limited* [2011] JRC 027, [15]–[16.]

[8] See eg *HM Viscount v Treanor* (1969) JJ 1243, 1245.

[9] J Kelleher 'The Sources of Jersey Contract Law' (1999) 3 *Jersey Law Review* 1.

[10] On this, see J Bell, *French Legal Cultures* (Butterworths, London, 2001) 72–76; N Duxbury, *Jurists and Judges* (Oxford, Hart Publishing, 2001) 47–60; Ph Jestaz and C Jamin, 'L'entité doctrinale française' Dalloz.1997.Chronique 167; Ph Jestaz, and C Jamin, *La Doctrine* (Paris, Dalloz, 2004).

for the use of such sources in Jersey above.[11] This approach is also illustrative of the porous and open-textured approach to both norms and sources of law, and the way in which even secondary sources have been made use of in order to influence and form the law in this hybrid legal system.

As we have seen in this book, there are areas where the civil law heritage is apparent in Jersey, and that the Jersey law of contract is an example of this. Jersey lawyers will thus grapple on a daily basis with civil law concepts such as *cause* (rather than consideration) and *vices de consentement* such as *violence*, *dol* and *erreur*. The hybrid nature of the legal system has also had an impact *beyond* substantive law. We have thus argued that the mentality of a Jersey lawyer is distinctive, and we have examined and traced this feature throughout this book. Not only are the contract law concepts grounded in continental influences, but the language of the law is also reflective of that hybrid background. References thus abound to civil law terms or concepts, such as '*volonté*',[12] *prescription* (rather than limitation period),[13] '*deception d'outre moitié*',[14] '*lucrative*' and '*onéreuse*' transactions,[15] and so on.[16]

That distinctive approach is also apparent in the readiness of the Jersey courts and jurists to resort to comparative law sources, not as a vanity exercise or as simply a show of learning, but as a highly pragmatic method for identifying an optimal solution that is adaptable to local circumstances. We have seen that comparative law references are thus made *in extenso* in Jersey cases as a matter of course.[17] The distinctive mentality of Jersey lawyers is shown also through the many Jersey cases illustrating a mode of reasoning that is strikingly principle-based. We have thus remarked upon the ubiquity of maxims in many Jersey cases,[18] as well as the presence of underpinning precepts of the law.[19] This strikes a very different note to the casuistic methodology and approach of the English common lawyer.[20]

Our analysis of Jersey contract law has also revealed a very different underlying approach to contractual arrangements, which is reflective of a somewhat different philosophy underpinning contract law. This is shown in the conception of the

[11] See Chapter 2, at pp 12–15 above.

[12] *Cunningham v Sinel* [2011] JRC 015, [18.]

[13] *Mendonca v Le Boutillier* 1997 JLR 142.

[14] See Chapter 5 above.

[15] *Re Esteem Settlement*, unreported, 17 January 2002, [297].

[16] See generally Chapter 2 above.

[17] See eg the case of *Attorney General v Foster* 1989 JLR 70 (upheld by the Court of Appeal: 1992 JLR 6) in which, in a sophisticated comparative analysis, reference was made to a series of legal systems which derived from the common sources of Roman law, including Scottish and South African law.

[18] Which have been described by one local commentator as 'sacred' principles: see Le Gros (n 6) 350.

[19] There is a detectable preference for reasoning from such principles as a basic starting point of analysis of a legal problem. Many examples of this can found in the case law, such as the judgments in *Incat Equatorial Guinee Ltd v Luba Freeport Ltd* 2010 JLR 287 (concerning the maxim of *la convention fait la loi des parties*, [22]) or *Flynn v Reid* [2012] JRC 100 (concerning *volonté or* 'true consent', [21]). For a recent example of such an approach, see *Fogarty v St Martin's Cottage Limited* [2015] JRC 068.

[20] See Chapter 2, at pp 28–30 above.

role of the court, in the sense that Jersey judges will intervene in certain circumstances to re-evaluate the equilibrium of a contractual arrangement, through the notion of *lesion*, or potentially even through the notion of *cause*,[21] a much more malleable tool than its common law cousin of consideration.[22] These examples illustrate that in a number of spheres of contract law, the Jersey judiciary is prepared to take a more interventionist role than would be readily assumed in a common law context, and to some extent this reveals deeper differences.[23] This accords also with broader, contextual factors in Jersey in terms of the desire to scrutinise the fairness of contractual bargains,[24] explained perhaps by its geography, demographics and the fact that, as a micro-jurisdiction, overall fairness is as important a consideration as pure economic efficiency within the contractual sphere. From this perspective, it is striking how prominently terminology with a moral dimension, such as 'fraud', 'dolus', 'déception', 'lésion' or bad faith, is found in Jersey law.[25]

These features make the jurisdiction of Jersey a fascinating example of comparative law in action, and in many ways quite an unusual mixture of civil law and common law influences within a European context.[26] And yet the openness to non-orthodox sources, the use of comparative law and the combined, interlacing influences of both civil and common law sources may also have a more general relevance. The increasingly heterogeneous and interconnected legal environment globally, as well as the heightened polycentric and transnational nature of legal issues, has thus entailed that policy-makers, lawyers and the judiciary are grappling with a series of more complex issues, referring to heterogeneous sources, including official as well as non-official sources.[27] In that sense, the themes explored in this book may also have a more general resonance.

[21] See Chapter 4, at pp 73–82 above.

[22] This phenomenon is also reflected in other recent cases, such as the *Doorstop* case, where the Royal Court was prepared, under the cover of the control of penalty clauses, to rewrite the level of contractual interest rates which it considered to be appropriate: *Doorstop Ltd v Gillman and Lepervier Holdings Ltd* [2012] JRC 199.

[23] In one comparative law study, it has been argued that 'French contract law is both more "moral" and more dogmatic; English contract law is both more "economic" and more pragmatic' (D Harris and D Tallon, 'Conclusions' in *Contract Law Today: Anglo-French Comparisons* (Oxford, Clarendon Press, 1989) 386.

[24] This distinctive approach may also derive from the *esprit* of Norman Customary law: see eg S Poirey, 'L'Esprit of Norman Customary Law' in P Bailhache (ed), *A Celebration of Autonomy: 1204–2004, 800 Years of Channel Islands' Law* (St Helier, Jersey Law Review, 2004) 17.

[25] From a comparative perspective, see the discussion in Harris and Tallon (n 23) 386.

[26] Albeit though not of course unique: see generally S Farran, E Orucu and S Patrick, *A Study of Mixed Legal Systems: Endangered, Entrenched or Blended* (Farnham, Ashgate Publishing, 2014); VV Palmer, *Mixed Jurisdictions Worldwide: The Third Legal Family* (Cambridge, CUP, 2012).

[27] See on this generally G-P Calliess and P Zumbansen, *Rough Consensus and Running Code* (Oxford, Hart Publishing, 2010).

## B. Comparative Law Lessons

The jurisdiction of Jersey may be seen as illustrating key modern themes of comparative law. This is a hybrid legal system which has drawn upon both civil and common law influences in shaping its law of contract; and the Jersey case law is replete with references to foreign sources and doctrinal writing, making for a rich and heterogeneous set of sources, and an interesting example of the practical use of comparative law during the forensic process. As we have seen, these very features of Jersey law have both proved to make this jurisdiction unusual and distinctive, but have also posed a series of challenges: indeed, we have seen that the modern construct of Jersey contract law has by no means followed a smooth path. Many voices have been critical of the status quo, and we will review the reform options below, which itself will give rise to comparative law reflections.

The Jersey system provides some interesting comparative law insights. It first underlines the importance of the contextual approach in comparative law. The past, present and future of Jersey law contract depends upon, and is intricately linked to, its specific context. One cannot understand the system—or for that matter reform it—without taking full account of that context, in terms of history, sources, procedure, *mentalité*, as well as substantive law. As we have seen, this is most clearly illustrated in the sphere of sources. In recent times, it has, however, been suggested by certain stakeholders in Jersey that there is a strong, almost inexorable, pull towards the common law in general, and English law in particular. The close ties with the United Kingdom provide cultural and economic reasons to draw upon the stock of ideas and concepts of the common law, as does the fact that the members of the Jersey legal profession (as well as a majority of Court of Appeal judges) are primarily educated at English universities and law schools,[28] before undertaking training in the Channel Islands. Certain cases illustrate that attraction for Albion, and the enactment of recent legislation in Jersey reinforces this tendency.[29]

The resort to English law in this area is, however, highly questionable, and arguments can be made that it is important to take account of the specific context in this sense. For instance, the Jersey Law Commission in its Final Report on the Jersey Law of Contract observed that: '[I]t is noteworthy that English law has in recent years influenced Jersey contract case law. It is questionable, however, from a strict jurisprudential view, whether there are any circumstances when English law should be followed.'[30] Indeed, in some recent cases, the Jersey judiciary has

[28] See on this generally A Binnington, 'The Law of Contract—Which Way?' in Bailhache (n 24) 61.

[29] Such as the Supply of Goods and Services (Jersey) Law 2009 given the fact that the 2009 Law is based upon English statutes: T Hanson, 'An Introduction to the Supply of Goods and Services (Jersey) Law 2009' (2009) 13 *Jersey Law Review* 336.

[30] Jersey Law Commission, *Consultation Paper: The Jersey Law of Contract* (Consultation Paper No 5, February 2002) para 7. Available at: www.lawcomm.gov.je/Contract.htm.

indicated a more sceptical attitude to English law sources. In the case of *Incat Equatorial Guinee Ltd v Luba Freeport Ltd*, the judge responded robustly to an attempt by one party to rely upon English sources.[31] In another decision, *Sutton v Insurance Corporation of the Channel Islands Limited*, it was held that: '[I]t appears to us that the Court should be cautious to declare the Law of Jersey by abstracting principles from the Law of England which have been drawn fundamentally from a different approach to the law of contract.'[32]

It is true that such legal transplants from English law, if taken in isolation, can present disadvantages. The original DNA of the law of Jersey is that of Norman customary law. Jersey clearly has its origins in the civil law. This is not just a historical particularity, but also impacts, on the language, concepts, legal reasoning and structures of the Jersey law of contract, as we have seen throughout this book. Clearly there are issues relating to accessibility of materials,[33] which are particularly acute for Norman customary law, but which apply in a similar manner to modern French-language materials, given that the familiarity with French language is decreasing, even within the Jersey legal profession. However, it is difficult to escape the conclusion that, given the background, Jersey contract law has a good deal in common with the civil law in terms of substance, terminology, legal reasoning as well as *mentalité*.

It is important not to underestimate this importance of the civil law influence: indeed, it is quite difficult to see how Jersey lawyers can properly look to the common law for guidance on topics such as the classification and categorisation of contracts, given the presence of the distinction between between lucrative/onerous transactions,[34] the notion of potestative contractual conditions (*conditions potestatives*),[35] or more fundamentally when the doctrine of consideration is absent from Jersey law. This latter example is a very important one. The existence of *cause* in Jersey rather than the doctrine of consideration is not just expressive of a preference for civil law concepts, it is also a product of broader circumstances. In a legal system such as Jersey, which does not possess an instrument of deed which can be deployed so as to circumvent the exigencies of the doctrine of consideration, the preference for the notion of *cause* is perhaps understandable. As we have seen, this concept allows for the deployment of transactions such as promises of gifts, due to the broader circumstances of the cases, such as an *intention libérale*.[36]

[31] *Incat Equatorial Guinee Ltd v Luba Freeport Ltd* [2010] JRC 0834, [24].

[32] *Sutton v Insurance Corporation of the Channel Islands Limited* [2011] JRC 027, [45].

[33] See generally P Hodge, 'The Value of the Civilian Strand' in Bailhache (n 24) 41.

[34] See *Re Esteem Settlement*, unreported, 17 January 2002, in which the Royal Court explained that a lucrative transaction ('aliénations faites pour cause lucrative') consisted of an alienation to a volunteer, whereas an onerous transaction concerned 'an alienation made for value' ('aliénations faites pour cause onéreuse') (para 298).

[35] Namely contractual obligations which depend for their fulfilment purely on the will of one of the parties. See *Groom v Stock* (1965) JJ 429, 434.

[36] See generally Chapter 4, at pp 73–82.

Similar comments could also be made about the distinctively subjective civilian approach which is premised upon the parties' own consent, a notion that was underlined by the Court of Appeal as a centrepiece of the law of Jersey.[37] This is very different to the common law approach and, as we have seen,[38] has defined many of the constituent elements of Jersey contract law.

Jersey also illustrates the strengths and vulnerabilities[39] of a small jurisdiction geographically located between two larger neighbouring states, France and the United Kingdom. This situation has itself been given expression in constitutional terms through, on the one hand the evolving constitutional relationship with the sovereign power, the United Kingdom,[40] and, on the other, in terms of Jersey's relationship with the European Union.[41] Those relationships are not frozen in time and the political relationship may also impact upon legal traditions. Sir Philip Bailhache, a previous Bailiff of the island,[42] has thus noted that hand in hand with a slowly developing political autonomy, there has also been 'a greater interest on the part of the courts to rediscover the roots of the Island's jurisprudence',[43] leading him to argue that: 'It is difficult to avoid the conclusion that they are related, and that a greater political autonomy helps to support the independence of a country's legal system.'[44]

Another point to underline is that Jersey contract law could also be relevant in a wider European context. At first glance, this might seem an incongruous argument to make given the somewhat disjointed relationship which Jersey maintains with the European project: indeed Jersey is not per se part of the European Union.[45] However, there are reasons for thinking that the Jersey experience in the sphere of

[37] The Court of Appeal in *O'Brien v Marett* was unambiguous on this point: '[T]he Jersey law of contract determines *consent* by use of the subjective theory of contract' (*O'Brien v Marett* [2008] JCA 178, [55]). See, however, the recent decision of the Jersey Court of Appeal in *Home Farm Developments Ltd v Le Sueur* [2015] JCA 242, which has generated some uncertainty on this issue. See discussion above in Chapter 3, at pp 44–47.

[38] Ibid.

[39] The terminology is drawn from Bailhache (n 4) 110.

[40] See variously R Falle, 'Jersey and the UK: A Choice of Destiny (1)' (2004) 8 *Jersey Law Review* 321; J Kelleher, 'Jersey and the UK: A Choice of Destiny (2)' (2004) 8 *Jersey Law Review* 337; A Binnington, 'Jersey and the UK: A Choice of Destiny (3)' (2004) 8 *Jersey Law Review* 345; P Bailhache, 'One or Two Steps from Sovereignty' (2009) 13 *Jersey and Guernsey Law Review* 252.

[41] P Johnson, 'The Genesis of Protocol 3: The Channel Islands and the EEC' (2013) 17 *Jersey and Guernsey Law Review* 254; A Sutton, 'Jersey's Changing Constitutional Relationship with Europe' (2005) 9 *Jersey and Guernsey Law Review* 14.

[42] The Bailiff is President of the Royal Court in Jersey and is also civic head of the Island with responsibility for official communication with the UK authorities. The bailiff is also the President of the States Assembly.

[43] Bailhache (n 4) 109.

[44] Ibid.

[45] For a historical view, see Johnson (n 41). The relationship is, however, subtle. Although not a Member State, nor an associate member of the European Union, Jersey may nevertheless (depending on the subject matter) be required to implement certain EU Regulations or Directives. See generally Sutton (n 41).

contract law represents an instructive one for European private law. The hybrid nature of the Jersey legal system illustrates the challenges of accommodating the features of a modern contract law system by drawing upon competing common law and civil law influences. The resultant fusion has, as we have seen, provided challenges for the coherence and consistency of the law. Unsuccessful transplants have been made (many examples can be given—but the unhappy introduction of a form of misrepresentation to vitiate a contract is illustrative of this tendency).[46] Inconsistencies are rife (such as in the sphere of remedies,[47] or in relation to the law on *vices de consentement*[48]); cherry-picking is often in evidence; and legal certainty could be better served (such as the role and place of good faith).[49] There are also some striking omissions in contract law, in particular in respect of consumer protection. And yet, there is an evident attempt on the part of policy-makers and the judiciary to attempt to strive for a contract law that is clear, modern and equitable, and which is consonant with the very particular history and culture of this mixed jurisdiction. It is within this distinctive comparative law context that the reform options for Jersey will now be considered.

## II. Reforming the Jersey Law of Contract

### A. Introduction

As we have already seen, the current position of Jersey contract law has been subject to a degree of criticism notably due to the lack of consistency in sources and the impact that this has had on legal certainty.[50] When the Jersey Law Commission was asked to examine the position of Jersey contract law, it concluded that Jersey contract law had failed to keep pace with changing times, and that it thus needed to be made more accessible and updated. The Commission identified the following causes of continuing uncertainty: difficulties in accessing Norman texts, language issues relating to texts in Norman or modern French, uncertainty as to the current law and complexities associated with applying ancient concepts.[51]

Given the perceived inadequacy of the status quo, reform of the law of contract has long been on the agenda in Jersey. Various methods of reform have been

[46] See Chapter 5 above.
[47] See further Chapter 7 above.
[48] See further Chapter 5 above.
[49] See Chapter 3 above, at pp 55–58.
[50] Many commentators have accepted that the status quo is inadequate. Hanson has thus argued that the 'Jersey law of contract is in urgent need of reform and clarification' (T Hanson, 'Jersey's Contract Law: A Question of Identity?' (2005) 9 *Jersey Law Review* 126, [32]. See generally the section on the Jersey law of contract in Bailhache (n 4) 57–101.
[51] Jersey Law Commission (n 30).

proposed, including incremental development through case law,[52] the codification of the Jersey law of contract,[53] or even the wholesale transplantation of English law by statute.[54] Alternative comparative law sources of inspiration have been put forward. Professor Rosalie Jukier of McGill University has suggested that Jersey may learn from Quebec's experience. Although Professor Jukier recognises that it would not be appropriate to adopt or transplant the Quebec Civil Code into Jersey, she argues that it might provide insights 'as a jurisdiction which has successfully adapted and modernized its civilian legal system'.[55]

In the Jersey Law Commission's Consultation Paper on the reform of Jersey contract law, published in 2002, the Commission concluded that there was a series of current difficulties associated with the position of the Jersey law of contract, as we have already seen. The Commission thus proposed three alternative solutions for rectifying the current state of affairs, namely: (i) maintaining the current approach of developing the law through case law but encouraging 'the Jersey courts to apply the Jersey law of contract as expounded by the earlier writers on Norman law and jurists such as Pothier but developing the law by analogy with concepts drawn from English and French law'; (ii) the codification of Jersey contract law; or (iii) incorporation of English law by statute.

After consultation, the Jersey Law Commission concluded that the most practicable solution to existing problems was to adopt a statutory framework for the law of contract, and that it was preferable to base that upon a model used in another jurisdiction.[56] A number of such jurisdictions were considered, such as the Quebec Civil Code and the US Uniform Commercial Code, but it was instead recommended that Jersey adopt a statute based on the Indian Contract Act 1872.[57] The latter was seen as suitable and interesting as it was a stand-alone model, defining the Indian law of contract without reference to an entire code of laws.[58] This somewhat esoteric proposal was not taken up with much enthusiasm within Jersey. It is perhaps understandable that a nineteenth-century relic of the British Empire was not generally seen as the ideal solution for twenty-first-century Jersey. Whilst it is fair to say that the Law Commission recognised that some adaptation was

[52] Jersey Law Commission, *Report on the Law of Contract* (Topic Report No 10, February 2004) para 4.

[53] This was one option considered by A Binnington et al, 'The Way(s) Forward: Contract Law in Guernsey and Jersey' (panel discussion at the Contract Law of the Channel Islands at the Crossroads conference hosted by the Institute of Law, Jersey, 15 October 2010).

[54] See further discussion below.

[55] R Jukier, 'Contract Law: What Can Jersey Learn from the Quebec Experience?' (2011) 15 *Jersey and Guernsey Law Review* 131.

[56] Jersey Law Commission (n 52) para 6.

[57] Ibid, para 7: 'We recommend that a statutory framework be adopted for the Jersey law of contract and that the Indian Contract Act of 1872 be used as a model, incorporating where necessary those aspects of our existing law which are peculiar to Jersey as opposed to England and which are found to be worthy of retention.'

[58] For a detailed analysis of this Act, see S Tofaris, *A Historical Study in the Indian Contract Act 1872* (PhD Thesis, University of Cambridge, 2011).

required for the Jersey context, it may also have underestimated the work required to take account of Jersey's civil law heritage.

Since the Law Commission's report, very little has actually transpired in terms of reform, setting aside the enactment of the Sales of Goods-inspired legislation.[59] Recently, the Government of Jersey announced in 2015 that it was seeking to evaluate the current and future position of the Jersey law of contract with a view to reform.[60] Impetus thus seems to be growing for a renewed reform attempt. Two of the main proposed instruments for reform are a Restatement of Jersey Contract Law or a Codification of the Law of Contract. In the following section, these proposals will be examined in further detail.

## B. A Restatement of Jersey Contract Law

### *(i) The Notion of a Restatement*

One method for reforming the Jersey law of contract is by means of a restatement of contract law in Jersey. This was explicitly considered by the Government of Jersey in its evaluation of the current and future position of the Jersey law of contract.[61] The restatement model is primarily associated with the United States, where Restatements of the Law are a set of treatises on legal subjects that seek to inform judges and lawyers about general principles of common law. A short word will be said about the restatement model in general before we analyse the specific application to Jersey.

The Restatements of the Law was the first project of the American Law Institute (ALI),[62] founded in 1923, in response to a perceived uncertainty and complexity in US law. The first Restatements were intended to address 'basic legal subjects' and to 'tell judges and lawyers what the law was'.[63] Work on the first Restatement took place between 1923 and 1944, and the project attempted to clarify nine broad subject areas of law: agency, conflict of laws, contracts, judgments, property, restitution, security, torts, and trusts.[64] The final draft of the first Restatement was approved at the ALI Annual meeting in May 1942.

[59] Supply of Goods and Services (Jersey) Law 2009.

[60] A seminar was thus run in conjunction with the Jersey Institute of Law on 11 November 2015 entitled 'Presentation on the Current and Future Position of the Jersey Law of Contract and the Opportunities Presented by a Re-statement.'

[61] Ibid.

[62] The ALI was conceived as a representative gathering of American jurists with the stated mission 'to promote the clarification and simplification of the law and its better adaptation to social needs, to secure the better administration of justice and to encourage and carry on scholarly and scientific legal work'.

[63] KD Adams, 'The Folly of Uniformity? Lessons from the Restatement Movement' (2004) 33 *Hofstra Law Review* 423, 433.

[64] Two other subject areas, business associations and sales of land, were explored but never officially adopted by the ALI.

Restatements only have persuasive authority: a decision was taken by the ALI early on, and followed since then, not to pursue codification of the common law through the Restatements. Whilst the Restatements are thus secondary sources, the reputation of the ALI and the esteem in which the Restatements are generally held has meant that the Restatements have had a significant impact on the law. Restatements have thus influenced the development of the law in a substantial manner.[65] Indeed, the ALI has itself stated that: 'Many Institute publications have been accorded an authority greater than that imparted to any legal treatise, an authority more nearly comparable to that accorded to judicial decisions.'[66] In advance of the drafting process, Cardozo prophesied the impact of the Restatement as follows:

> something less than a code and something more than a treatise. It will be invested with unique authority, not to command, but to persuade. It will embody a composite thought and speak a composite voice. Universities and bench and bar will have had a part in its creation.[67]

Debate has occurred about the exact objective of the Restatements and in particular whether the goal is meant to be that of stating existing law or rather promoting desirable change in the law.[68] That tension between normative or merely descriptive roles has never really been entirely resolved.[69] Many scholars have argued that clarification inevitably involves a normative purpose,[70] and that the very nature of restating the law necessarily requires some change in the law.[71] The US Restatements are not without their critics, however, including prominent US jurists such as Richard Posner.[72] Criticism has been directed at the membership of the ALI, its mission and goals, its perceived insularity, and its conservatism in the face of proposed reform.[73]

[65] Adams (n 63) 436.

[66] See www.ali.org/about-ali/how-institute-works/ (last accessed 17 February 2016).

[67] B Cardozo, *The Growth of the Law* (New Haven, Yale University Press, 1924) 9.

[68] DB Massey, 'How the American Law Institute Influences Customary Law: The Reasonableness Requirement of the Restatement of Foreign Relations Law' (1997) 22 *Yale Journal of International Law* 419, 421.

[69] Massey, ibid, however notes that 'After pursuing the [descriptive] approach during its first two decades the ALI changed course and began to adopt rules supported by a minority of jurisdictions when the majority rules seemed less sound' (421).

[70] J Gordley, 'European Codes and American Restatements: Some Difficulties' (1981) 81 Columbia Law Review 140, 140.

[71] Adams (n 63) 435. One leading English commentary has noted that: '[T]he term "restatement" is used in a rather loose sense, since the process necessarily involves departures from at least some of the rules from which the restatement is drawn, not only because these differ from each other but also because of a concern to produce best solutions to typical problems in the light of experience' (R Goode, H Kronke and E McKendrick, *Transnational Commercial Law* (Oxford, OUP, 2011) para 14.04.

[72] See R Posner, *The Problematics of Moral and Legal Theory* (Cambridge, Harvard University Press, 1999) 304–07.

[73] As summarised by KD Adams in 'Blaming the Mirror: The Restatements and the Common Law' (2007) 40 *Indiana Law Review* 205.

Whilst the notion of a restatement is very much an American one, the concept has travelled beyond the borders of the United States.[74] An example of a European use of the restatement approach is the *Restatement of the English Law of Unjust Enrichment*, a project which was led by Professor Andrew Burrows in collaboration with a group of senior judges, academics, and legal practitioners.[75] Published by Oxford University Press in 2012, the *Restatement* was designed to enhance the understanding of the common law on unjust enrichment. The *Restatement* comprises a set of succinct rules, explained by a supporting commentary that sets out the law in England and Wales on unjust enrichment. It is to be noted that *A Restatement of the English Law of Contract* is currently being undertaken by Professor Burrows and team.[76]

### *(ii) A Restatement in Jersey*

Whilst it is true that the process of understanding the law in Jersey does not involve the multijurisdictional rules which are in encountered in the US, it is nonetheless submitted that the restatement model is an approach which might be particularly well suited to the Jersey law context. A Jersey Restatement would draw together the current principles underlying Jersey contract law into a set of clear, accessible and succinct rules. There would be real and appreciable benefits to be gained from setting out the Jersey law of contract in one place, in clear and accessible form. This would further the objective of legal certainty by allowing contracting parties to have greater clarity as to the rules governing agreements subject to Jersey law. It would be more readily understandable to ordinary consumers. From a business perspective, a clearer framework for the law of contract would facilitate the work of legal advisors providing advice on Jersey contract law, and must surely make it more feasible to contract under the Jersey law of contract than is currently the case.

It is also submitted that the methodology of a restatement could be adapted to the Jersey legal environment. Jersey lawyers are used to referring to authoritative guides or treatises which set out general principles of the area of the law in the form not dissimilar to a restatement.[77] The Restatement would seek simply to record the current state of the law, fill in any lacunae and clarify where ambiguity may lie. The drafting of the Restatement could be structured so as to allow for input from the various stakeholders in this area, and that work would in turn be both reflected in the substantive provisions of the Restatement, as well as in the accompanying commentary. The supporting commentary to the

[74] There are examples of international restatement projects in the sphere of contract law, such as the Unidroit *Principles of International Commercial Contracts* and the separate European project of the *Principles of European Contract Law*.

[75] A Burrows, *Restatement of the English Law of Unjust Enrichment* (Oxford, OUP, 2012).

[76] A. Burrows, *A Restatement of the English Law of Contract* (Oxford, OUP, 2016).

[77] See Chapter 2 above.

Restatement would provide interested parties with an explanation and authority for the various propositions, including references to case law, legislation and secondary sources (including the older Jersey commentaries) where relevant. The format of the Restatement thus allows one to give prominence to the rich sources of Jersey contract law whilst enhancing predictability and certainty. Where those responsible for the Restatement have, in the process of drafting, had to iron out inconsistencies in the current law, or provide clarification through a principled interpretation of the law,[78] then this could be fully explained in the supporting commentary. It is important to note that the Restatement would not be a binding document, so the drafting of the Restatement would not prevent the courts from interpreting and developing the law as they see fit. The Restatement would thus both clarify and present the current Jersey customary law *acquis*, whilst allowing for the law to evolve further.

There have been concerns voiced about the adoption of a restatement model of reform. Given the current lack of clarity in many areas of contract law, it might be felt that a mere restatement is not ambitious enough in either its scope or extent of reform. Indeed, arguments might be made that Jersey law needs rewriting rather than merely restating, and that a soft law instrument with an unclear legal status would not redress the fundamental inadequacies of the current position. This viewpoint has some substance and it is recognised that a more ambitious reform approach might be necessary, albeit though that a restatement could be a useful precursor to reform by codification.

### *(iii) Clarification by Codification*

Codification is a much more ambitious process. The premise of such an approach is that an entirely new piece of legislation should be enacted in a codified structure which sets a clear difference with the pre-existing regime.[79] The codification of the Jersey law of contract has long been considered within Jersey as a reform option. As we have already noted, the Jersey Law Commission examined the codification of Jersey contract law. In so doing, it explored the alternative possibilities of using a model from another jurisdiction or drawing upon the current, pre-existing law and thereby 'codify[ing] the Jersey law as it stands today'.[80] The Law Commission did, however, recognise various disadvantages of such an approach, in particular that the process of codification would likely take a long time and involve considerable effort. It ultimately thus dismissed the codification of the existing law 'as we believe that it is likely to take many years, during which the present unsatisfactory

[78] This was the approach of Professor Burrows in his project, which he describes as a 'principled' or 'progressive' restatement: Burrows (n 75) x.

[79] This is not just a feature of civilian systems—codification has been a perennial topic in the common law world: see the excellent overview of N Andrews, *Contract Law* (Cambridge, CUP, 2015) ch 22.

[80] Jersey Law Commission (n 52) para 4.

state of affairs will no doubt continue'.[81] The Law Commission instead advocated adopting a 'statutory framework for the law of contract', and that statutory framework was to be based upon 'a model used in another jurisdiction'.[82] It would seem from the deliberate use of the terminology of 'statutory framework' rather than codification that the former option was somewhat different to the latter, though no explanation of this was given, and somewhat confusingly the concept of reform by 'statutory framework' was not actually mentioned in the Law Commission's original options for reform![83]

Whilst it is true that time and effort would be required in codifying the existing law of contract in Jersey, it might be that the Law Commission overestimated those difficulties, and correspondingly underestimated the difficulties of drawing upon a pre-existing external model. As to codifying the existing law of contract, it is clear that this would require a degree of effort in terms of encapsulating in codified form the pre-existing rules in Jersey. Despite the uncertainty about sources, and the fact that the case law on Jersey contract law has been relatively sparse, many of the key aspects of the law of contract are relatively clear, and recent case law has clarified this. There are a number of important principles or maxims underpinning the Jersey law of contract.[84] Many features of Jersey contract law flows from these notions, in particular the primacy of the contracting parties' consent in the formation of contracts, with the Jersey courts repeatedly referring to the need to show a 'meeting of minds' between the parties.[85] The subjective approach,[86] with its focus on the actual intentions of the parties at the time of contracting, rather than an objective approach often associated with the common law, has had an impact on many areas of contract law, including the formation of a contract, the factors vitiating a contract (*vice de consentement*), the effects of a contract between the parties, and the position of remedies. Clarification will, however, be needed in various areas, such as the role and place of good faith, the composite elements of *vice de consentement* (in particular the role of misrepresentation and the extent of *dol par réticence*), the remedies of *résolution* and specific performance. Supplementary provisions will also need to be added in areas such as consumer protection (in respect of unfair contract terms, distance selling, etc).

If, on the other hand, codification was to be premised on an external model, following the recommendation of the Jersey Law Commission, then careful

[81] Ibid, para 6.

[82] Ibid, para 6.

[83] See the Jersey Law Commission's *Consultation Paper on the Jersey Law of Contract* (2002).

[84] See further Chapter 3.

[85] See eg *Bennett v Lincoln* 2005 JLR 125; *Cronin and Luce v Gordon-Bennet* 2003 JLR N22.

[86] The Court of Appeal in *O'Brien v Marett* was unambiguous on this point: '[T]he Jersey law of contract determines *consent* by use of the subjective theory of contract' (*O'Brien v Marett* [2008] JCA 178, [55]). See, however, the recent decision of the Jersey Court of Appeal in *Home Farm Developments Ltd v Le Sueur* [2015] JCA 242, which has generated some uncertainty on this issue. See discussion below in Chapter 3, at pp 44–46 above.

consideration would have to be given as to the appropriate model. Some brief discussion can be found in the Law Commission's 2004 Report, in which consideration is given to whether Jersey might codify the works of Pothier, or instead draw upon the Quebec Civil Code or the US Uniform Commercial Code.[87] Whilst the preference of the Jersey Law Commission seemed to be for the Indian Contract Act 1872 (which itself has been used as basis for reform in other parts of the world),[88] there are are, however, other potential models. It was a particular shame that no reference was made by the Jersey Law Commission to the many international projects in the sphere of contract law.[89] Over and above those reference points, there have also been national attempts to reform contract law in countries with comparable legal systems:[90] codification of contract law has been much discussed in Australia;[91] the Dubai International Financial Centre has enacted contract law rules representing a non-English codification of (predominantly) English contract law;[92] and the English and Scottish Law Commissions combined to produce a draft Contract Code in the 1970s, and whilst the project was never completed, draft versions of the Code have been published.[93]

If Jersey was to proceed with a codification project, then a series of issues would need to be broached. First, any new legislation would need to be context

[87] Jersey Law Commission (n 52) para 6.

[88] As recorded by Andrews (n 79) para 22.14.

[89] See generally: Ch Twigg-Flesner, *The Europeanisation of Contract Law* (London, Routledge-Cavendish, 2008). An early precursor was the *Principles of European Contract Law* (PECL) prepared by the Commission on European Contract Law and coordinated by Professor Lando (also known as the Lando Commission). *Principles of European Contract Law, Parts I and II*, The Commission on European Contract Law, prepared by O Lando, ed H Beale (Kluwer Law International, 1999); *Principles of European Contract Law, Part III*, ed O Lando, A Prüm, E Clive, R Zimmerman (Kluwer Law International, 2003). The text of the Principles is available online: http://frontpage.cbs.dk/law/commission_on_european_contract_law/. Another prominent example is the *Common Frame of Reference*. In that respect, the Study Group on a European Civil Code (SGECC) and the Research Group on EC Private Law (Acquis Group) prepared a Draft Common Frame of Reference, in respect of which a definitive version was released in 2008: *Principles, Definitions and Model Rules of European Private Law, Draft Common Frame of Reference (DCFR), Outline Edition, The Study Group on a European Civil Code, The Research Group on EC Private Law* (Acquis Group), prepared by Ch Von Bar, E Clive, H Schulte-Nölke, H Beale, J Herre, J Huet, M Storme, S Swann, P Varul, A Veneziano, ed F Zoll (Sellier European Law Publlishers, 2009).

[90] There are also codification or recodification projects ongoing in non-common law jurisdictions, such as France (as we have seen above, at 6) as well as Japan: H. Sono, 'Integrating Consumer Law into the Civil Code; A Japanese Attempt at Re-codification' in M Keyes and T Wilson, *Codifying Contract Law: International and Consumer Law Perspectives* (Farnham, Ashgate Publishing, 2014).

[91] In 2012, the Australian government undertook a public consultation exploring the scope for reforming Australian contract law: www.ag.gov.au/Consultations/Pages/ReviewofAustraliancontractlaw.aspx (last accessed 14 December 2015), though this process has now seemingly stalled: see generally W Swain, 'Contract Codification in Australia: Is it Necessary, Desirable and Possible?' (2014) 36 *Sydney Law Review* 131.

[92] For further details and a text of the legislation, see: www.difc.ae/legal-database (last accessed 17 February 2016).

[93] H MacGregor, *Contract Code: Drawn up on Behalf of the English Law Commission* (Milan, Giuffre Editore, 1993).

compatible. It would thus need to be compatible with fundamental principles of Jersey law, namely the principle of *la convention fait la loi des parties,* as well as the primacy of the contracting parties' consent in the formation of contracts and *volonté.* Given that the subjective approach is now an important feature of Jersey law,[94] it would seem difficult to derogate from such an approach which, as we have seen, has impacted on many areas of Jersey contract law. From that perspective, the gravitational and commercial pull of English contract law should be resisted. Not only would a wholescale adoption of English law be problematic in terms of history, tradition, sources, concepts and practicalities, there may be other reasons as well not to follow this path. As Lord Hope put it:

> [I]t would seem unwise … to adopt wholesale the entirety of English contract law. In so many respects it is out of keeping with that of most, if not all, of the other jurisdictions who wish to be part of the European project: as to its requirement for consideration, its rejection of the broad notions of good faith and reasonableness and its exclusion of evidence of pre-contractual negotiations, for example. It may look attractive today. That may not be so fifty years on from now, when so much more will have been done to encourage harmonisation along the lines favoured by the current generation of code-makers.[95]

Second, account needs to be taken of the specific legal and socio-legal context in Jersey. An example of this is the issue of *cause*/consideration. The existence of *cause* in Jersey rather than the doctrine of consideration is not just expressive of a preference for the civil law concept, it is also a product of broader factual circumstances. In a legal system such as Jersey, which does not possess an instrument of deed that can be deployed so as to circumvent the exigencies of the doctrine of consideration, the preference for the notion of cause is perhaps understandable, as we have seen above. Such an approach also reflects a different underlying approach to the contractual arrangement, and a different conception of the role of the court, in the sense that we have seen above.[96] Jersey judges will thus intervene in certain circumstances to re-evaluate the equilibrium of a contractual arrangement, through the notion of *lésion*, or potentially even through the notion of *cause adéquate*, which reflects the particularities of this island jurisdiction.

Third, it would be important that any such transplant was structured so that the graft was accepted, in medical terms, by the surrounding tissue. Drafting would need therefore to be consonant with Jersey tort law, property law and quasi-contracts so that there were no uneven edges or wrinkles within the broader area of obligations. Compatibility will need also to be ensured with the Jersey law

[94] *O'Brien v Marett* [2008] JCA 178, [55]. See, however, the recent decision of the Jersey Court of Appeal in *Home Farm Developments Ltd v Le Sueur* [2015] JCA 242, which has generated some uncertainty on this issue. See discussion above in Chapter 3, at 44–46 above.

[95] Lord Hope, 'The Role of the Judge in Developing Contract Law' (2011) 15 *Jersey and Guernsey Law Review* 6, 19.

[96] See Chapter 2, at pp 31–32.

notions and concepts found therein, such as *voisinage*.[97] Particular care would need to be taken in deciding upon the appropriate drafting style so that the advantages of codification were gained whilst being sensitive to the particular features and approach of statutory drafting in Jersey.[98]

Fourth, there are also considerations of tradition and mindset or *mentalité*. The customary law tradition in Jersey has very much been of a slow development of rules incrementally over time through the case law method. The adoption of a code would be a radical departure from the past tradition in the Jersey law of obligations, which in many ways has prioritised a slow evolutionary model.[99] There have, however, been some examples of codification within differing legal systems,[100] and there is some precedent in Jersey for such an approach. In the Jersey law of trusts, the Trusts (Jersey) Law 1984 was enacted as a comprehensive piece of legislation on trust law (albeit not as a codification of the law of trusts).[101]

If these considerations were united, then a Jersey Contract Code could indeed be crafted into a state-of-the-art piece of legislation drawing upon both common law and civil traditions to create an efficient modern approach to contract law which embraces the best of techniques from different legal systems. The aim would be to provide greater clarity and certainty as to current contract law, to the benefit of all stakeholders.[102] If that was achieved, it would be looked to by many other jurisdictions and law reform bodies worldwide, as representing an innovative legislative instrument, and even potentially as a reference point in contract law reform.[103] Any such reform would need to reconcile the hybrid nature of the Jersey legal system. It would thus have the added attraction of being a pioneering reform instrument marrying both civil and common law influences, thereby leveraging the influence of this microjurisdiction beyond its island shores, and also proving the importance of a jurisdiction which is illustrative of comparative law in action.

[97] Whereby a neighbour must not use his property so as to damage neighbouring property: see *Rockhampton Apartment Limited v Gale and Clarke* 2007 JLR 332; *Fogarty v St Martin's Cottage Limited* [2015] JRC 068. *Voisinage* has been characterised as an arising from quasi-contract: *Classic Herd Limited v Jersey Milk Marketing Board* 2014 (2) JLR 487, [16.] See generally R MacLeod, 'Voisinage and Nuisance' (2009) 13 *Jersey and Guernsey Law Review* 274.

[98] This has not always been the case, eg see the reference to 'with or without seal' in the Supply of Goods and Services Law 2009, Art 13(1).

[99] There is an abundant literature on this theme, but for a stimulating recent contribution, see G Samuel, 'All that Heaven Allows: Are Transnational Codes a "Scientific Truth" or are They Just a Form of Elegant "Pastiche"?' in P-G Monateri, *Methods of Comparative Law* (Cheltenham, Edward Elgar, 2012).

[100] This is not just a feature of civilian systems—codification has been a perennial topic in the common law world: see the excellent overview of Andrews (n 79) ch 22.

[101] See *Mubarak v Mubarak, re IMK Family Trust* 2008 JLR 250, [64].

[102] For an excellent consideration of these issues, see R Halson, 'A Common Lawyer's Perspective on Contract Codes' (2011) *Jersey and Guernsey Law* Review 150.

[103] See discussion of codification in this context: Keyes and Wilson (n 90).

# INDEX